who is

WONDER WOMAN?

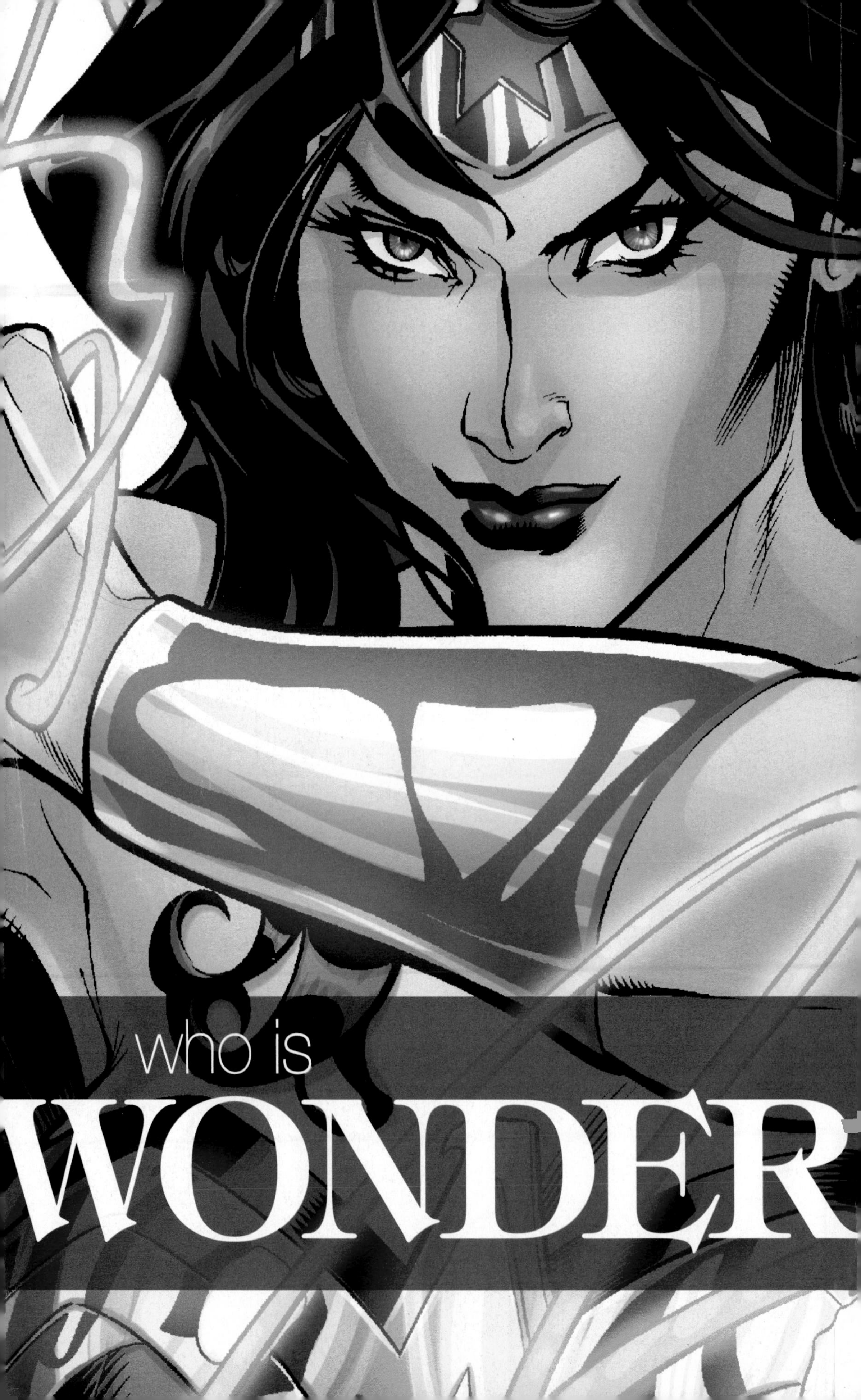
who is
WONDER

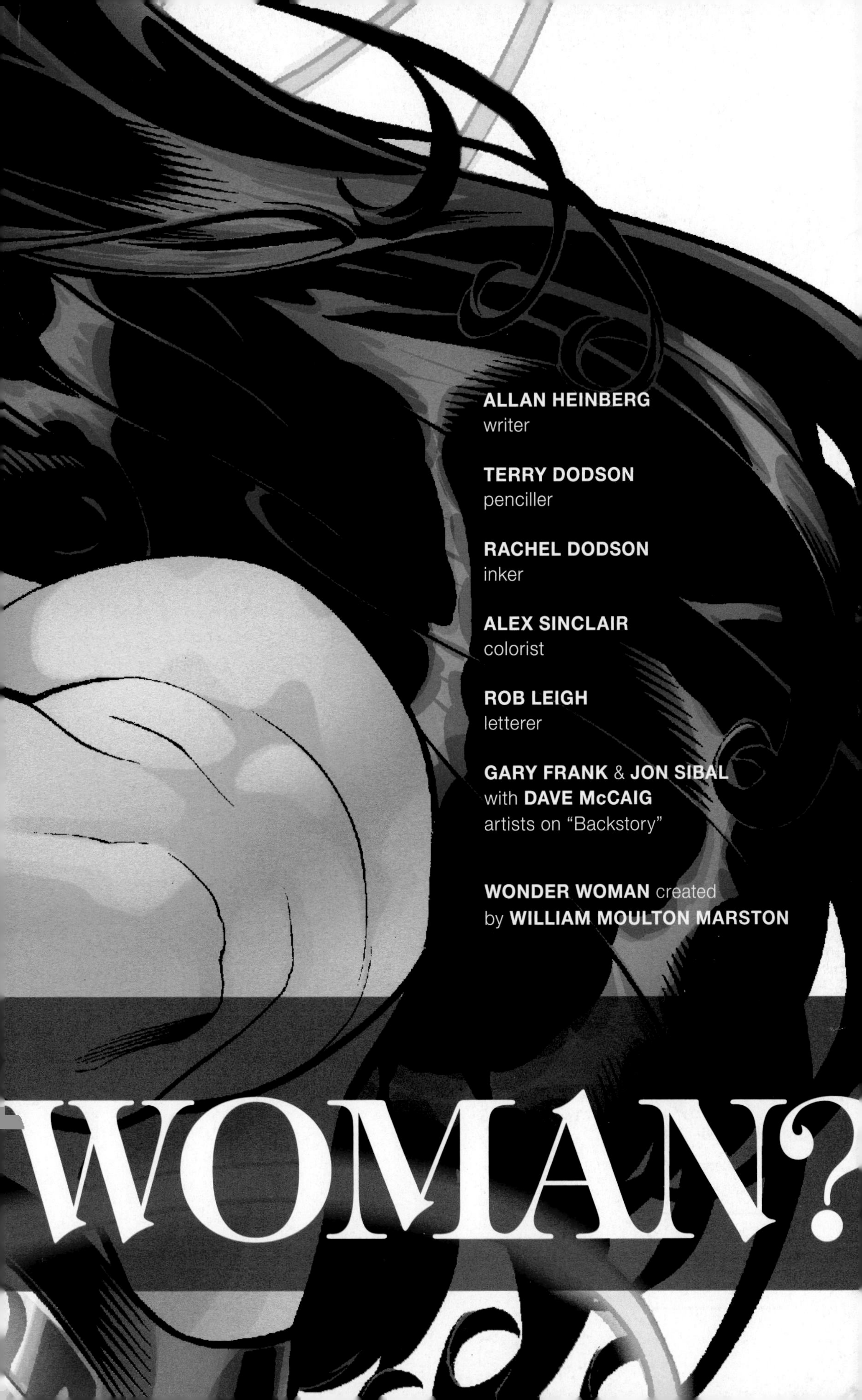
WOMAN?

ALLAN HEINBERG
writer

TERRY DODSON
penciller

RACHEL DODSON
inker

ALEX SINCLAIR
colorist

ROB LEIGH
letterer

GARY FRANK & **JON SIBAL**
with **DAVE McCAIG**
artists on "Backstory"

WONDER WOMAN created
by **WILLIAM MOULTON MARSTON**

MATT IDELSON editor – original series
NACHIE CASTRO associate editor – original series
JEB WOODARD group editor – collected editions
STEVE COOK design director – books
MONIQUE GRUSPE publication design

BOB HARRAS senior vp – editor-in-chief, dc comics

DIANE NELSON president
DAN DiDIO publisher
JIM LEE publisher
GEOFF JOHNS president & chief creative officer
AMIT DESAI executive vp – business & marketing strategy,
direct to consumer & global franchise management
SAM ADES senior vp – direct to consumer
BOBBIE CHASE vp – talent development
MARK CHIARELLO senior vp – art, design & collected editions
JOHN CUNNINGHAM senior vp – sales & trade marketing
ANNE DePIES senior vp – business strategy, finance & administration
DON FALLETTI vp – manufacturing operations
LAWRENCE GANEM vp – editorial administration & talent relations
ALISON GILL senior vp – manufacturing & operations
HANK KANALZ senior vp – editorial strategy & administration
JAY KOGAN vp – legal affairs
THOMAS LOFTUS vp – business affairs
JACK MAHAN vp – business affairs
NICK J. NAPOLITANO vp – manufacturing administration
EDDIE SCANNELL vp – consumer marketing
COURTNEY SIMMONS senior vp – publicity & communications
JIM (SKI) SOKOLOWSKI vp – comic book specialty sales & trade marketing
NANCY SPEARS vp – mass, book, digital sales & trade marketing

WONDER WOMAN: WHO IS WONDER WOMAN?

DC Comics, 2900 West Alameda Ave., Burbank, CA 91505
Printed by LSC Communications, Salem, VA, USA. 3/24/17. First Printing.
ISBN: 978-1-4012-7233-3

Library of Congress Cataloging-in-Publication Data is available.

PEFC Certified

Printed on paper from
sustainably managed
forests, controlled
sources

PEFC/29-31-337   www.pefc.org

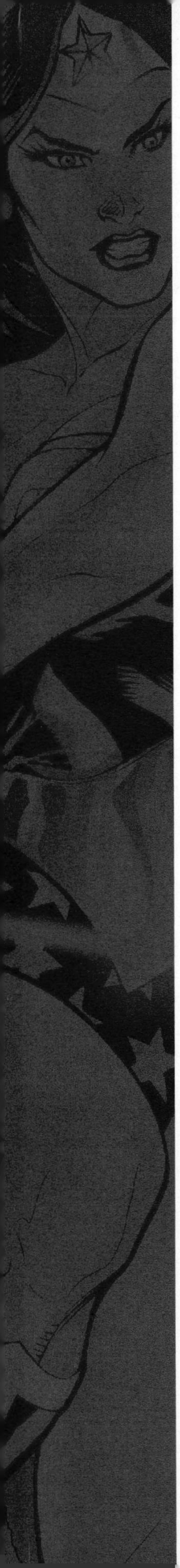

who is wonder woman?

It's a question that creators have been struggling, and often failing, to answer for more than sixty years. While she shares the iconic stature of characters like Batman and Superman, Wonder Woman has enjoyed far fewer truly memorable storylines than either of those characters, and not for lack of trying.

But nobody ever said wrestling an Amazon was supposed to be easy.

I think Wonder Woman is so hard to write because she's so full of contradictions. A warrior who loves peace? A champion for women's dignity who runs around in star-studded little blue underpants? And don't get me started on a goddess with the gift of flight needing an invisible jet to get around town...

To understand all of this duality, you probably have to start with Wonder Woman's creator, Dr. William Moulton Marston, an ingenious inventor whose groundbreaking lie detector machine was the inspiration for the Lasso of Truth (or was it the other way around?).

Marston was a trailblazing modern feminist theorist, as well as a man involved in what some might consider an anachronistic quasi-polygamist relationship with two women. He cared deeply about the idea of women's liberation, which he often explored through tales of bondage and submission. Marston wanted to create a role model for young girls, while also appealing to the desires of his male readers.

Rather than ignoring seeming inconsistencies like these, writer Allan Heinberg chose to embrace them, and it's why his complex Wonder Woman storyline is destined to be remembered as a classic.

I first became aware of Allan's writing on the Marvel series *Young Avengers*, where he demonstrated his reverent affection for and deep understanding of old characters, but also his trademark inventiveness and bold willingness to take these heroes in unexpected new directions.

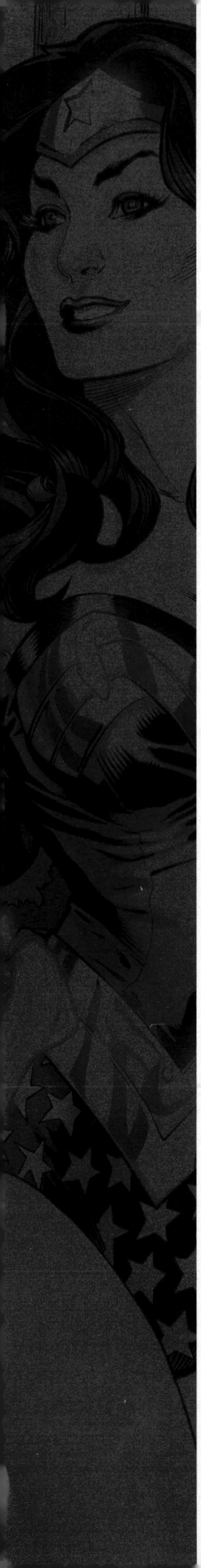

He brings all of those gifts and more to this arc, particularly with a final twist that I won't spoil here, a game-changer for "Diana Prince" and her alter ego that I think makes Wonder Woman even *more* interesting than her male colleagues in the upper echelons of DC's pantheon.

I also loved getting to know Wonder Woman through a brilliantly constructed supporting cast, especially forgotten old favorites like Nemesis, who Allan and friends infuse with new life.

And speaking of those friends, not enough can be said about Terry and Rachel Dodson, maybe the most talented couple in the history of comics. They're two of the few artists who understand that sexy doesn't always mean cheesecake and that femininity never means weakness. Whether it's the spectacle of an epic action scene or the drama of a quiet rooftop conversation, their storytelling is consistently a wonder to behold.

All of these elements combine to make a story that was always worth waiting for when it was first serialized, but one that really soars now that it can finally be read start to finish in one beautiful collection.

And for those of you still wondering just who the hell Wonder Woman really is?

Turn the page.

BRIAN K. VAUGHAN
December 2007

Along with being a writer-producer on the television series Lost*, Vaughan is the co-creator of Y: THE LAST MAN,* Saga*, EX MACHINA and PRIDE OF BAGHDAD. He once wrote a story about Batman villain Clayface* eating *Wonder Woman, which only he thinks is destined to be remembered as a classic.*

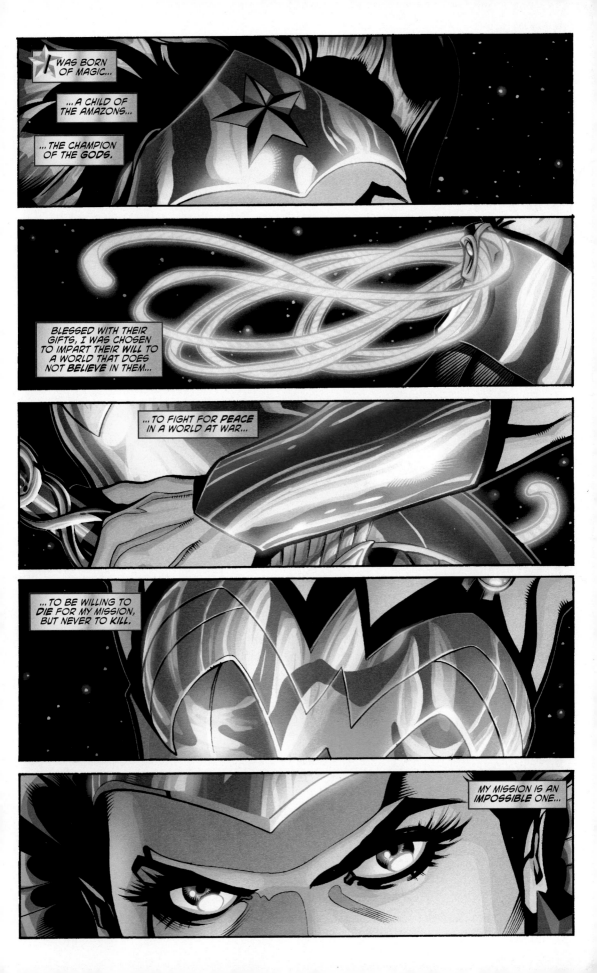

I WAS BORN OF MAGIC...

...A CHILD OF THE AMAZONS...

...THE CHAMPION OF THE GODS.

BLESSED WITH THEIR GIFTS, I WAS CHOSEN TO IMPART THEIR WILL TO A WORLD THAT DOES NOT *BELIEVE* IN THEM...

...TO FIGHT FOR *PEACE* IN A WORLD AT WAR...

...TO BE WILLING TO *DIE* FOR MY MISSION, BUT NEVER TO KILL.

MY MISSION IS AN IMPOSSIBLE ONE...

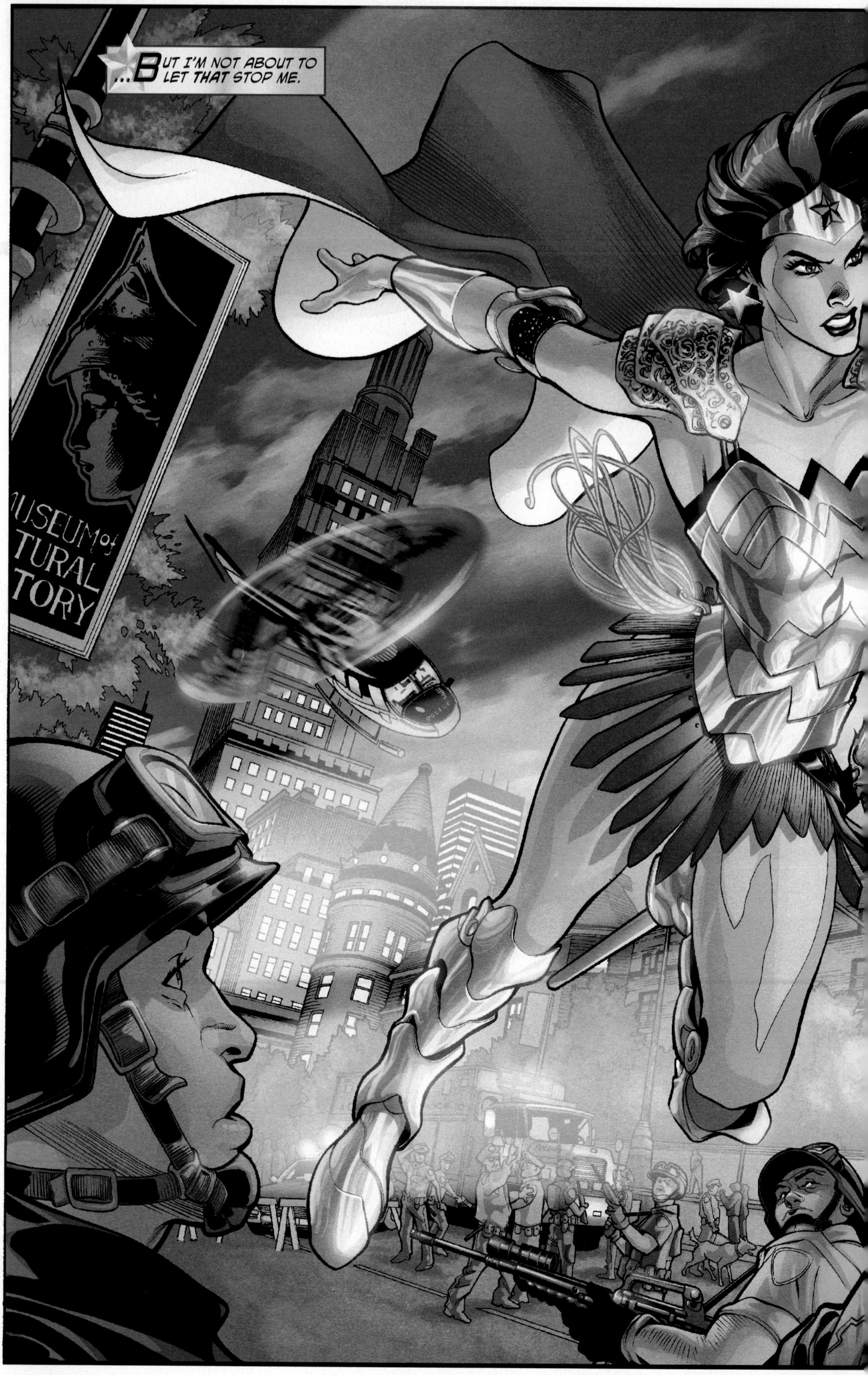
...BUT I'M NOT ABOUT TO LET THAT STOP ME.
MUSEUM of
TURAL
TORY

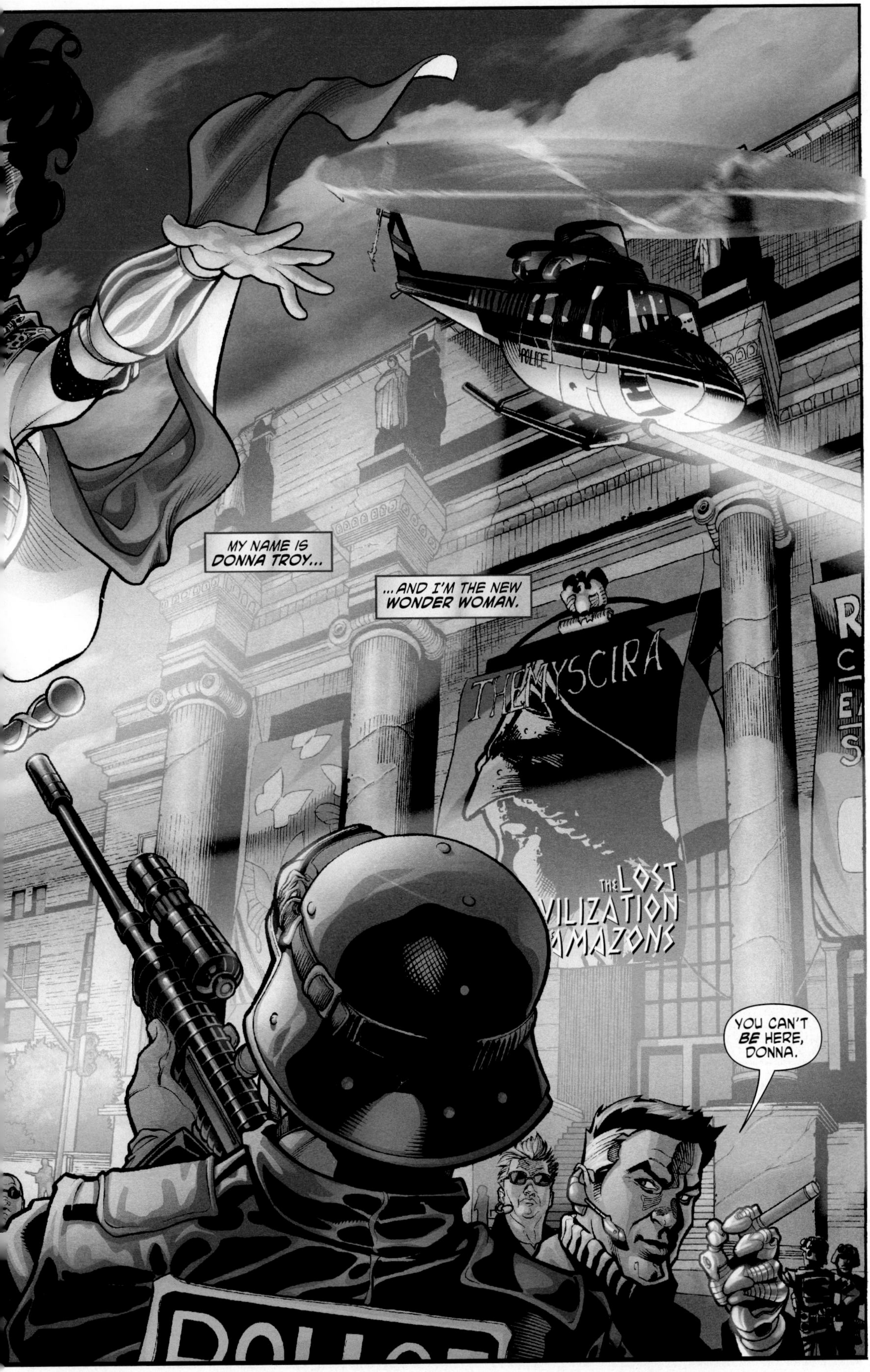
MY NAME IS DONNA TROY...
...AND I'M THE NEW WONDER WOMAN.
POLICE
THEMYSCIRA
THE LOST
VILIZATION
AMAZONS
YOU CAN'T BE HERE, DONNA.

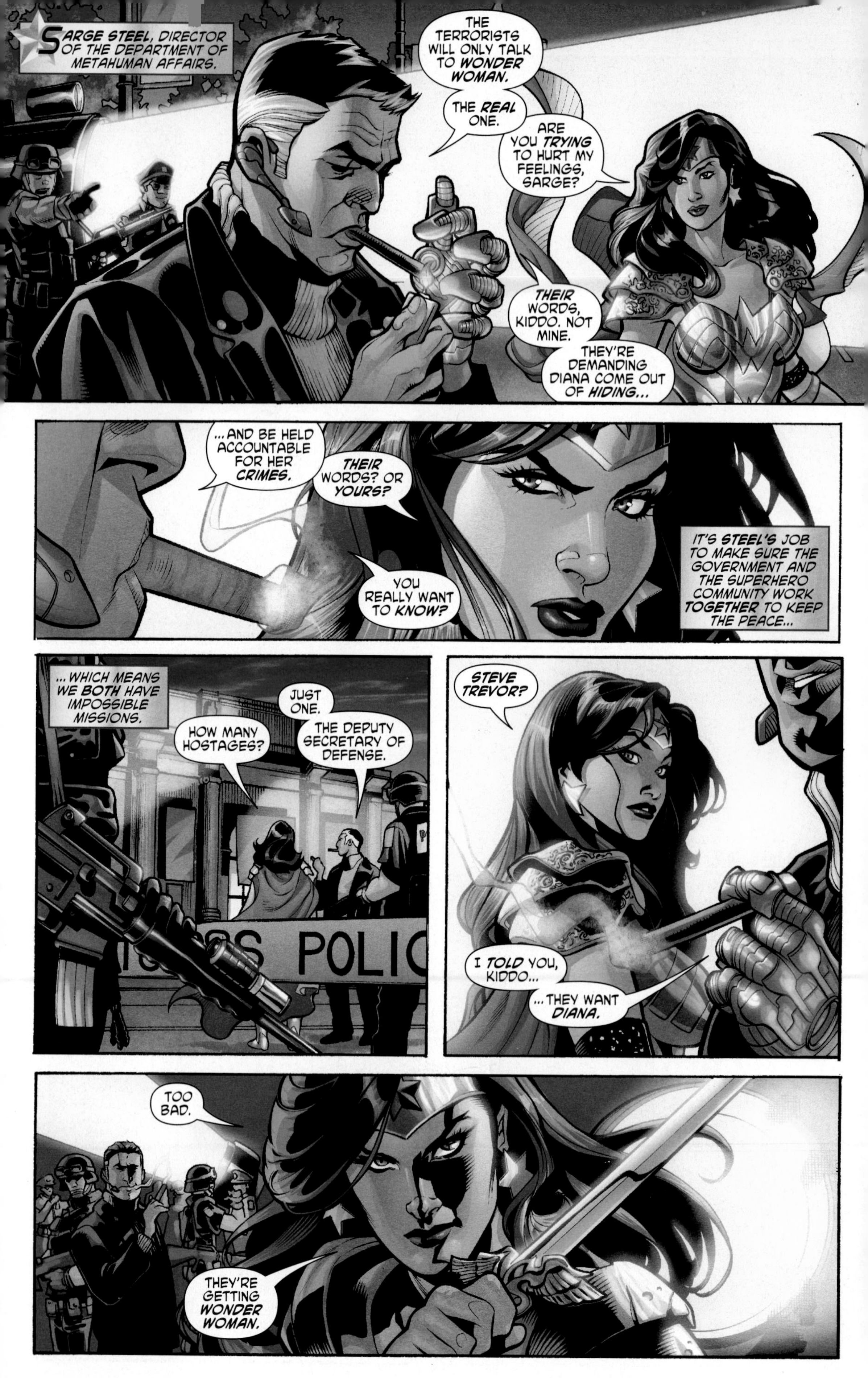
SARGE STEEL, DIRECTOR OF THE DEPARTMENT OF METAHUMAN AFFAIRS.
THE TERRORISTS WILL ONLY TALK TO WONDER WOMAN.
THE REAL ONE.
ARE YOU TRYING TO HURT MY FEELINGS, SARGE?
THEIR WORDS, KIDDO. NOT MINE.
THEY'RE DEMANDING DIANA COME OUT OF HIDING...
...AND BE HELD ACCOUNTABLE FOR HER CRIMES.
THEIR WORDS? OR YOURS?
YOU REALLY WANT TO KNOW?
IT'S STEEL'S JOB TO MAKE SURE THE GOVERNMENT AND THE SUPERHERO COMMUNITY WORK TOGETHER TO KEEP THE PEACE...
...WHICH MEANS WE BOTH HAVE IMPOSSIBLE MISSIONS.
HOW MANY HOSTAGES?
JUST ONE.
THE DEPUTY SECRETARY OF DEFENSE.
POLIC
STEVE TREVOR?
I TOLD YOU, KIDDO...
...THEY WANT DIANA.
TOO BAD.
THEY'RE GETTING WONDER WOMAN.

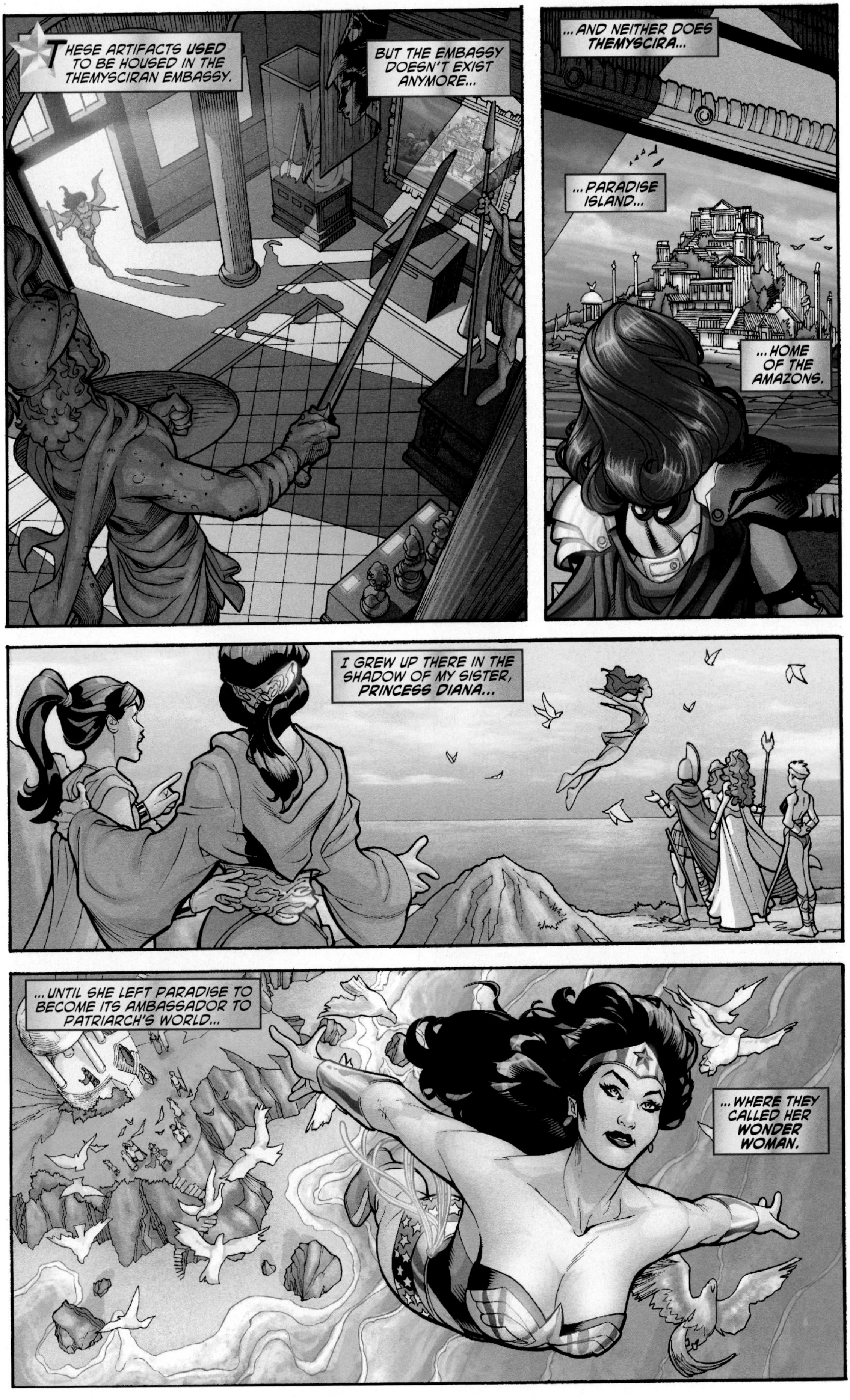
THESE ARTIFACTS USED TO BE HOUSED IN THE THEMYSCIRAN EMBASSY.
BUT THE EMBASSY DOESN'T EXIST ANYMORE...
...AND NEITHER DOES THEMYSCIRA...
...PARADISE ISLAND...
...HOME OF THE AMAZONS.
I GREW UP THERE IN THE SHADOW OF MY SISTER, PRINCESS DIANA...
...UNTIL SHE LEFT PARADISE TO BECOME ITS AMBASSADOR TO PATRIARCH'S WORLD...
...WHERE THEY CALLED HER WONDER WOMAN.

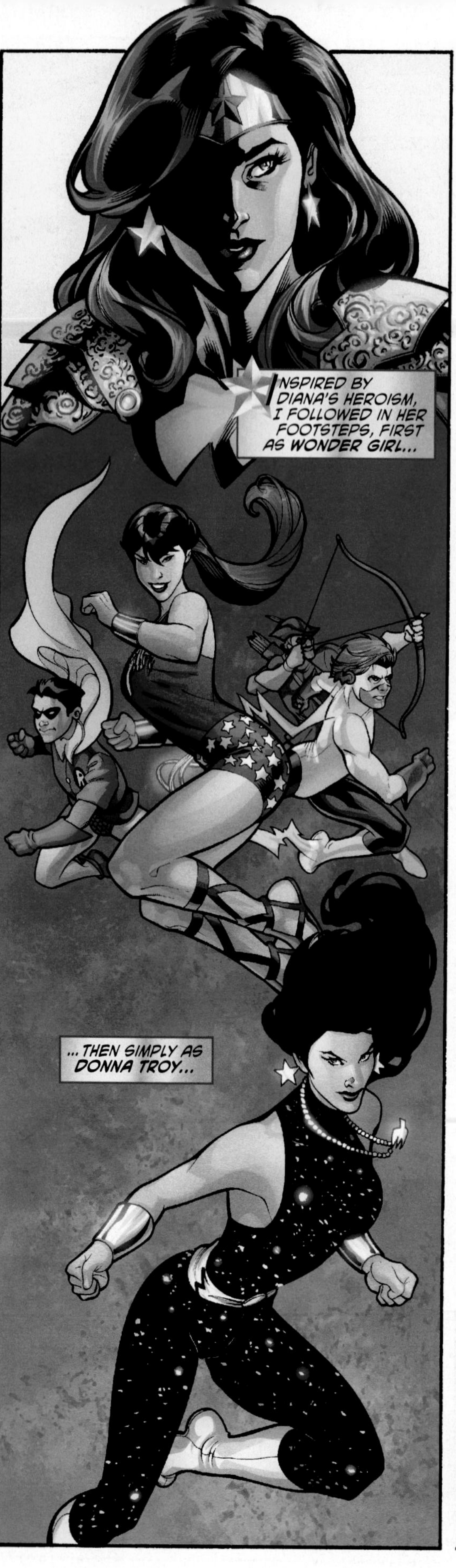
INSPIRED BY DIANA'S HEROISM, I FOLLOWED IN HER FOOTSTEPS, FIRST AS WONDER GIRL...
...THEN SIMPLY AS DONNA TROY...

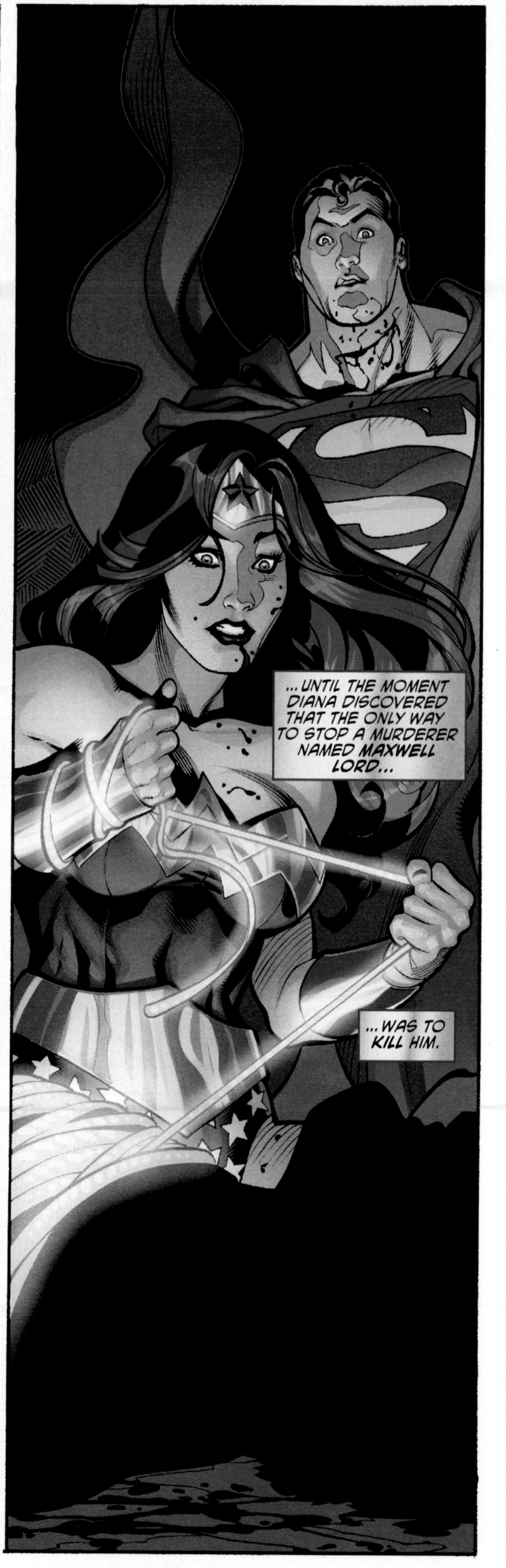
...UNTIL THE MOMENT DIANA DISCOVERED THAT THE ONLY WAY TO STOP A MURDERER NAMED MAXWELL LORD...
...WAS TO KILL HIM.

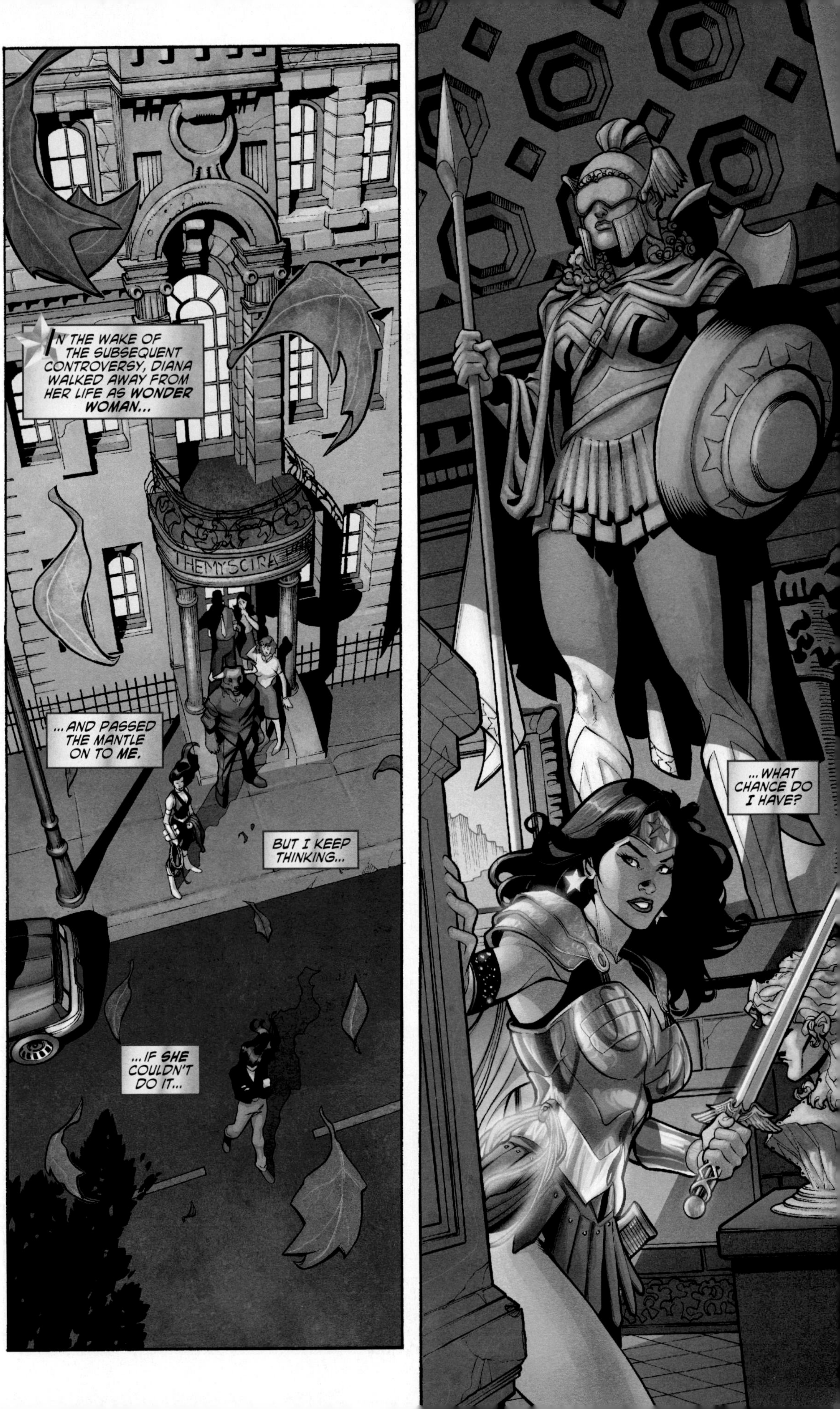
IN THE WAKE OF THE SUBSEQUENT CONTROVERSY, DIANA WALKED AWAY FROM HER LIFE AS WONDER WOMAN...
THEMYSCIRA
...AND PASSED THE MANTLE ON TO ME.
BUT I KEEP THINKING...
...IF SHE COULDN'T DO IT...
...WHAT CHANCE DO I HAVE?

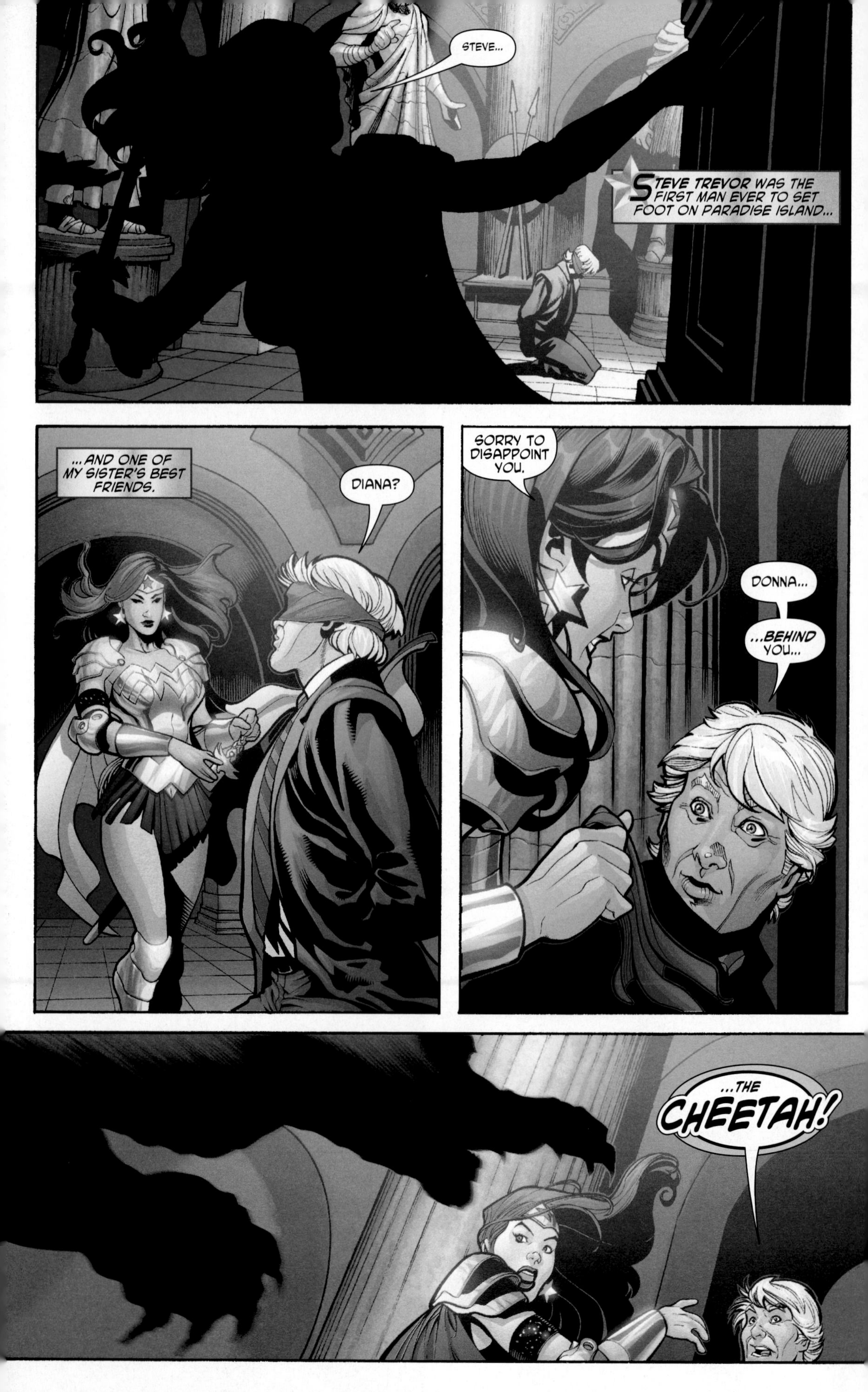
STEVE...
STEVE TREVOR WAS THE FIRST MAN EVER TO SET FOOT ON PARADISE ISLAND...
...AND ONE OF MY SISTER'S BEST FRIENDS.
DIANA?
SORRY TO DISAPPOINT YOU.
DONNA...
...BEHIND YOU...
...THE CHEETAH!

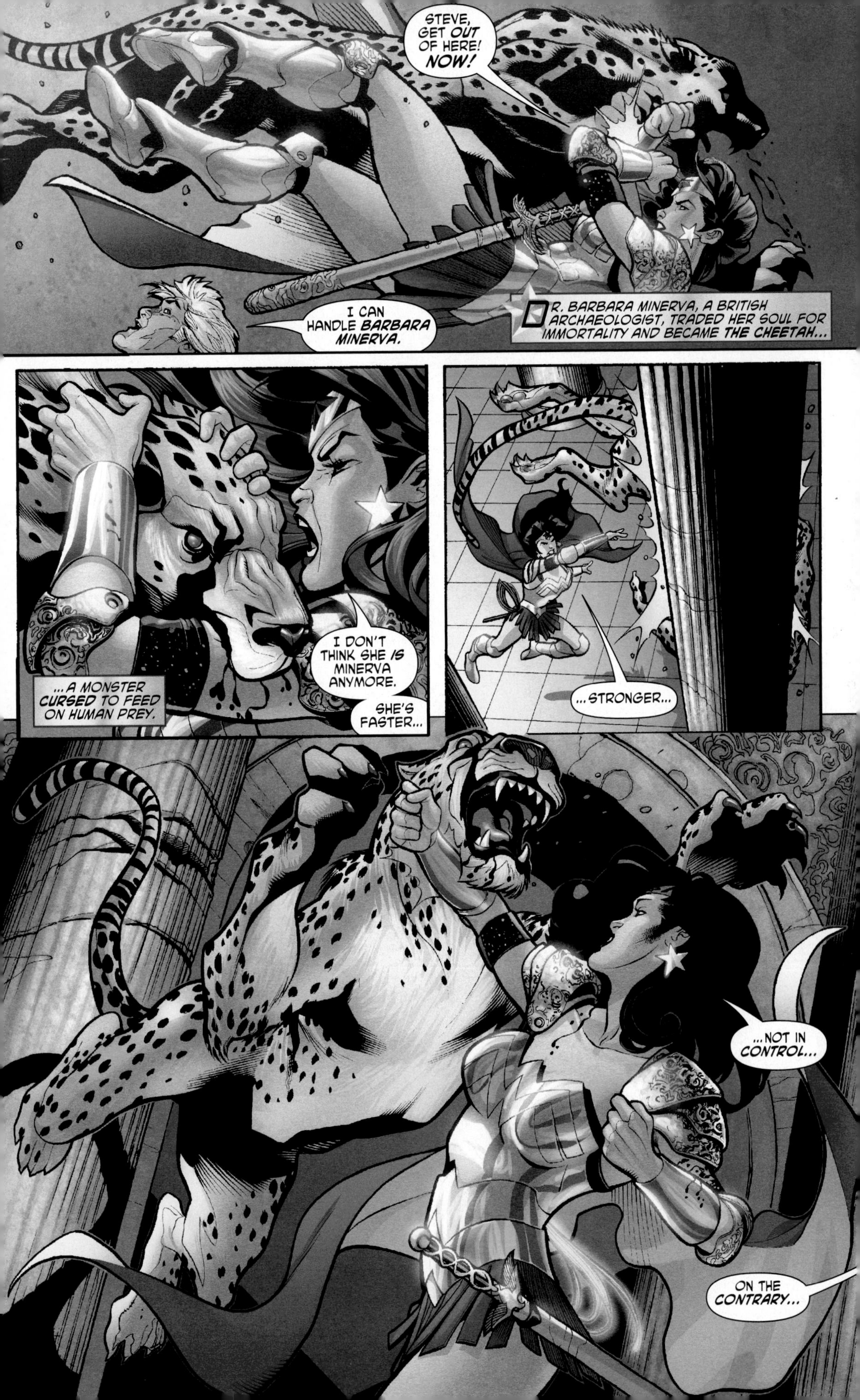
STEVE, GET OUT OF HERE! NOW!
I CAN HANDLE BARBARA MINERVA.
DR. BARBARA MINERVA, A BRITISH ARCHAEOLOGIST, TRADED HER SOUL FOR IMMORTALITY AND BECAME THE CHEETAH...
...A MONSTER CURSED TO FEED ON HUMAN PREY.
I DON'T THINK SHE IS MINERVA ANYMORE.
SHE'S FASTER...
...STRONGER...
...NOT IN CONTROL...
ON THE CONTRARY...

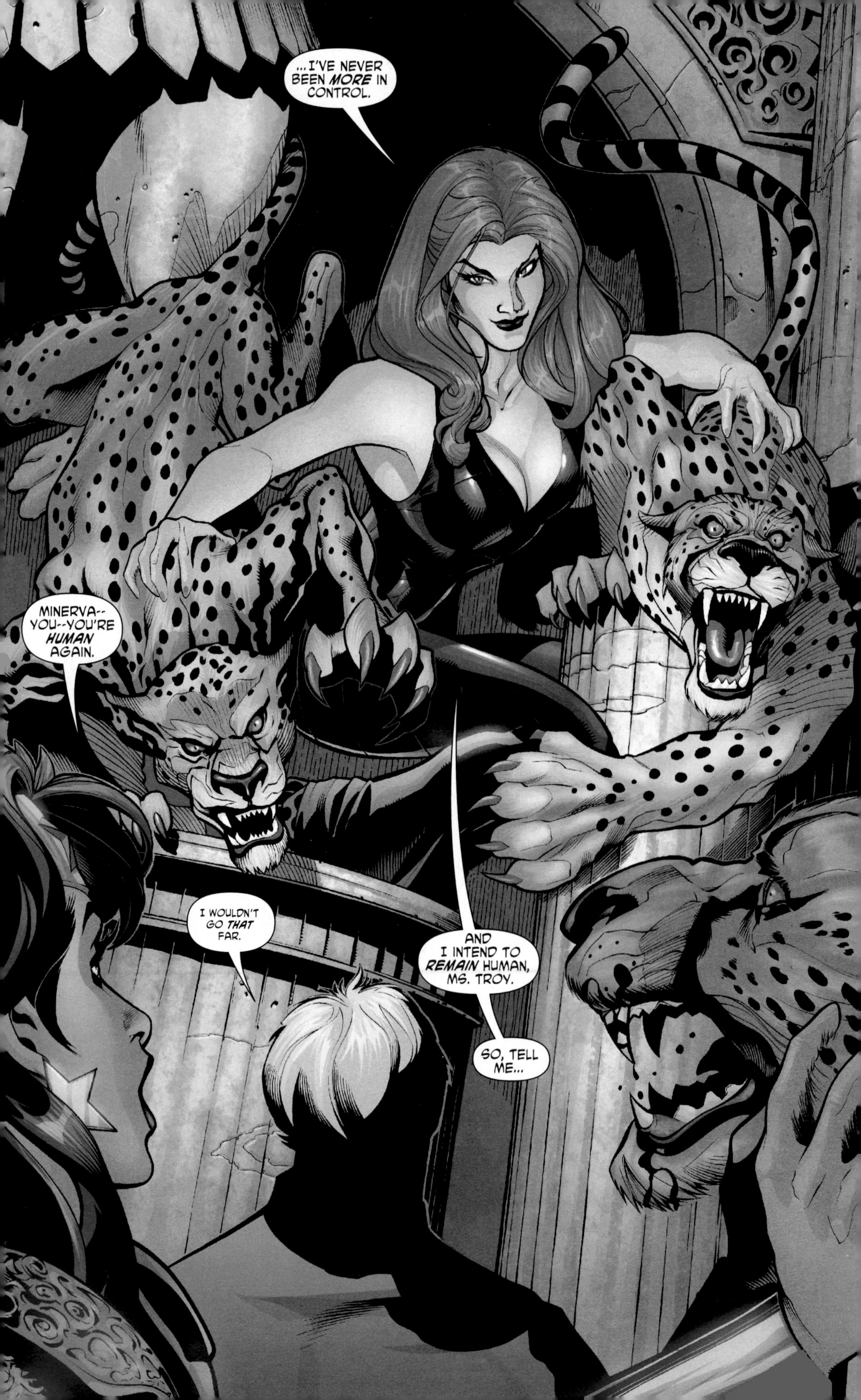
...I'VE NEVER BEEN MORE IN CONTROL.
MINERVA-- YOU--YOU'RE HUMAN AGAIN.
I WOULDN'T GO THAT FAR.
AND I INTEND TO REMAIN HUMAN, MS. TROY.
SO, TELL ME...

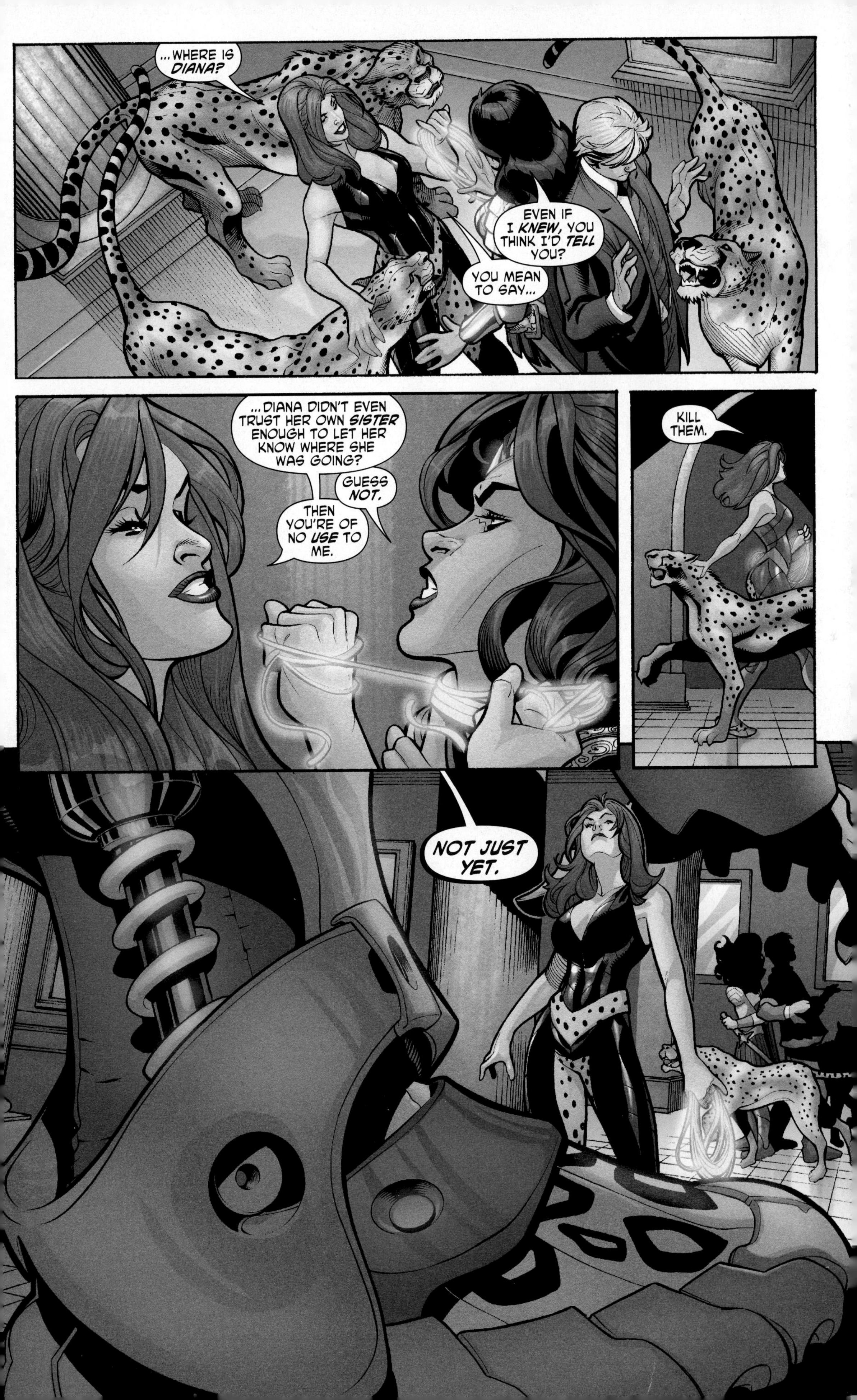
...WHERE IS DIANA?
EVEN IF I KNEW, YOU THINK I'D TELL YOU?
YOU MEAN TO SAY...
...DIANA DIDN'T EVEN TRUST HER OWN SISTER ENOUGH TO LET HER KNOW WHERE SHE WAS GOING?
GUESS NOT.
THEN YOU'RE OF NO USE TO ME.
KILL THEM.
NOT JUST YET.

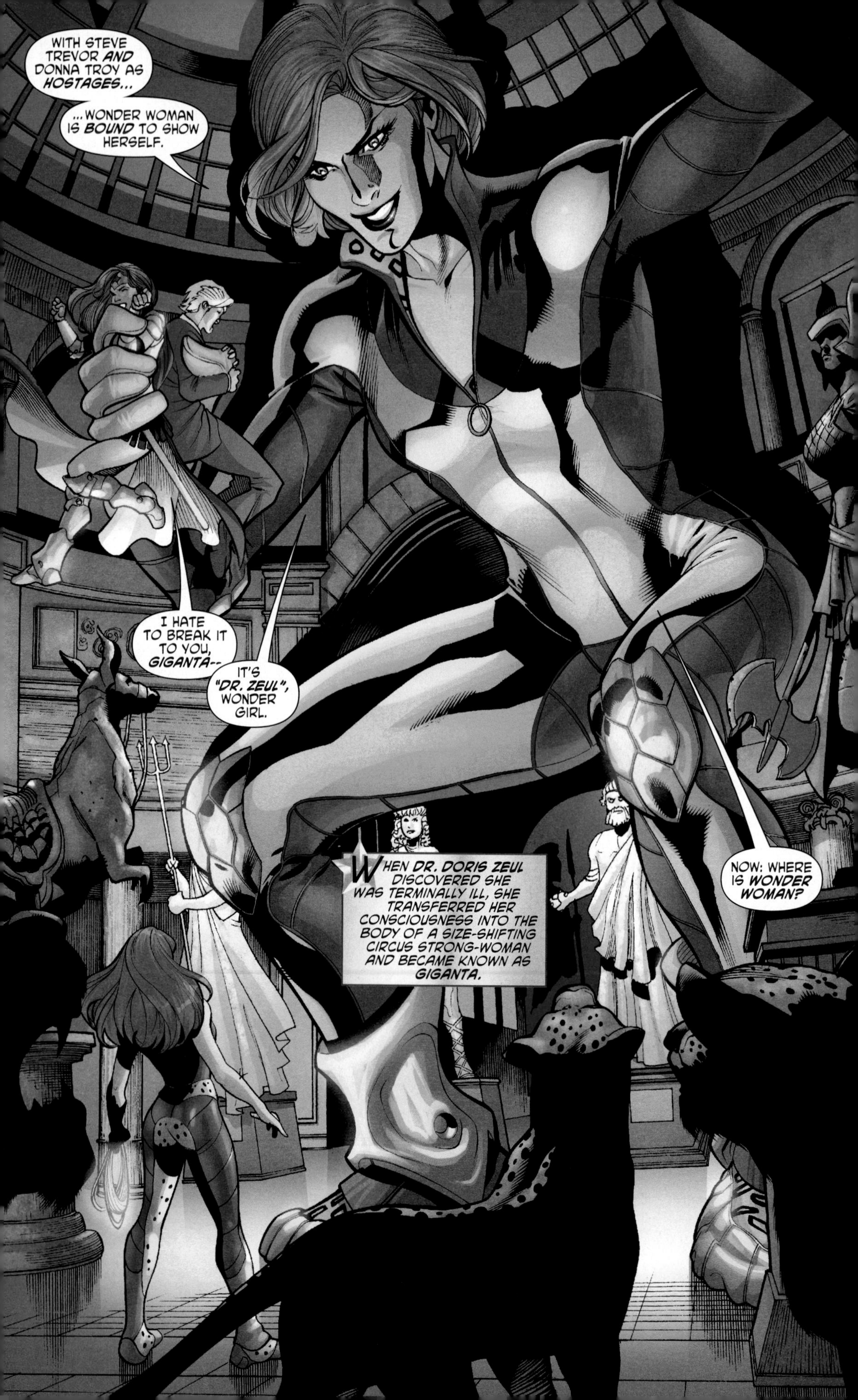
WITH STEVE TREVOR AND DONNA TROY AS HOSTAGES...
...WONDER WOMAN IS BOUND TO SHOW HERSELF.
I HATE TO BREAK IT TO YOU, GIGANTA--
IT'S "DR. ZEUL", WONDER GIRL.
WHEN DR. DORIS ZEUL DISCOVERED SHE WAS TERMINALLY ILL, SHE TRANSFERRED HER CONSCIOUSNESS INTO THE BODY OF A SIZE-SHIFTING CIRCUS STRONG-WOMAN AND BECAME KNOWN AS GIGANTA.
NOW: WHERE IS WONDER WOMAN?

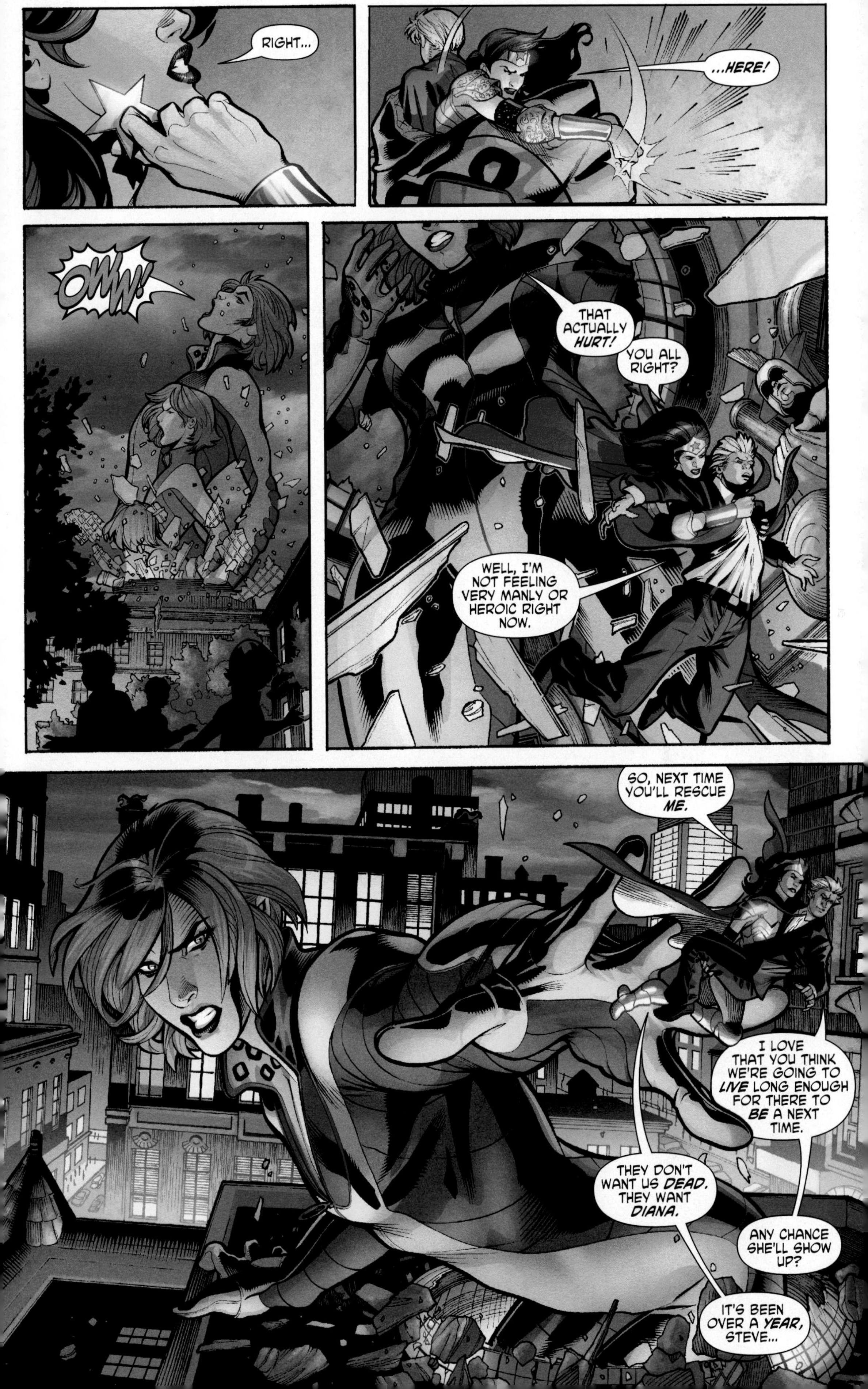
RIGHT...
...HERE!
OWW!
THAT ACTUALLY HURT!
YOU ALL RIGHT?
WELL, I'M NOT FEELING VERY MANLY OR HEROIC RIGHT NOW.
SO, NEXT TIME YOU'LL RESCUE ME.
I LOVE THAT YOU THINK WE'RE GOING TO LIVE LONG ENOUGH FOR THERE TO BE A NEXT TIME.
THEY DON'T WANT US DEAD. THEY WANT DIANA.
ANY CHANCE SHE'LL SHOW UP?
IT'S BEEN OVER A YEAR, STEVE...

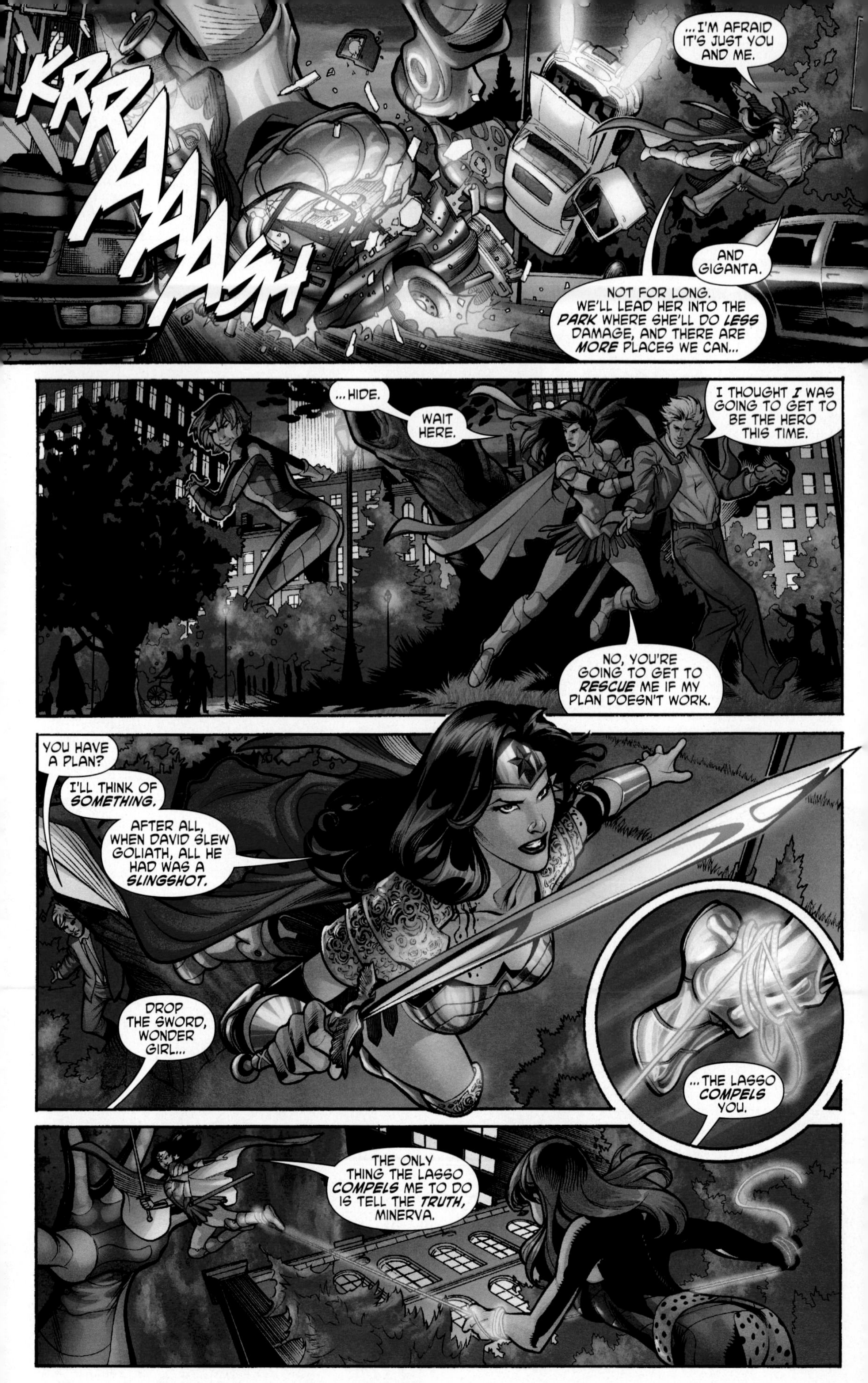
KRRAAASH
...I'M AFRAID IT'S JUST YOU AND ME.
AND GIGANTA.
NOT FOR LONG. WE'LL LEAD HER INTO THE PARK WHERE SHE'LL DO LESS DAMAGE, AND THERE ARE MORE PLACES WE CAN...
...HIDE.
WAIT HERE.
I THOUGHT I WAS GOING TO GET TO BE THE HERO THIS TIME.
NO, YOU'RE GOING TO GET TO RESCUE ME IF MY PLAN DOESN'T WORK.
YOU HAVE A PLAN?
I'LL THINK OF SOMETHING.
AFTER ALL, WHEN DAVID SLEW GOLIATH, ALL HE HAD WAS A SLINGSHOT.
DROP THE SWORD, WONDER GIRL...
...THE LASSO COMPELS YOU.
THE ONLY THING THE LASSO COMPELS ME TO DO IS TELL THE TRUTH, MINERVA.

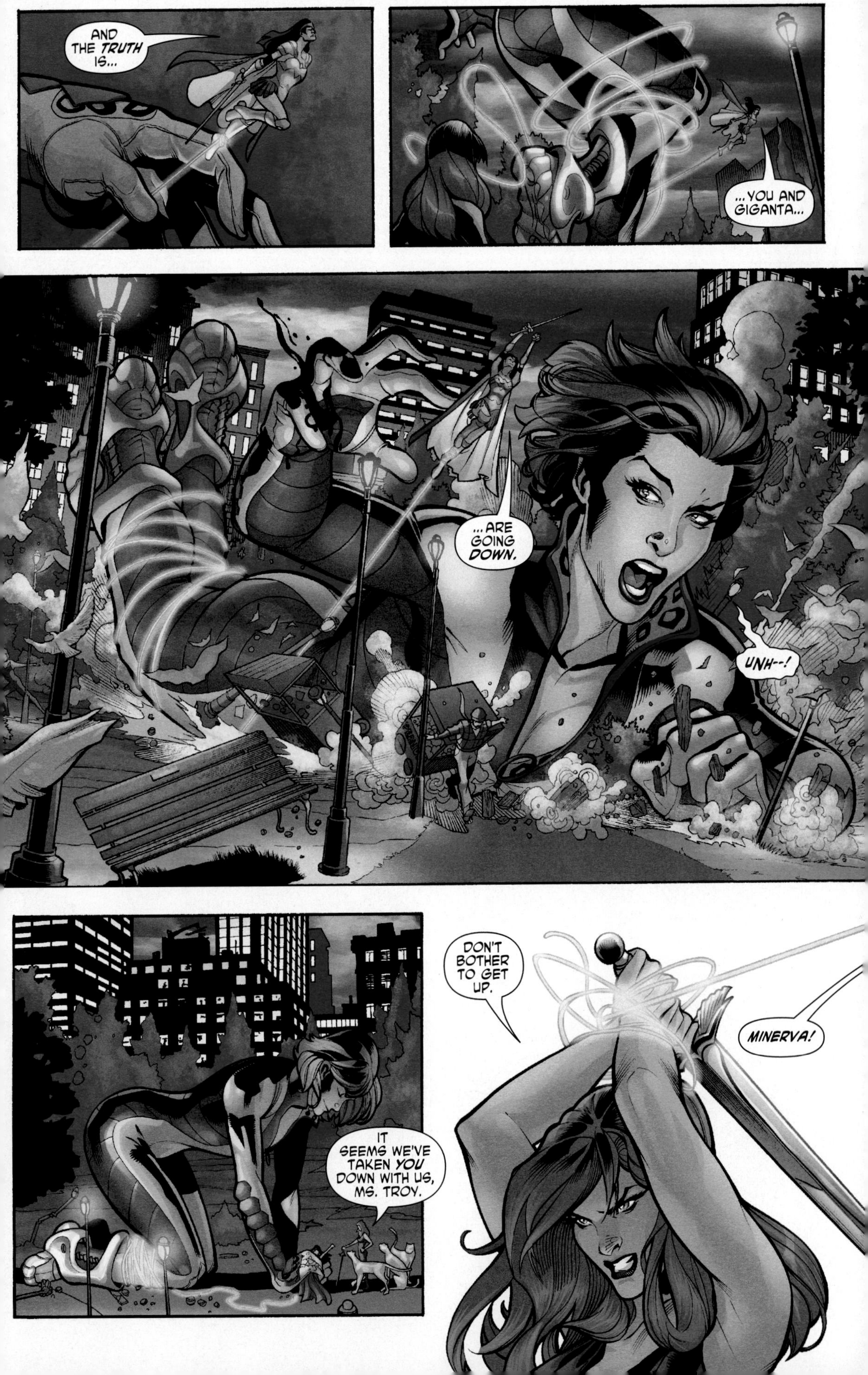
AND THE TRUTH IS...
...YOU AND GIGANTA...
...ARE GOING DOWN.
UNH--!
IT SEEMS WE'VE TAKEN YOU DOWN WITH US, MS. TROY.
DON'T BOTHER TO GET UP.
MINERVA!

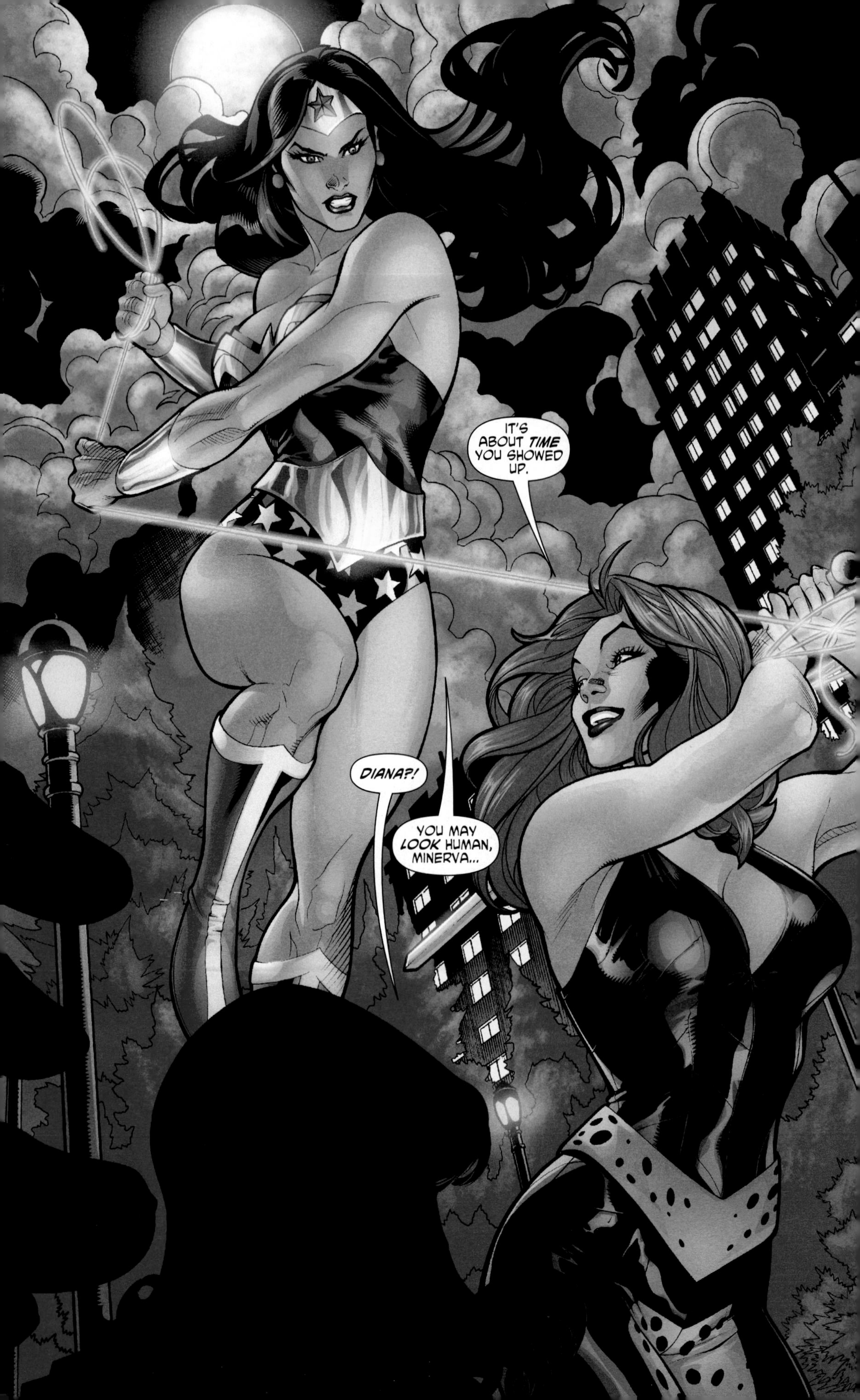

IT'S ABOUT *TIME* YOU SHOWED UP.
DIANA?!
YOU MAY *LOOK* HUMAN, MINERVA...

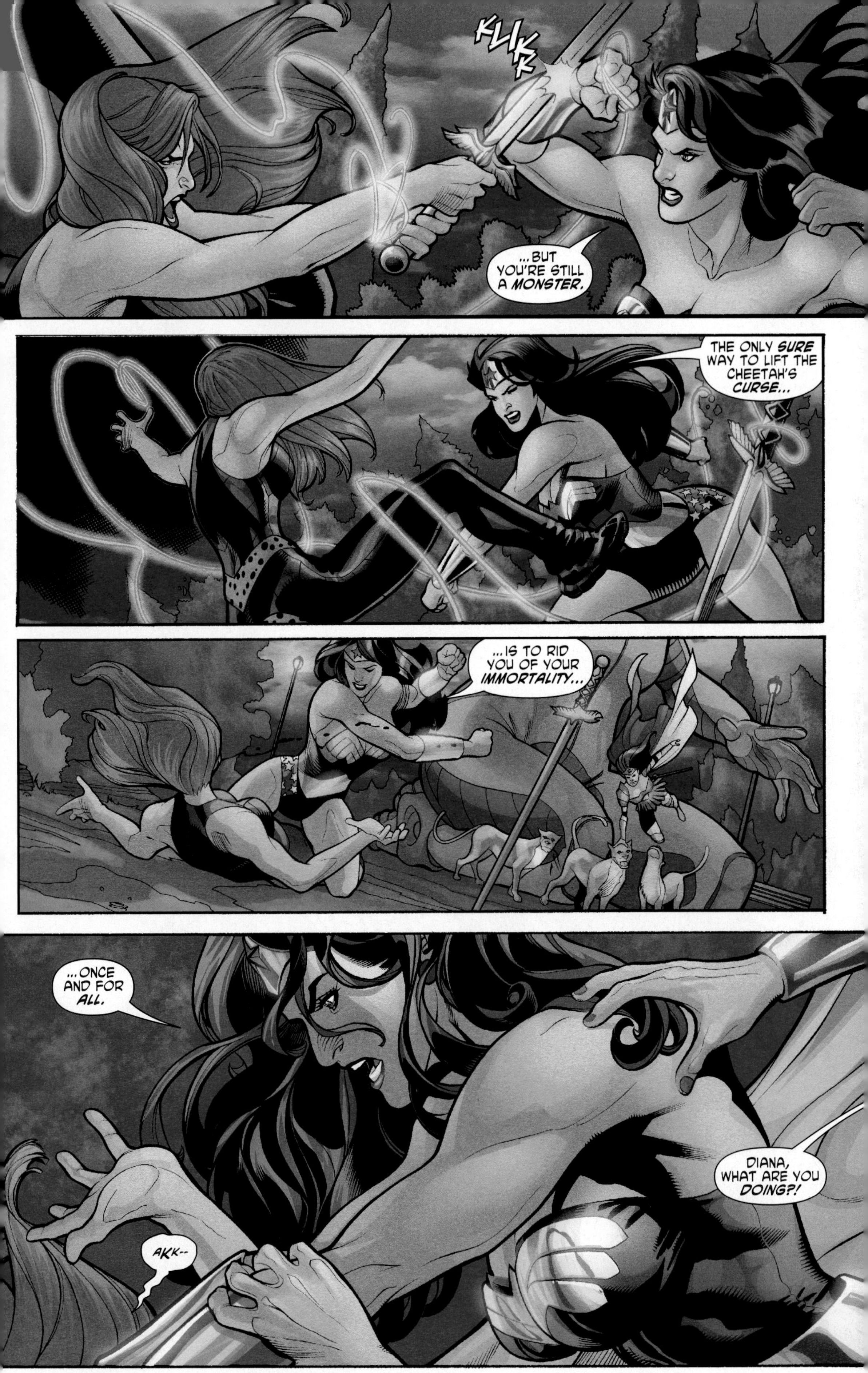
KLIKK
...BUT YOU'RE STILL A MONSTER.
THE ONLY SURE WAY TO LIFT THE CHEETAH'S CURSE...
...IS TO RID YOU OF YOUR IMMORTALITY...
...ONCE AND FOR ALL.
DIANA, WHAT ARE YOU DOING?!
AKK--

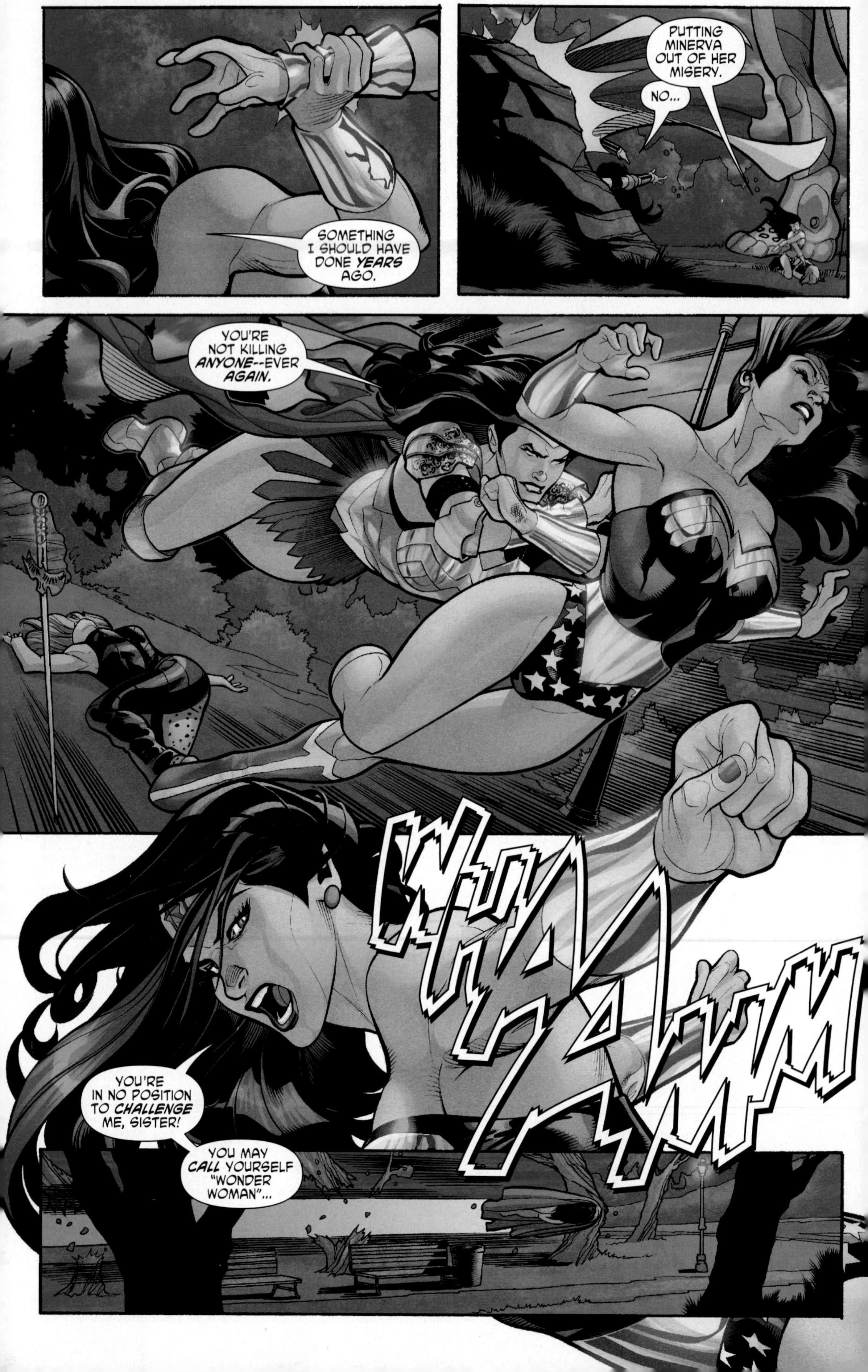
SOMETHING I SHOULD HAVE DONE YEARS AGO.
PUTTING MINERVA OUT OF HER MISERY.
NO...
YOU'RE NOT KILLING ANYONE--EVER AGAIN.
WHAMM
YOU'RE IN NO POSITION TO CHALLENGE ME, SISTER!
YOU MAY CALL YOURSELF "WONDER WOMAN"...

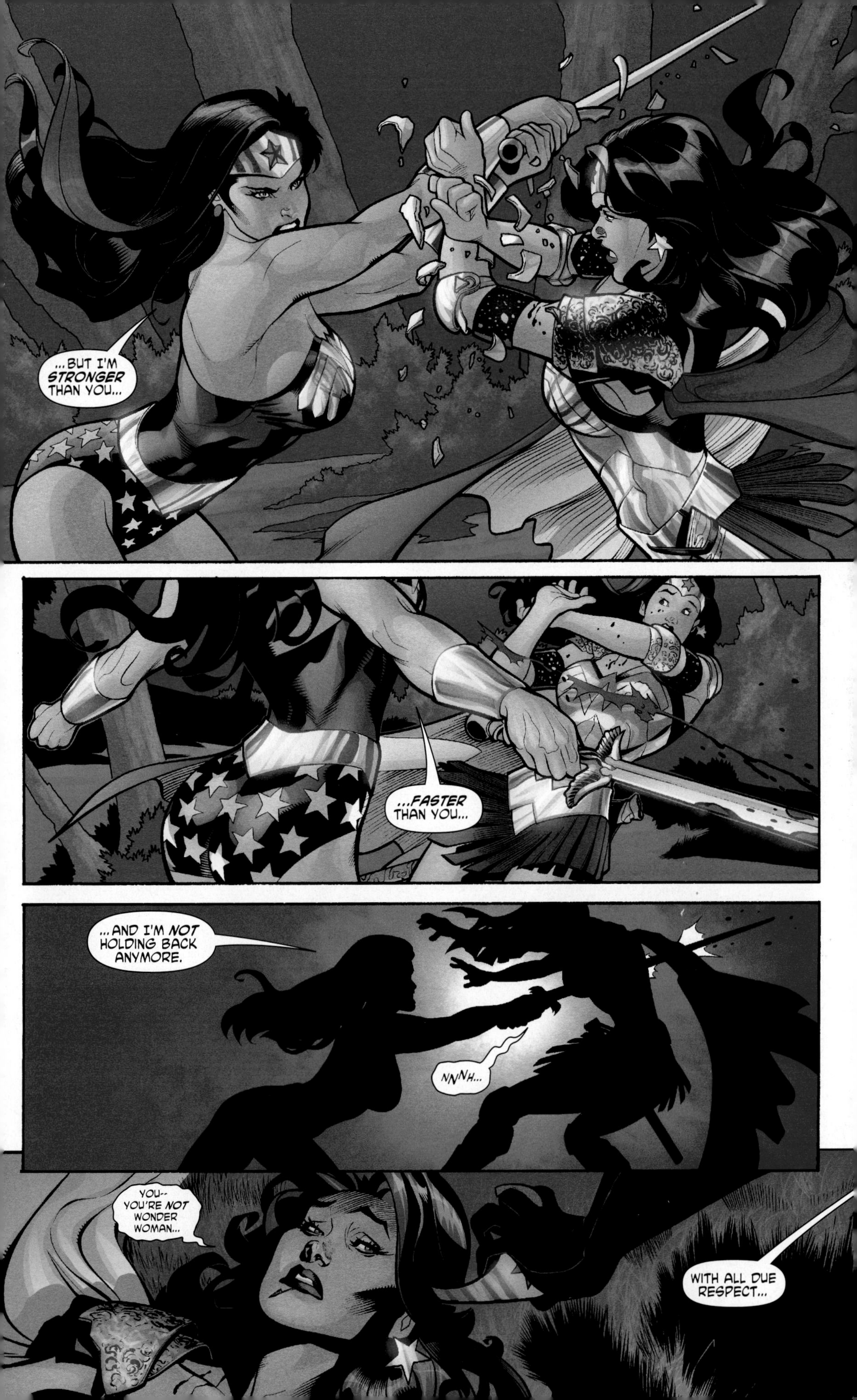
...BUT I'M STRONGER THAN YOU...
...FASTER THAN YOU...
...AND I'M NOT HOLDING BACK ANYMORE.
NNNH...
YOU-- YOU'RE NOT WONDER WOMAN...
WITH ALL DUE RESPECT...

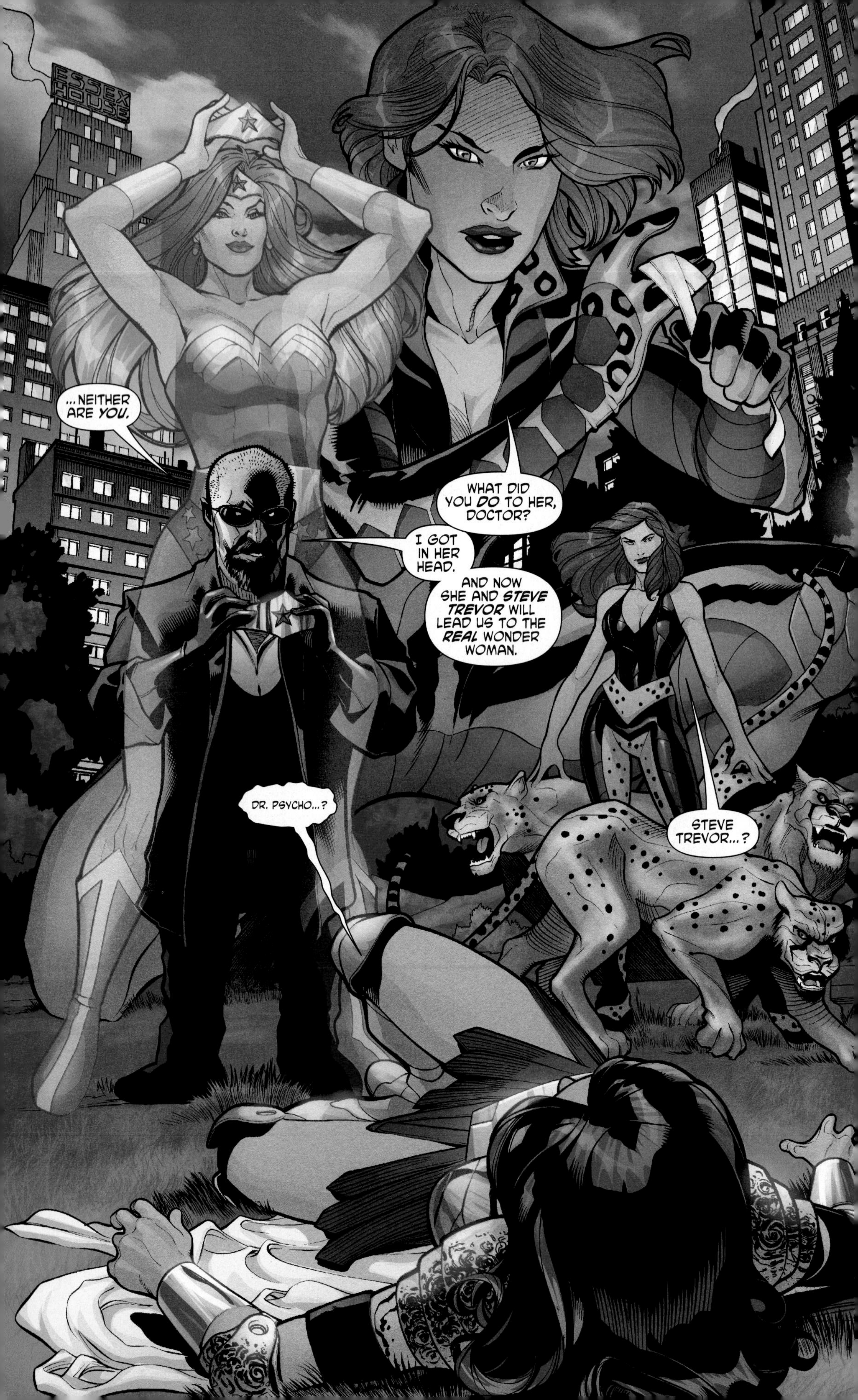
ESSEX HOUSE
...NEITHER ARE YOU.
WHAT DID YOU DO TO HER, DOCTOR?
I GOT IN HER HEAD.
AND NOW SHE AND STEVE TREVOR WILL LEAD US TO THE REAL WONDER WOMAN.
DR. PSYCHO...?
STEVE TREVOR...?

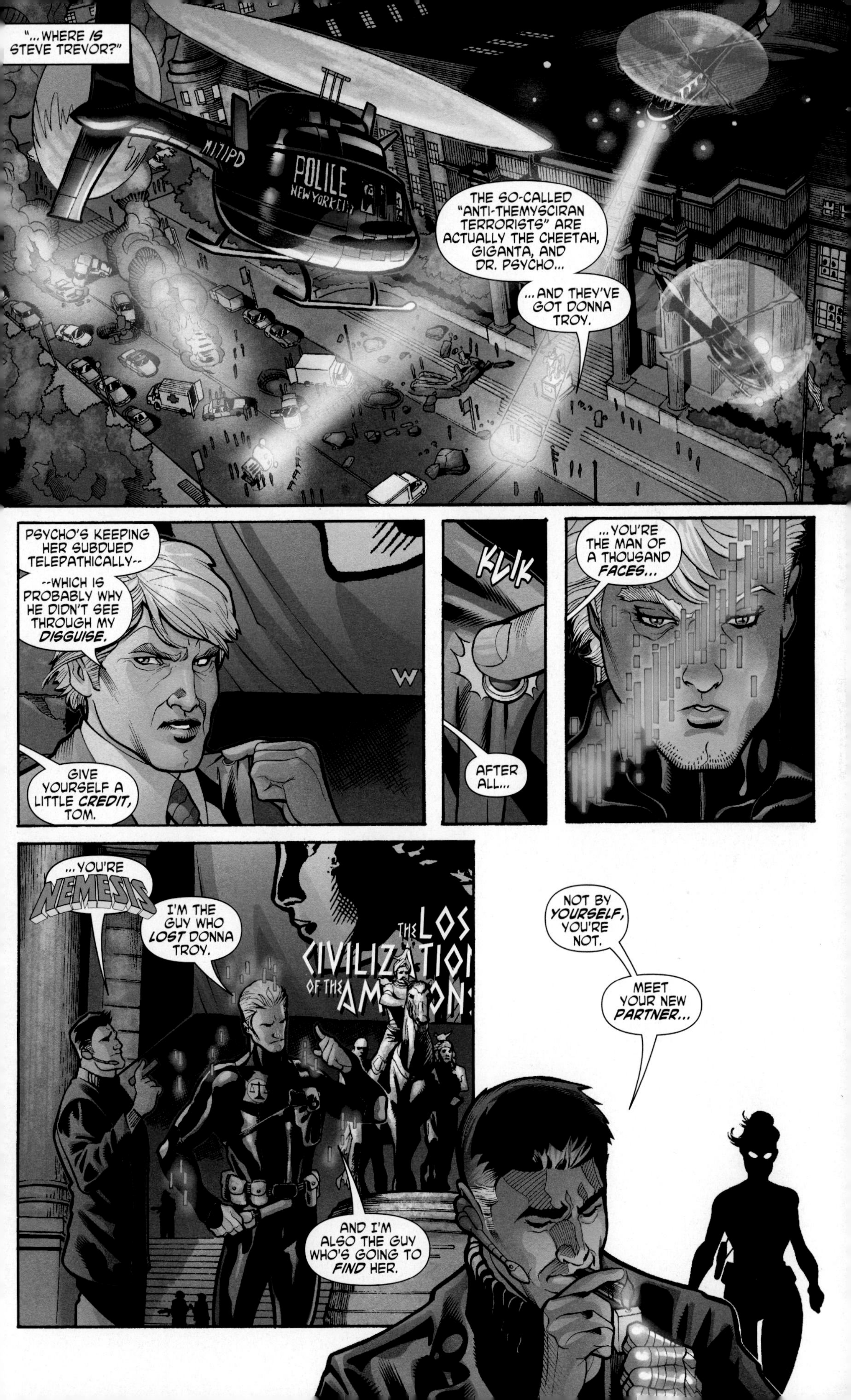
"...WHERE IS STEVE TREVOR?"
M17PD
POLICE NEW YORK CITY
THE SO-CALLED "ANTI-THEMYSCIRAN TERRORISTS" ARE ACTUALLY THE CHEETAH, GIGANTA, AND DR. PSYCHO...
...AND THEY'VE GOT DONNA TROY.
PSYCHO'S KEEPING HER SUBDUED TELEPATHICALLY--
--WHICH IS PROBABLY WHY HE DIDN'T SEE THROUGH MY DISGUISE.
GIVE YOURSELF A LITTLE CREDIT, TOM.
KLIK
AFTER ALL...
...YOU'RE THE MAN OF A THOUSAND FACES...
...YOU'RE NEMESIS
I'M THE GUY WHO LOST DONNA TROY.
THE LOS CIVILIZ ATION OF THE AM ONS
AND I'M ALSO THE GUY WHO'S GOING TO FIND HER.
NOT BY YOURSELF, YOU'RE NOT.
MEET YOUR NEW PARTNER...

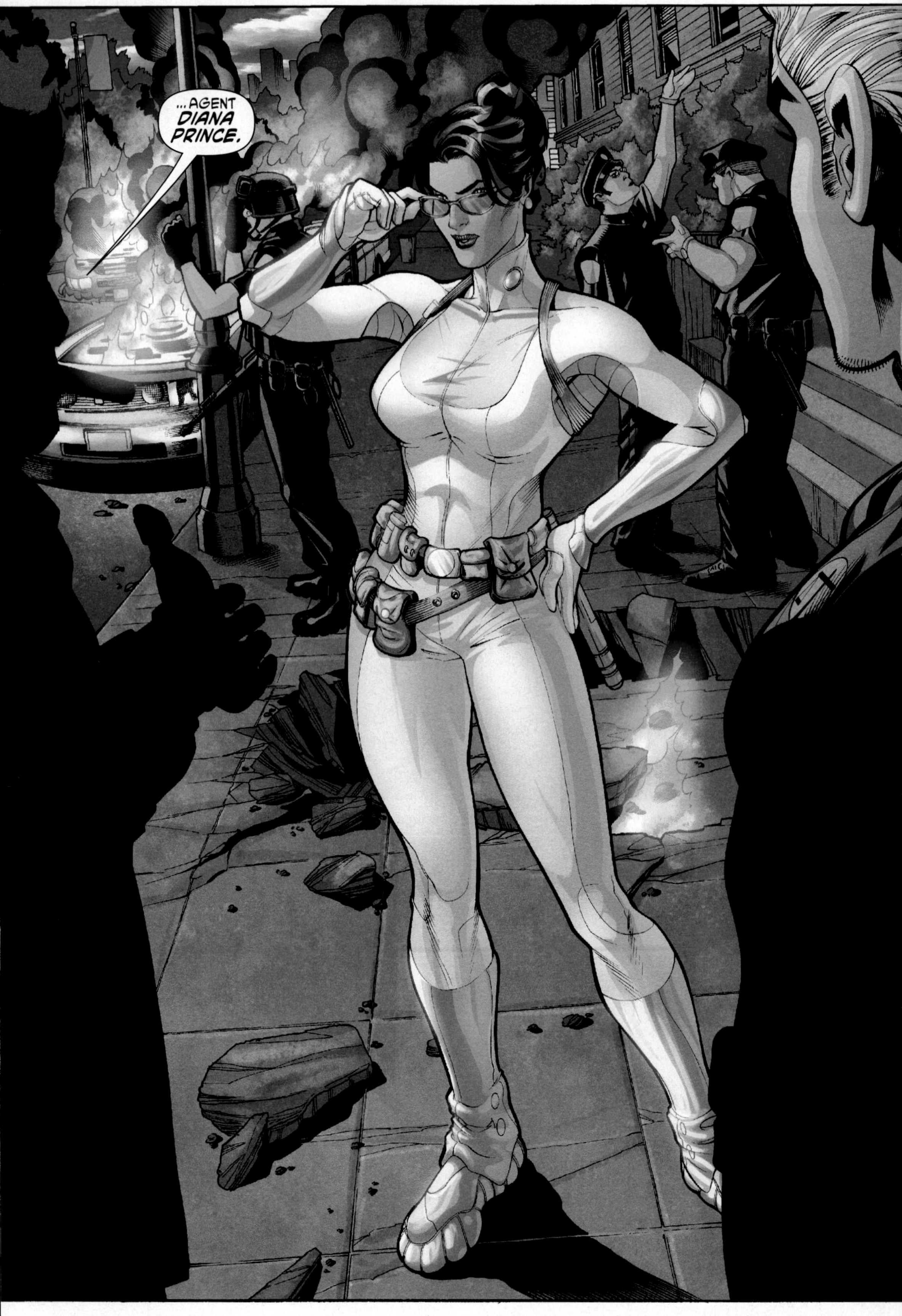
...AGENT DIANA PRINCE.

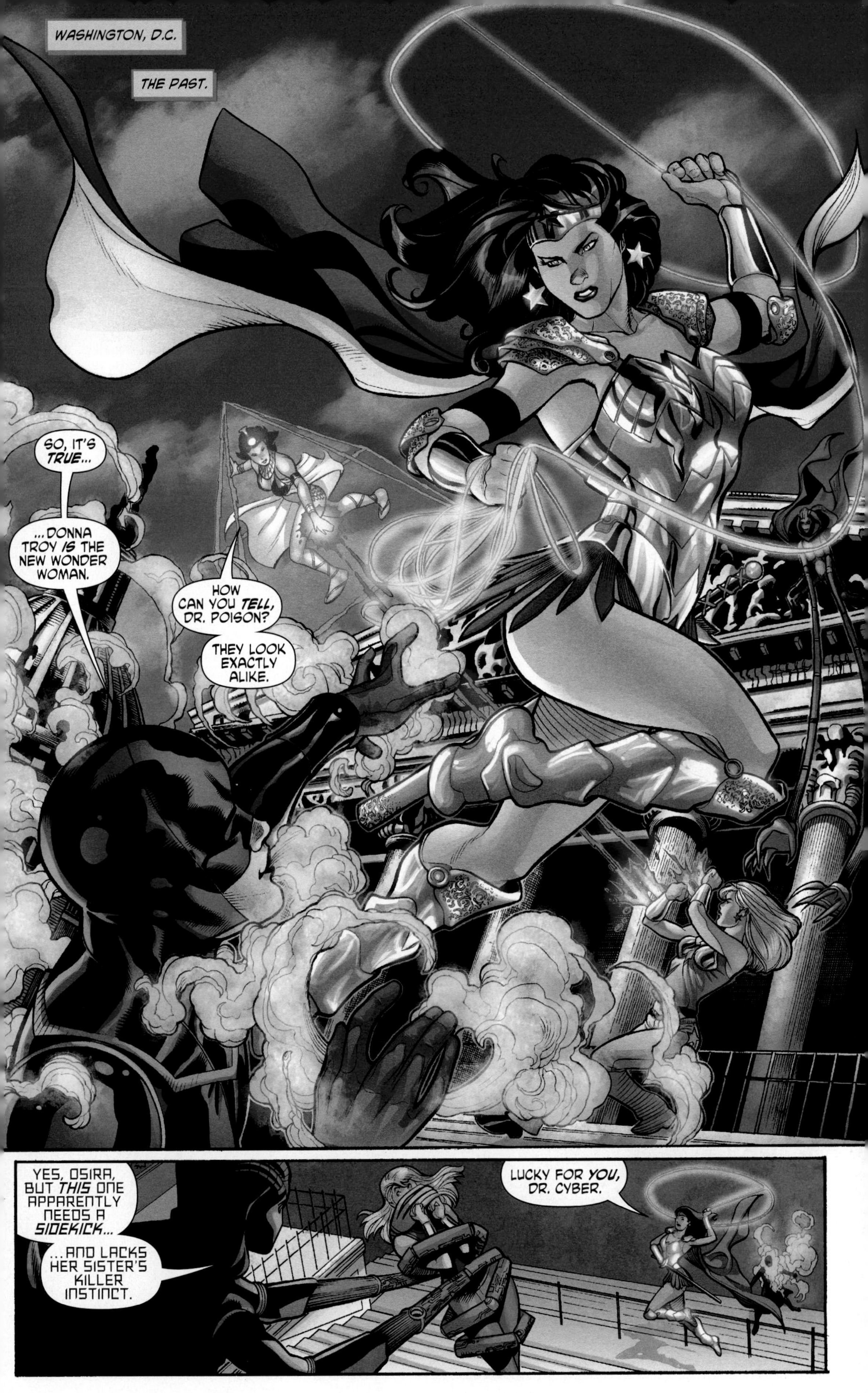
WASHINGTON, D.C.
THE PAST.
SO, IT'S TRUE...
...DONNA TROY IS THE NEW WONDER WOMAN.
HOW CAN YOU TELL, DR. POISON?
THEY LOOK EXACTLY ALIKE.
YES, OSIRA, BUT THIS ONE APPARENTLY NEEDS A SIDEKICK...
...AND LACKS HER SISTER'S KILLER INSTINCT.
LUCKY FOR YOU, DR. CYBER.

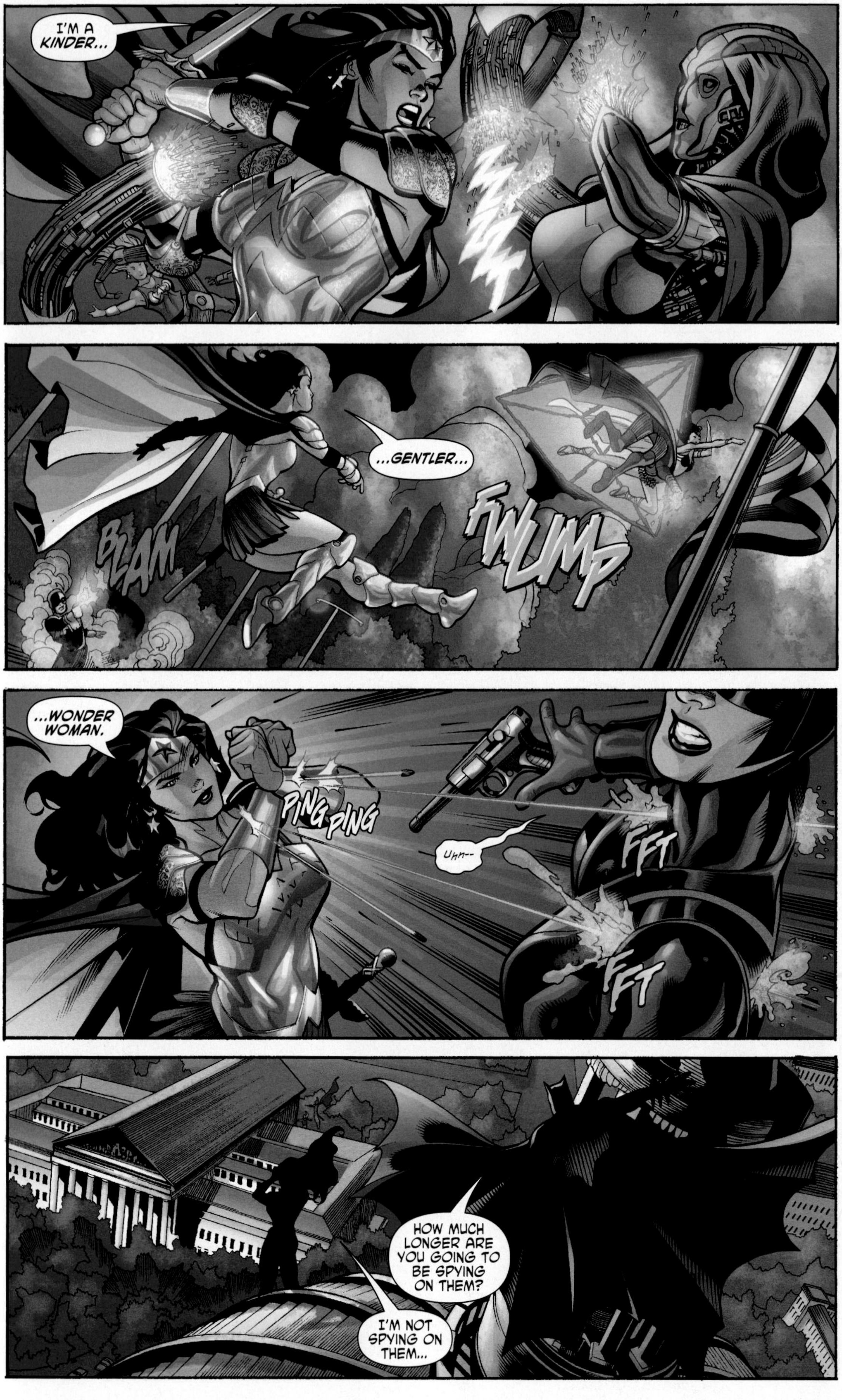

I'M A KINDER...
...GENTLER...
BLAM
FWUMP
...WONDER WOMAN.
PING PING
Uhn--
FFT
FFT
HOW MUCH LONGER ARE YOU GOING TO BE SPYING ON THEM?
I'M NOT SPYING ON THEM...

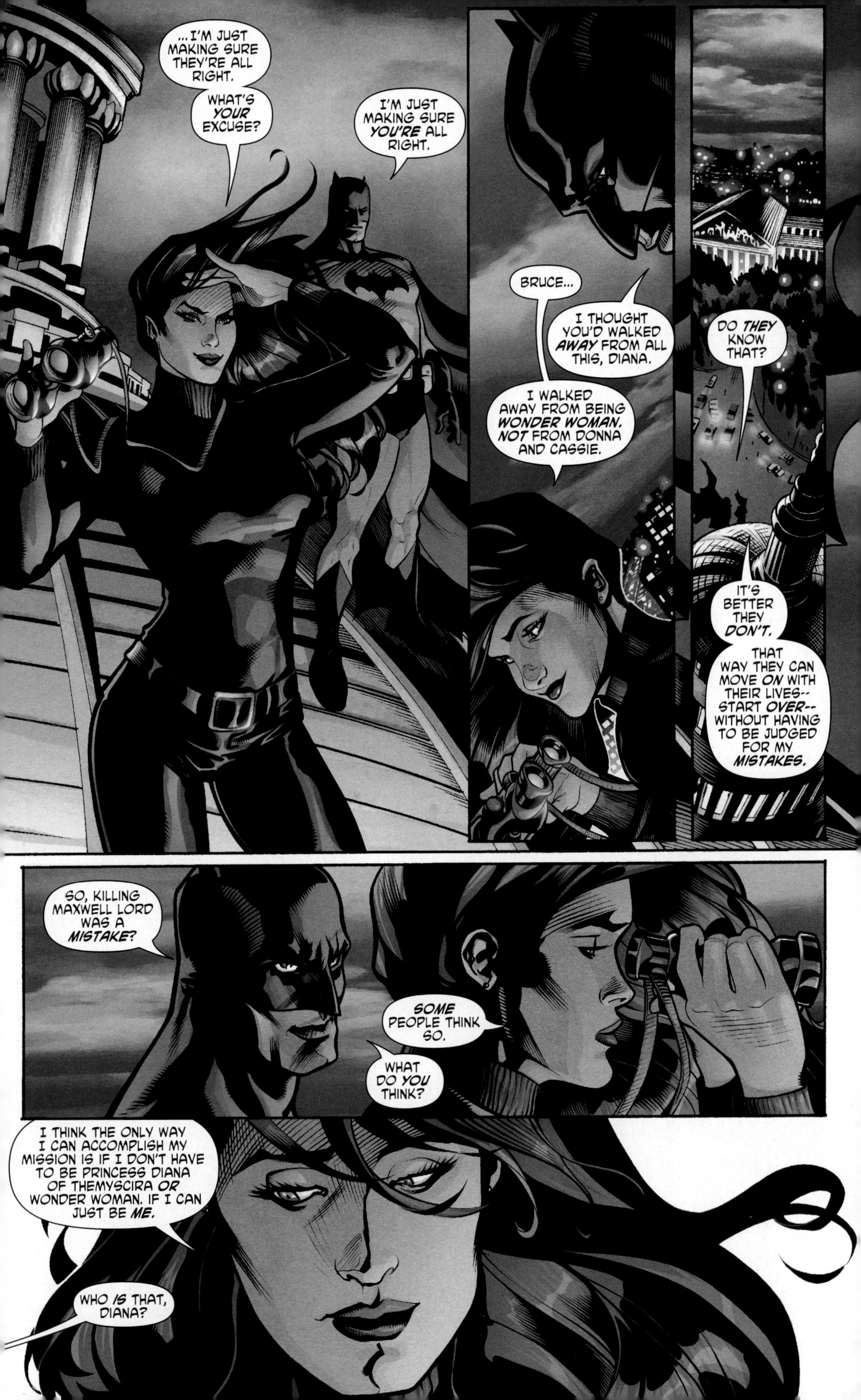
...I'M JUST MAKING SURE THEY'RE ALL RIGHT.
WHAT'S *YOUR* EXCUSE?
I'M JUST MAKING SURE *YOU'RE* ALL RIGHT.
BRUCE...
I THOUGHT YOU'D WALKED *AWAY* FROM ALL THIS, DIANA.
I WALKED AWAY FROM BEING *WONDER WOMAN. NOT* FROM DONNA AND CASSIE.
DO *THEY* KNOW THAT?
IT'S BETTER THEY *DON'T.*
THAT WAY THEY CAN MOVE *ON* WITH THEIR LIVES-- START *OVER*-- WITHOUT HAVING TO BE JUDGED FOR MY *MISTAKES.*
SO, KILLING MAXWELL LORD WAS A *MISTAKE?*
SOME PEOPLE THINK SO.
WHAT DO *YOU* THINK?
I THINK THE ONLY WAY I CAN ACCOMPLISH MY MISSION IS IF I DON'T HAVE TO BE PRINCESS DIANA OF THEMYSCIRA *OR* WONDER WOMAN. IF I CAN JUST BE *ME.*
WHO *IS* THAT, DIANA?

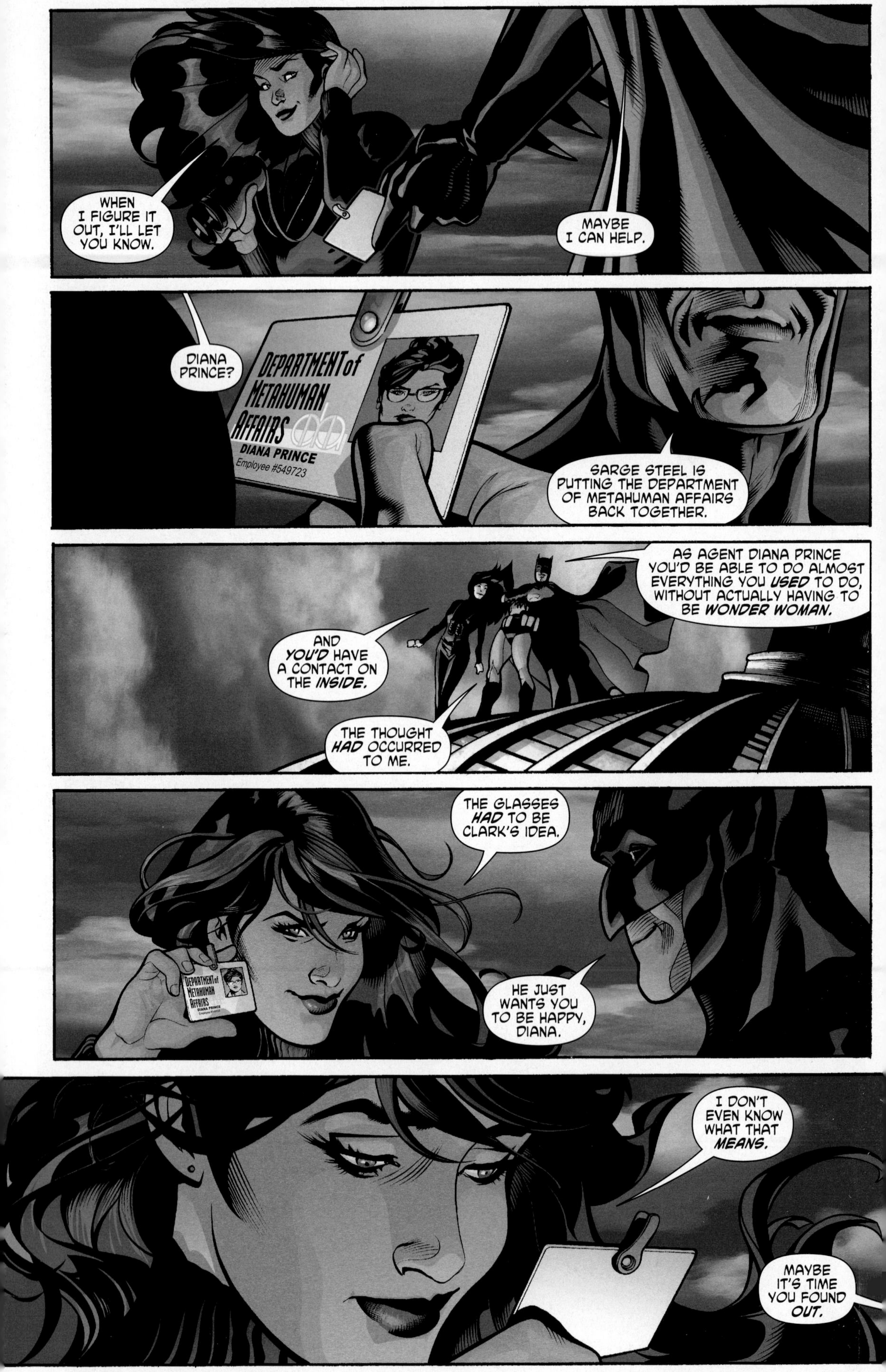
WHEN I FIGURE IT OUT, I'LL LET YOU KNOW.
MAYBE I CAN HELP.
DIANA PRINCE?
DEPARTMENT of METAHUMAN AFFAIRS
DIANA PRINCE
Employee #549723
SARGE STEEL IS PUTTING THE DEPARTMENT OF METAHUMAN AFFAIRS BACK TOGETHER.
AS AGENT DIANA PRINCE YOU'D BE ABLE TO DO ALMOST EVERYTHING YOU USED TO DO, WITHOUT ACTUALLY HAVING TO BE WONDER WOMAN.
AND YOU'D HAVE A CONTACT ON THE INSIDE.
THE THOUGHT HAD OCCURRED TO ME.
THE GLASSES HAD TO BE CLARK'S IDEA.
HE JUST WANTS YOU TO BE HAPPY, DIANA.
I DON'T EVEN KNOW WHAT THAT MEANS.
MAYBE IT'S TIME YOU FOUND OUT.

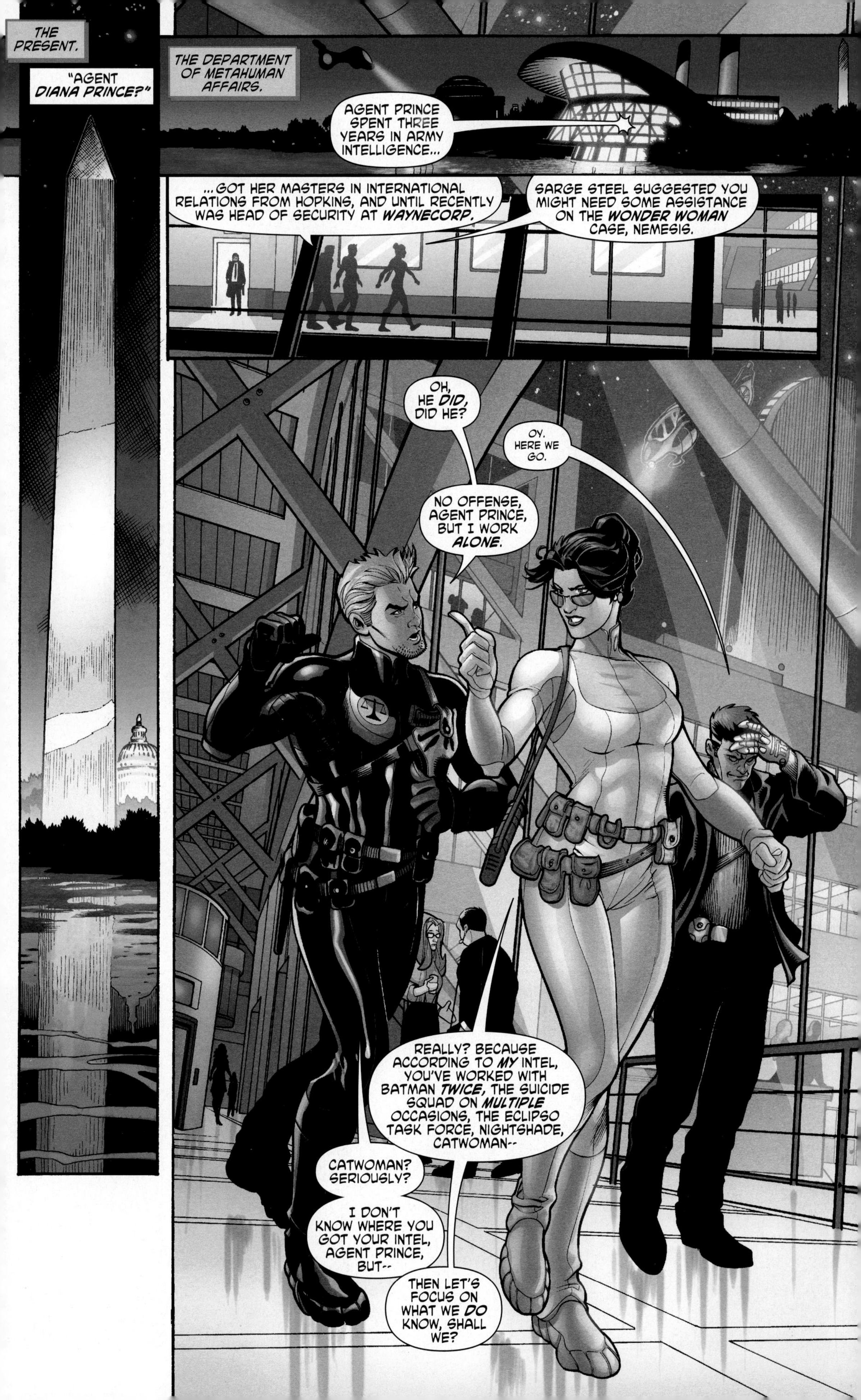
THE PRESENT.
"AGENT DIANA PRINCE?"
THE DEPARTMENT OF METAHUMAN AFFAIRS.
AGENT PRINCE SPENT THREE YEARS IN ARMY INTELLIGENCE...
...GOT HER MASTERS IN INTERNATIONAL RELATIONS FROM HOPKINS, AND UNTIL RECENTLY WAS HEAD OF SECURITY AT WAYNECORP.
SARGE STEEL SUGGESTED YOU MIGHT NEED SOME ASSISTANCE ON THE WONDER WOMAN CASE, NEMESIS.
OH, HE DID, DID HE?
OY. HERE WE GO.
NO OFFENSE, AGENT PRINCE, BUT I WORK ALONE.
REALLY? BECAUSE ACCORDING TO MY INTEL, YOU'VE WORKED WITH BATMAN TWICE, THE SUICIDE SQUAD ON MULTIPLE OCCASIONS, THE ECLIPSO TASK FORCE, NIGHTSHADE, CATWOMAN--
CATWOMAN? SERIOUSLY?
I DON'T KNOW WHERE YOU GOT YOUR INTEL, AGENT PRINCE, BUT--
THEN LET'S FOCUS ON WHAT WE DO KNOW, SHALL WE?

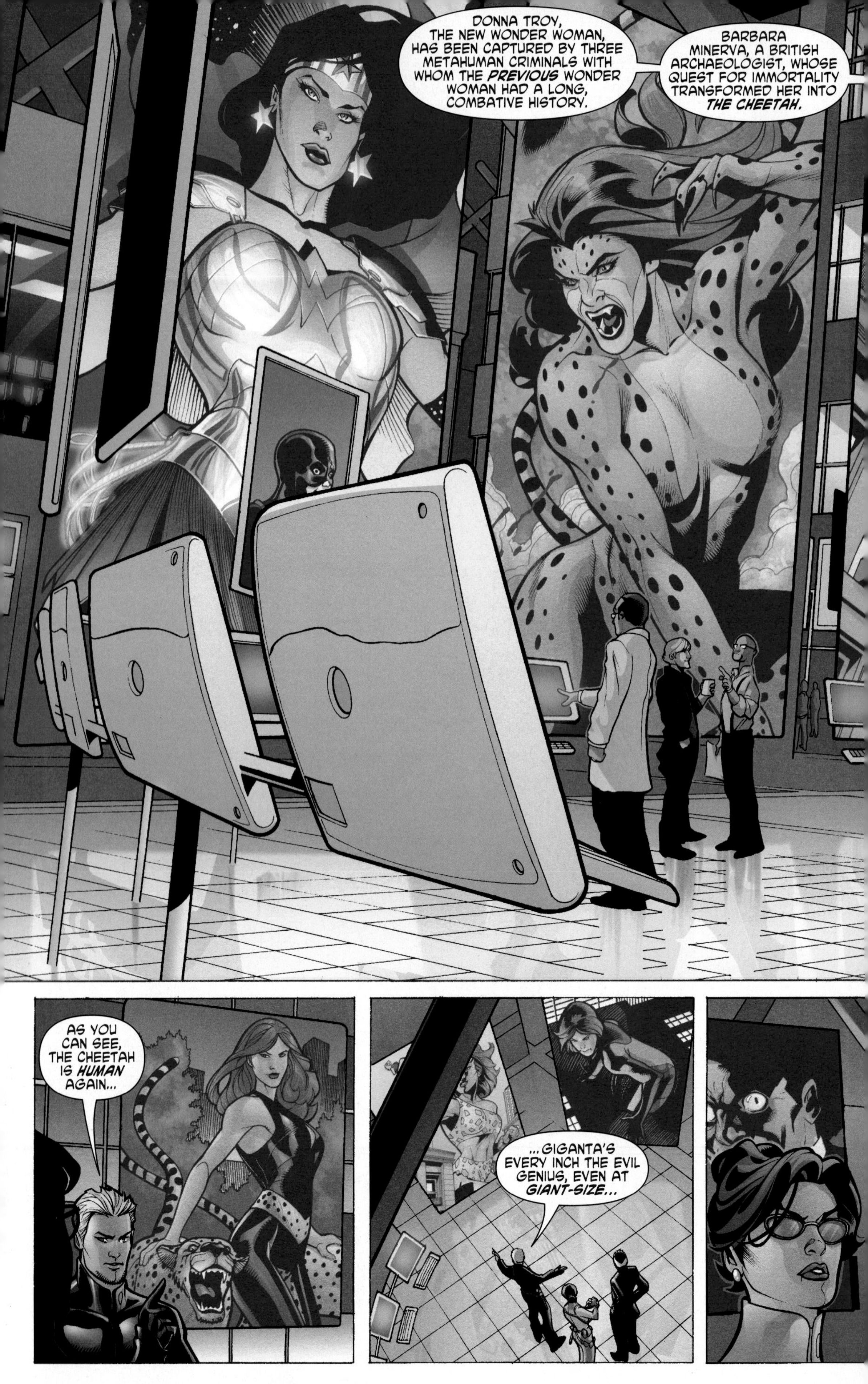
DONNA TROY, THE NEW WONDER WOMAN, HAS BEEN CAPTURED BY THREE METAHUMAN CRIMINALS WITH WHOM THE *PREVIOUS* WONDER WOMAN HAD A LONG, COMBATIVE HISTORY.
BARBARA MINERVA, A BRITISH ARCHAEOLOGIST, WHOSE QUEST FOR IMMORTALITY TRANSFORMED HER INTO ***THE CHEETAH.***
AS YOU CAN SEE, THE CHEETAH IS *HUMAN* AGAIN...
...GIGANTA'S EVERY INCH THE EVIL GENIUS, EVEN AT ***GIANT-SIZE...***

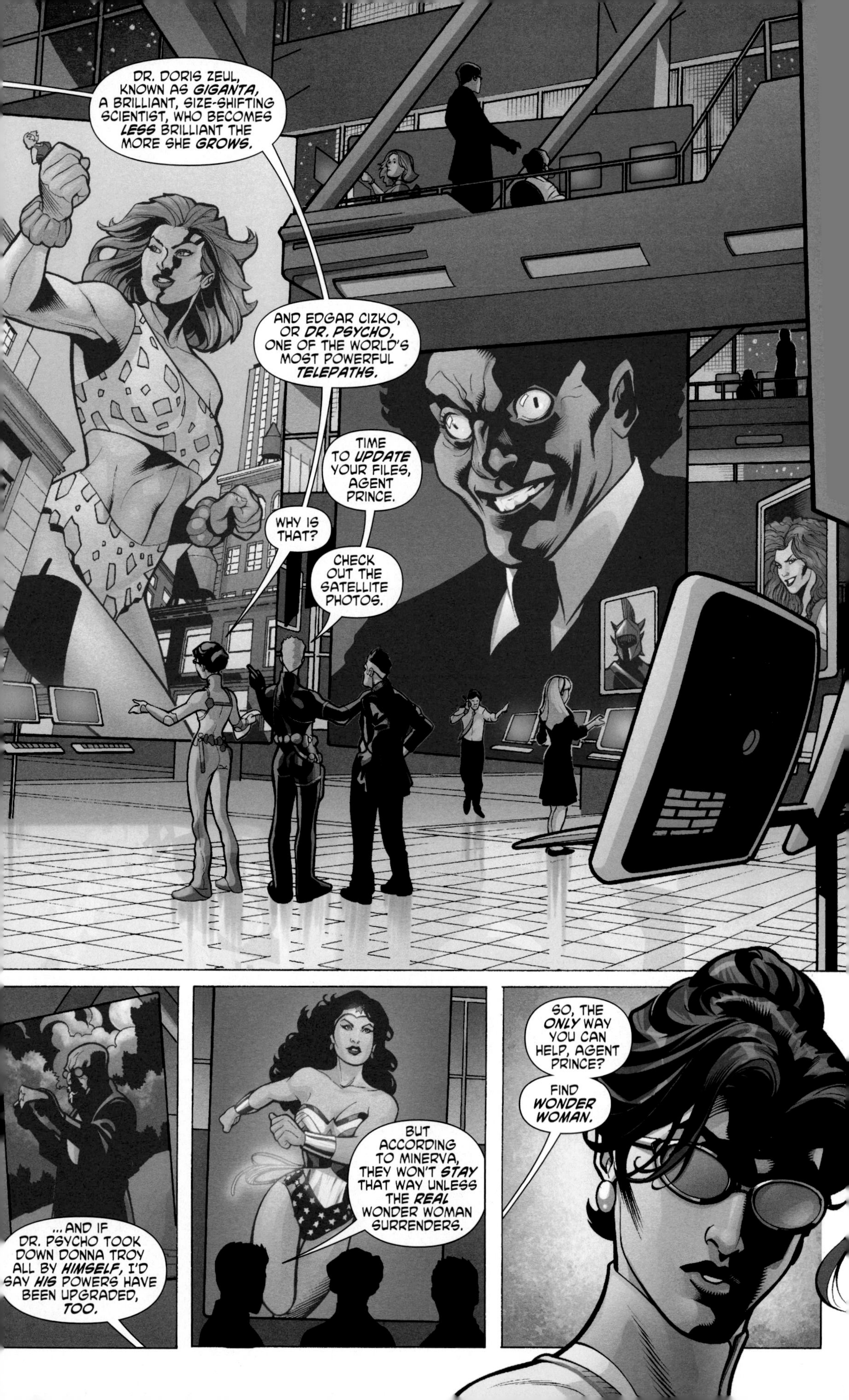
DR. DORIS ZEUL, KNOWN AS GIGANTA, A BRILLIANT, SIZE-SHIFTING SCIENTIST, WHO BECOMES LESS BRILLIANT THE MORE SHE GROWS.
AND EDGAR CIZKO, OR DR. PSYCHO, ONE OF THE WORLD'S MOST POWERFUL TELEPATHS.
TIME TO UPDATE YOUR FILES, AGENT PRINCE.
WHY IS THAT?
CHECK OUT THE SATELLITE PHOTOS.
...AND IF DR. PSYCHO TOOK DOWN DONNA TROY ALL BY HIMSELF, I'D SAY HIS POWERS HAVE BEEN UPGRADED, TOO.
BUT ACCORDING TO MINERVA, THEY WON'T STAY THAT WAY UNLESS THE REAL WONDER WOMAN SURRENDERS.
SO, THE ONLY WAY YOU CAN HELP, AGENT PRINCE?
FIND WONDER WOMAN.

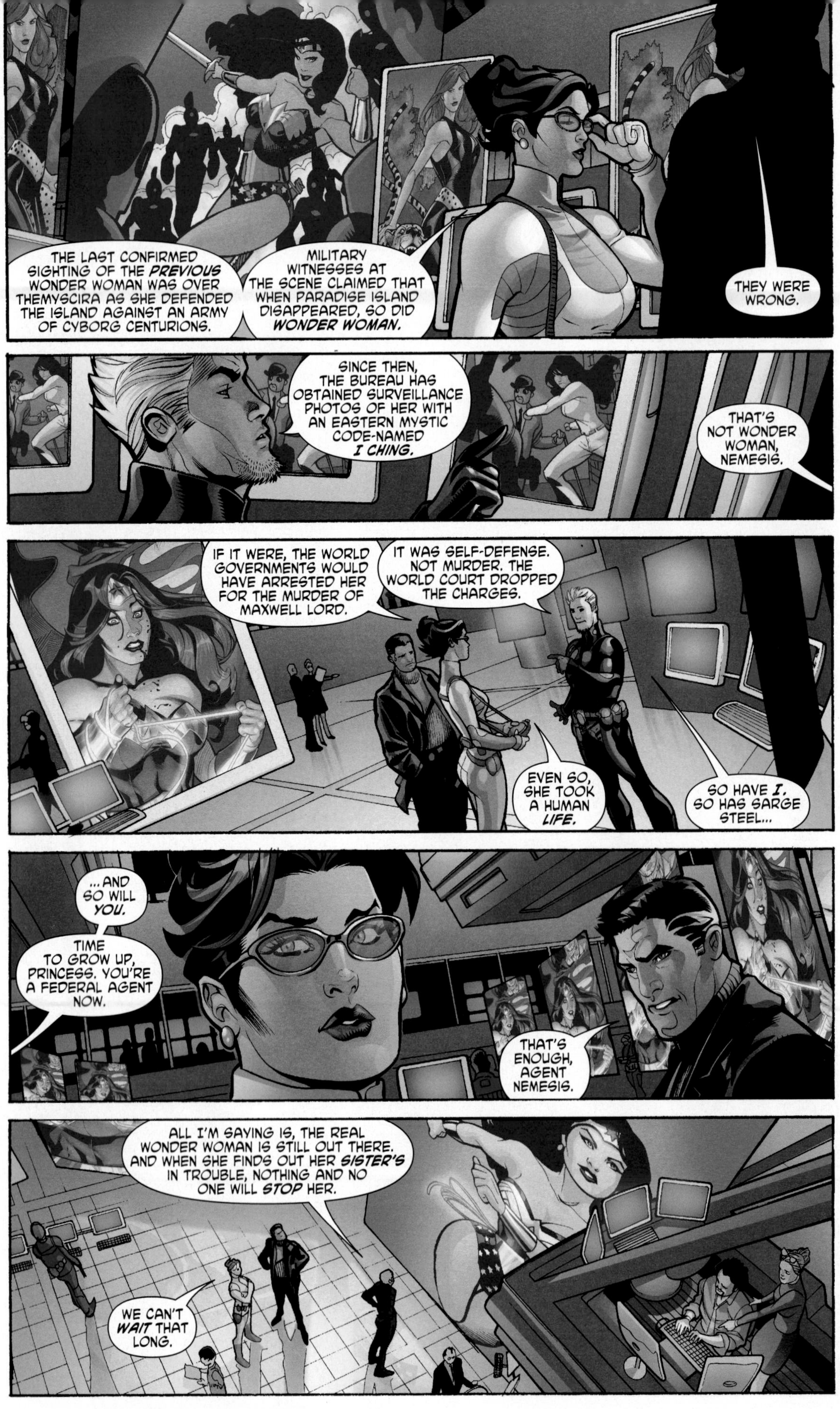
THE LAST CONFIRMED SIGHTING OF THE PREVIOUS WONDER WOMAN WAS OVER THEMYSCIRA AS SHE DEFENDED THE ISLAND AGAINST AN ARMY OF CYBORG CENTURIONS.
MILITARY WITNESSES AT THE SCENE CLAIMED THAT WHEN PARADISE ISLAND DISAPPEARED, SO DID WONDER WOMAN.
THEY WERE WRONG.
SINCE THEN, THE BUREAU HAS OBTAINED SURVEILLANCE PHOTOS OF HER WITH AN EASTERN MYSTIC CODE-NAMED I CHING.
THAT'S NOT WONDER WOMAN, NEMESIS.
IF IT WERE, THE WORLD GOVERNMENTS WOULD HAVE ARRESTED HER FOR THE MURDER OF MAXWELL LORD.
IT WAS SELF-DEFENSE. NOT MURDER. THE WORLD COURT DROPPED THE CHARGES.
EVEN SO, SHE TOOK A HUMAN LIFE.
SO HAVE I. SO HAS SARGE STEEL...
...AND SO WILL YOU.
TIME TO GROW UP, PRINCESS. YOU'RE A FEDERAL AGENT NOW.
THAT'S ENOUGH, AGENT NEMESIS.
ALL I'M SAYING IS, THE REAL WONDER WOMAN IS STILL OUT THERE. AND WHEN SHE FINDS OUT HER SISTER'S IN TROUBLE, NOTHING AND NO ONE WILL STOP HER.
WE CAN'T WAIT THAT LONG.

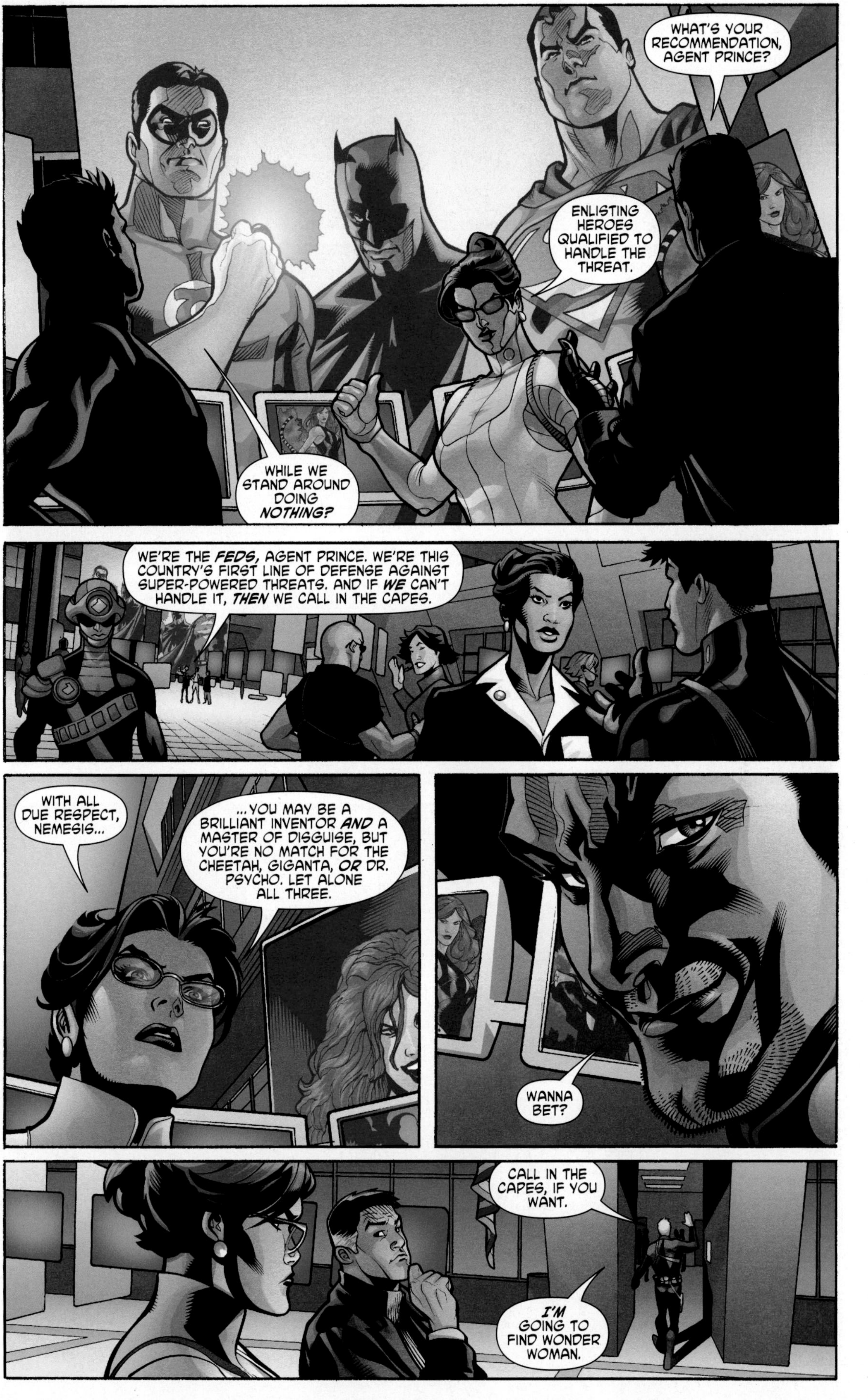
WHAT'S YOUR RECOMMENDATION, AGENT PRINCE?
ENLISTING HEROES QUALIFIED TO HANDLE THE THREAT.
WHILE WE STAND AROUND DOING *NOTHING?*
WE'RE THE *FEDS,* AGENT PRINCE. WE'RE THIS COUNTRY'S FIRST LINE OF DEFENSE AGAINST SUPER-POWERED THREATS. AND IF *WE* CAN'T HANDLE IT, *THEN* WE CALL IN THE CAPES.
WITH ALL DUE RESPECT, NEMESIS...
...YOU MAY BE A BRILLIANT INVENTOR *AND* A MASTER OF DISGUISE, BUT YOU'RE NO MATCH FOR THE CHEETAH, GIGANTA, *OR* DR. PSYCHO. LET ALONE ALL THREE.
WANNA BET?
CALL IN THE CAPES, IF YOU WANT.
I'M GOING TO FIND WONDER WOMAN.

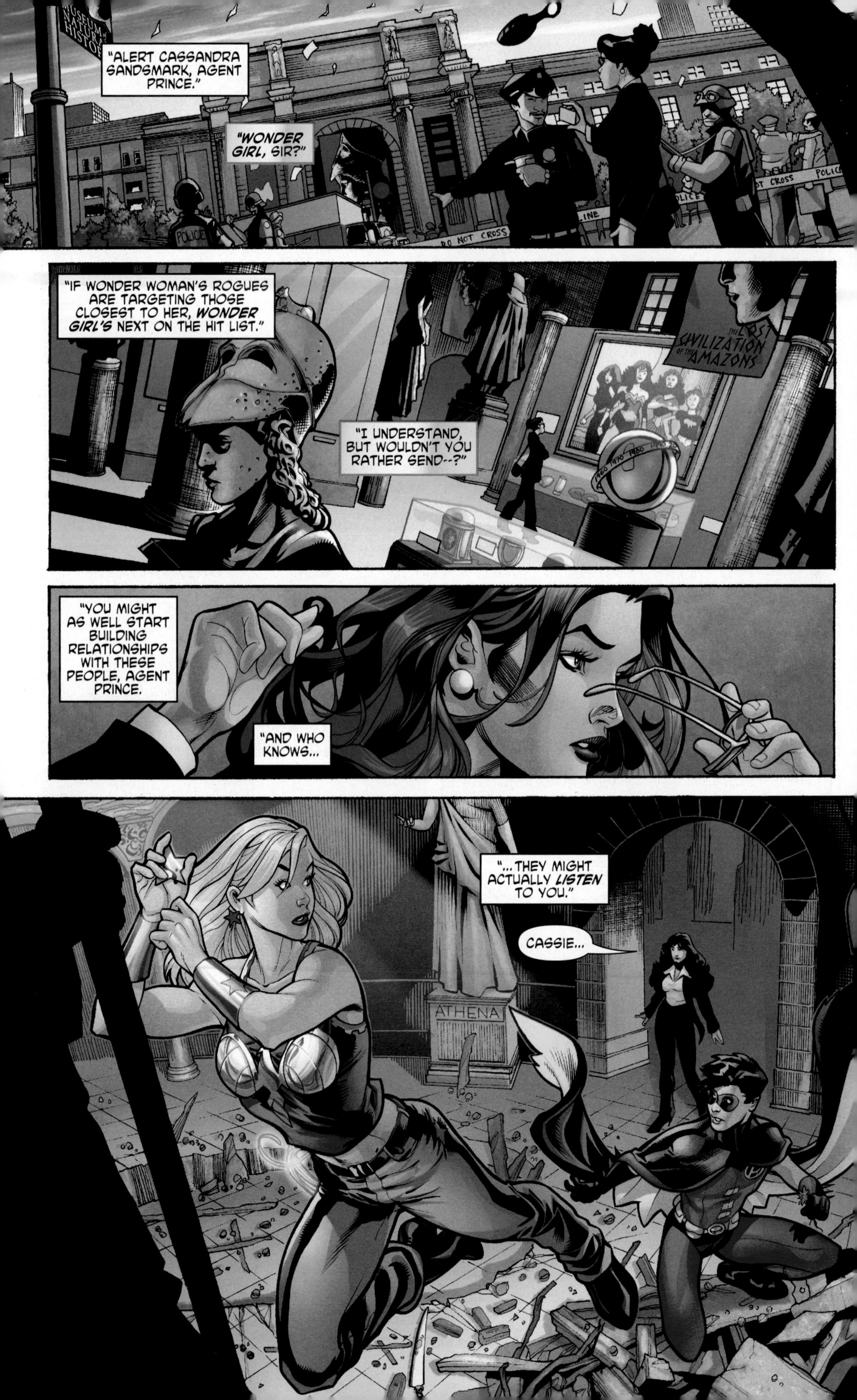

MUSEUM of NATURAL HISTO
"ALERT CASSANDRA SANDSMARK, AGENT PRINCE."
"WONDER GIRL, SIR?"
POLICE
DO NOT CROSS
LINE
POLICE
NOT CROSS
POLICE
"IF WONDER WOMAN'S ROGUES ARE TARGETING THOSE CLOSEST TO HER, WONDER GIRL'S NEXT ON THE HIT LIST."
THE LOST CIVILIZATION OF THE AMAZONS
"I UNDERSTAND, BUT WOULDN'T YOU RATHER SEND--?"
"YOU MIGHT AS WELL START BUILDING RELATIONSHIPS WITH THESE PEOPLE, AGENT PRINCE.
"AND WHO KNOWS...
"...THEY MIGHT ACTUALLY LISTEN TO YOU."
CASSIE...
ATHENA

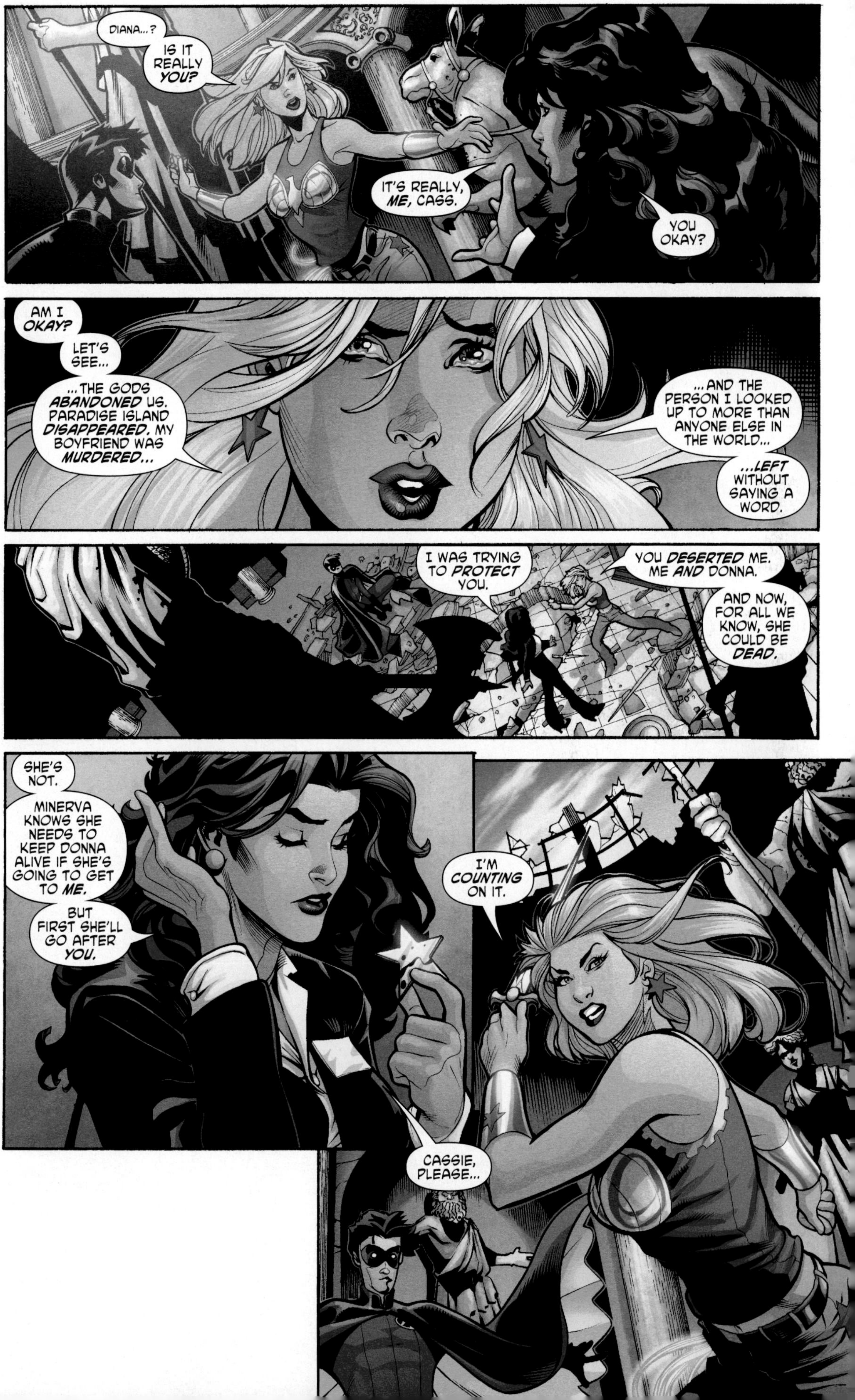
DIANA...?
IS IT REALLY YOU?
IT'S REALLY, ME, CASS.
YOU OKAY?
AM I OKAY?
LET'S SEE...
...THE GODS ABANDONED US. PARADISE ISLAND DISAPPEARED. MY BOYFRIEND WAS MURDERED...
...AND THE PERSON I LOOKED UP TO MORE THAN ANYONE ELSE IN THE WORLD...
...LEFT WITHOUT SAYING A WORD.
I WAS TRYING TO PROTECT YOU.
YOU DESERTED ME. ME AND DONNA.
AND NOW, FOR ALL WE KNOW, SHE COULD BE DEAD.
SHE'S NOT.
MINERVA KNOWS SHE NEEDS TO KEEP DONNA ALIVE IF SHE'S GOING TO GET TO ME.
BUT FIRST SHE'LL GO AFTER YOU.
I'M COUNTING ON IT.
CASSIE, PLEASE...

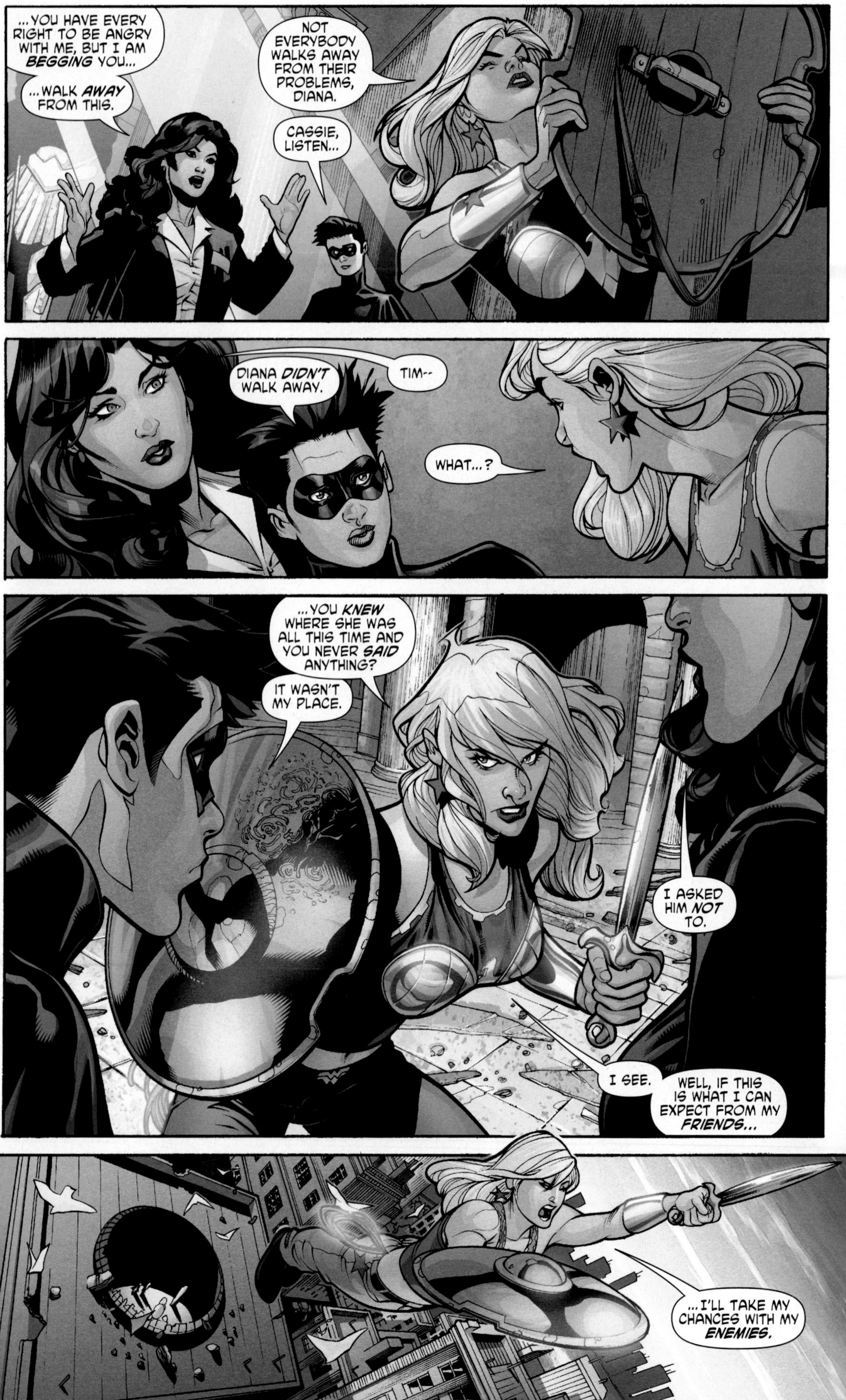
...YOU HAVE EVERY RIGHT TO BE ANGRY WITH ME, BUT I AM BEGGING YOU...
...WALK AWAY FROM THIS.
NOT EVERYBODY WALKS AWAY FROM THEIR PROBLEMS, DIANA.
CASSIE, LISTEN...
DIANA DIDN'T WALK AWAY.
TIM--
WHAT...?
...YOU KNEW WHERE SHE WAS ALL THIS TIME AND YOU NEVER SAID ANYTHING?
IT WASN'T MY PLACE.
I ASKED HIM NOT TO.
I SEE.
WELL, IF THIS IS WHAT I CAN EXPECT FROM MY FRIENDS...
...I'LL TAKE MY CHANCES WITH MY ENEMIES.

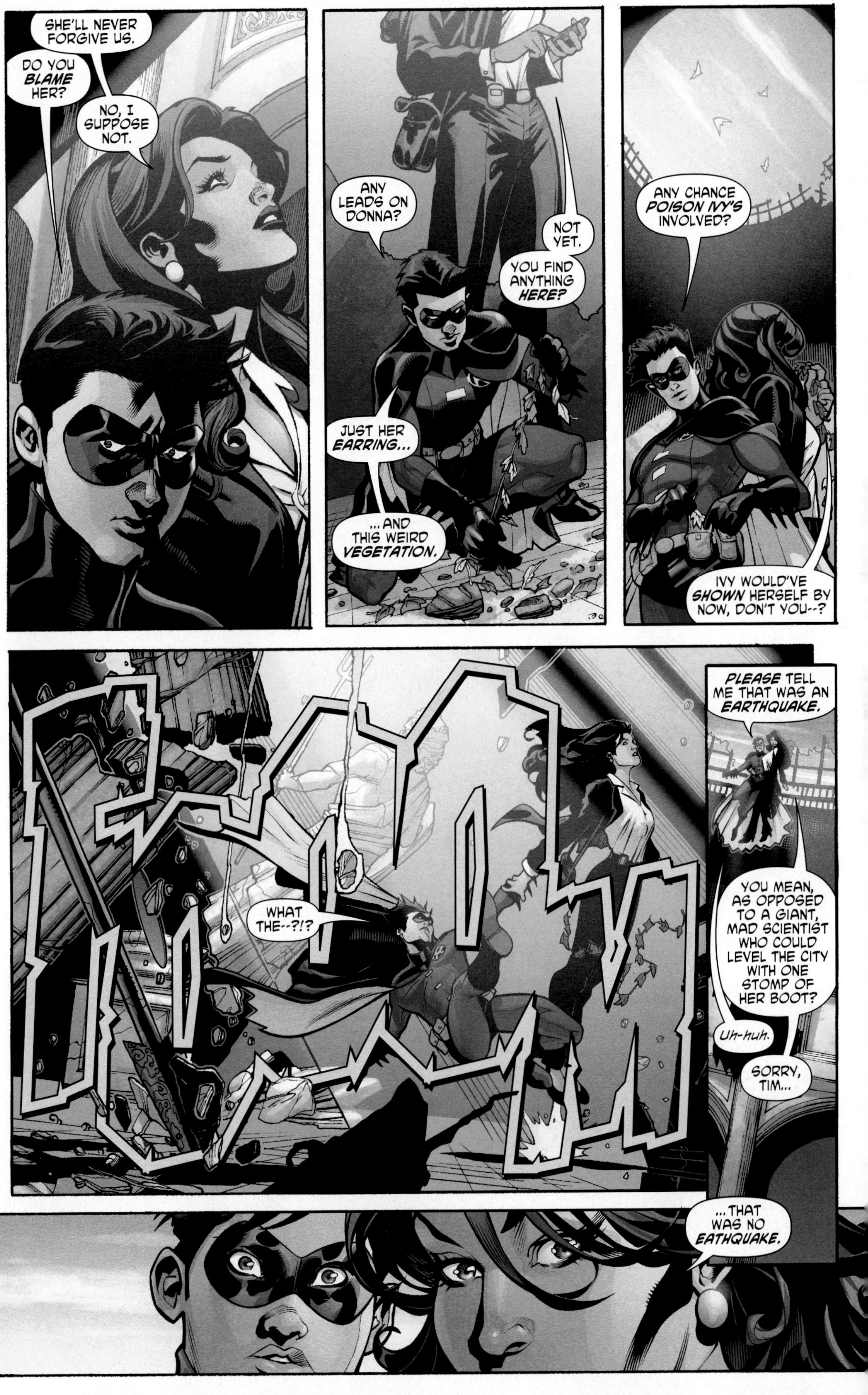
SHE'LL NEVER FORGIVE US.
DO YOU BLAME HER?
NO, I SUPPOSE NOT.
ANY LEADS ON DONNA?
NOT YET.
YOU FIND ANYTHING HERE?
JUST HER EARRING...
...AND THIS WEIRD VEGETATION.
ANY CHANCE POISON IVY'S INVOLVED?
IVY WOULD'VE SHOWN HERSELF BY NOW, DON'T YOU--?
WHAT THE--?!?
PLEASE TELL ME THAT WAS AN EARTHQUAKE.
YOU MEAN, AS OPPOSED TO A GIANT, MAD SCIENTIST WHO COULD LEVEL THE CITY WITH ONE STOMP OF HER BOOT?
Uh-huh.
SORRY, TIM...
...THAT WAS NO EATHQUAKE.

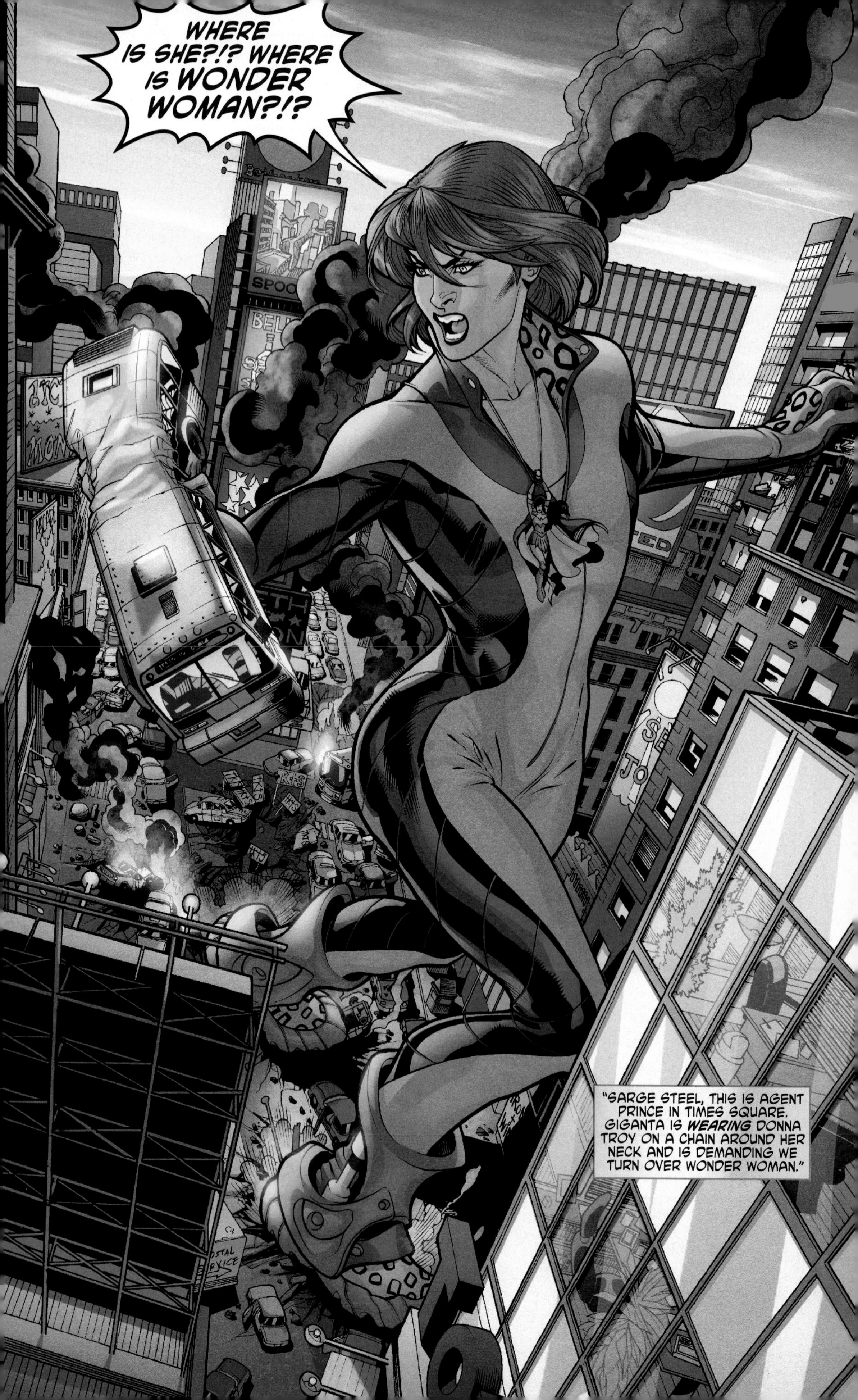
WHERE IS SHE?!? WHERE IS WONDER WOMAN?!?
"SARGE STEEL, THIS IS AGENT PRINCE IN TIMES SQUARE. GIGANTA IS WEARING DONNA TROY ON A CHAIN AROUND HER NECK AND IS DEMANDING WE TURN OVER WONDER WOMAN."

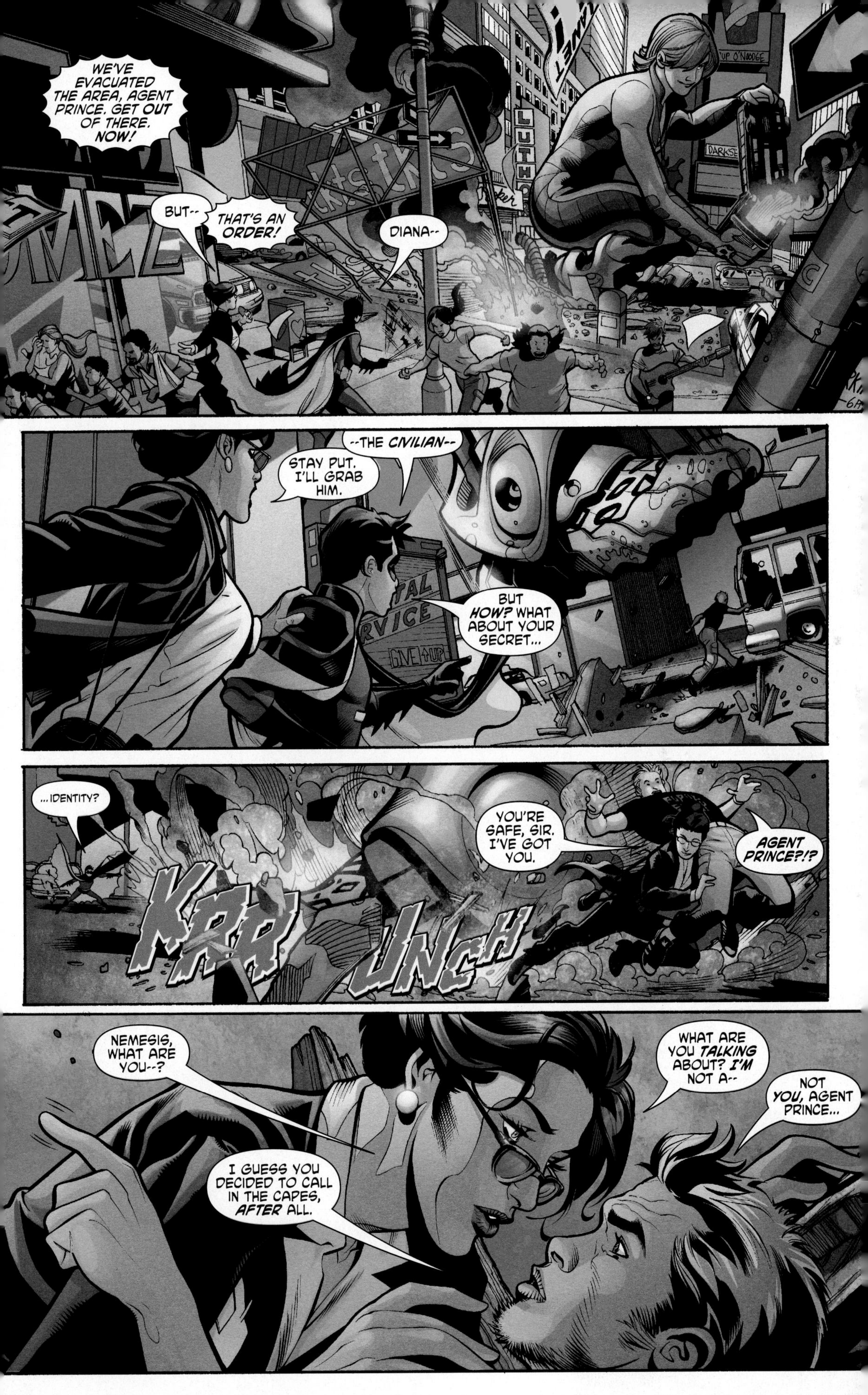
WE'VE EVACUATED THE AREA, AGENT PRINCE. GET OUT OF THERE. NOW!
BUT--
THAT'S AN ORDER!
DIANA--
--THE CIVILIAN--
STAY PUT. I'LL GRAB HIM.
BUT HOW? WHAT ABOUT YOUR SECRET...
...IDENTITY?
YOU'RE SAFE, SIR. I'VE GOT YOU.
AGENT PRINCE?!?
KRRUNCH
NEMESIS, WHAT ARE YOU--?
WHAT ARE YOU TALKING ABOUT? I'M NOT A--
NOT YOU, AGENT PRINCE...
I GUESS YOU DECIDED TO CALL IN THE CAPES, AFTER ALL.

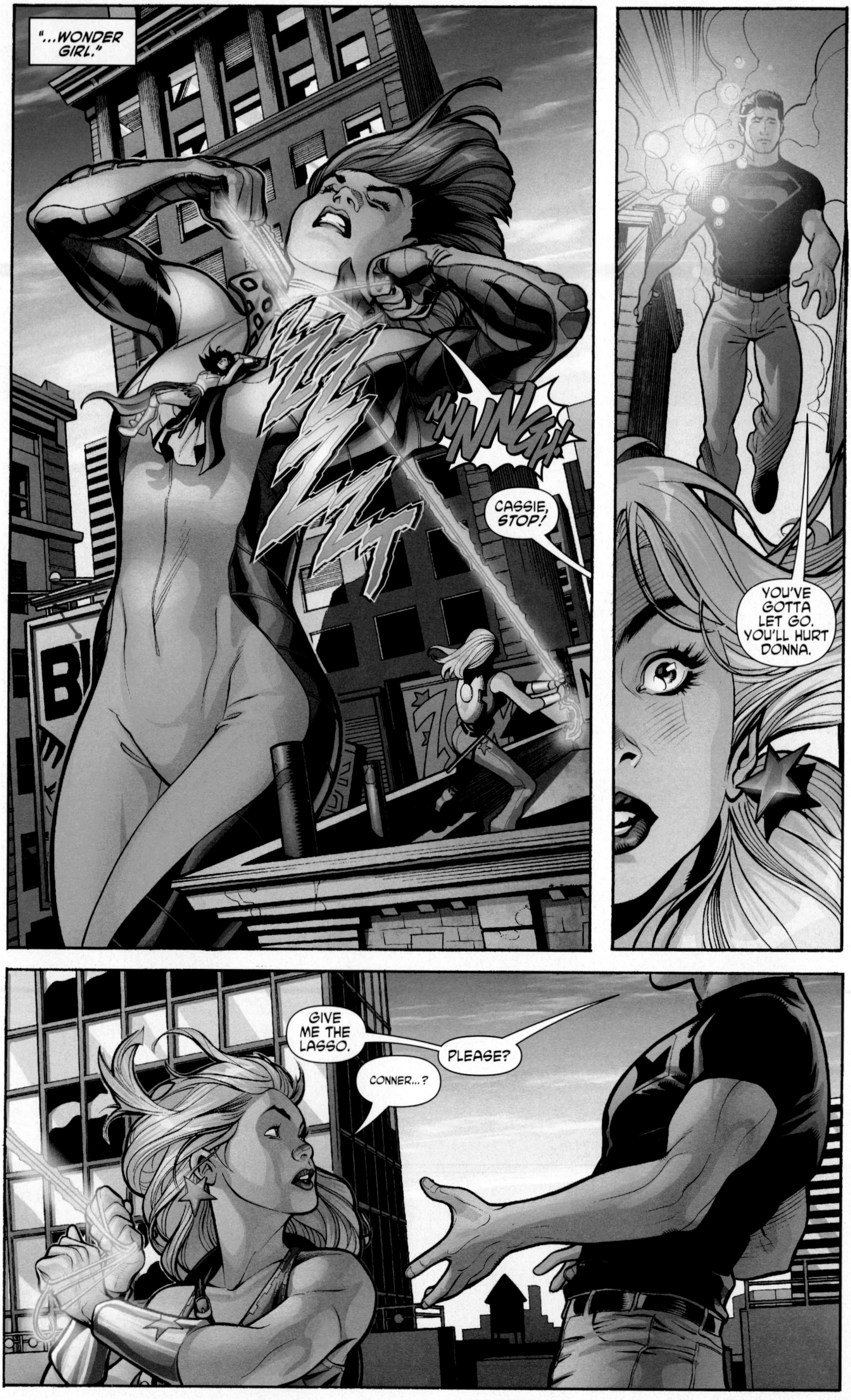
"...WONDER GIRL."
ZZZZT
NNNNNGH!
CASSIE, STOP!
YOU'VE GOTTA LET GO. YOU'LL HURT DONNA.
GIVE ME THE LASSO.
PLEASE?
CONNER...?

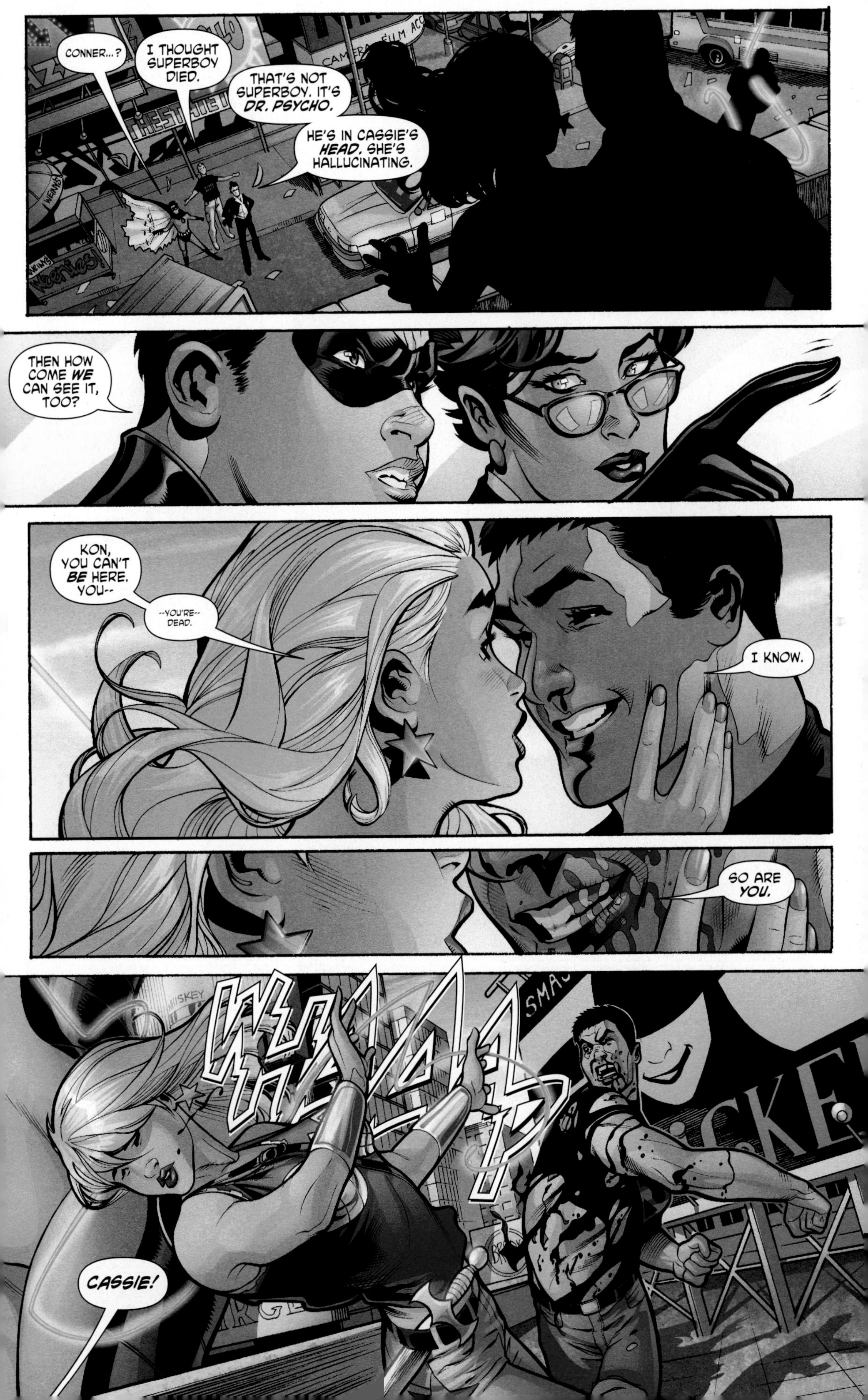
CONNER...?
I THOUGHT SUPERBOY DIED.
THAT'S NOT SUPERBOY. IT'S DR. PSYCHO.
HE'S IN CASSIE'S HEAD. SHE'S HALLUCINATING.
THEN HOW COME WE CAN SEE IT, TOO?
KON, YOU CAN'T BE HERE. YOU--
--YOU'RE-- DEAD.
I KNOW.
SO ARE YOU.
WHAM
CASSIE!

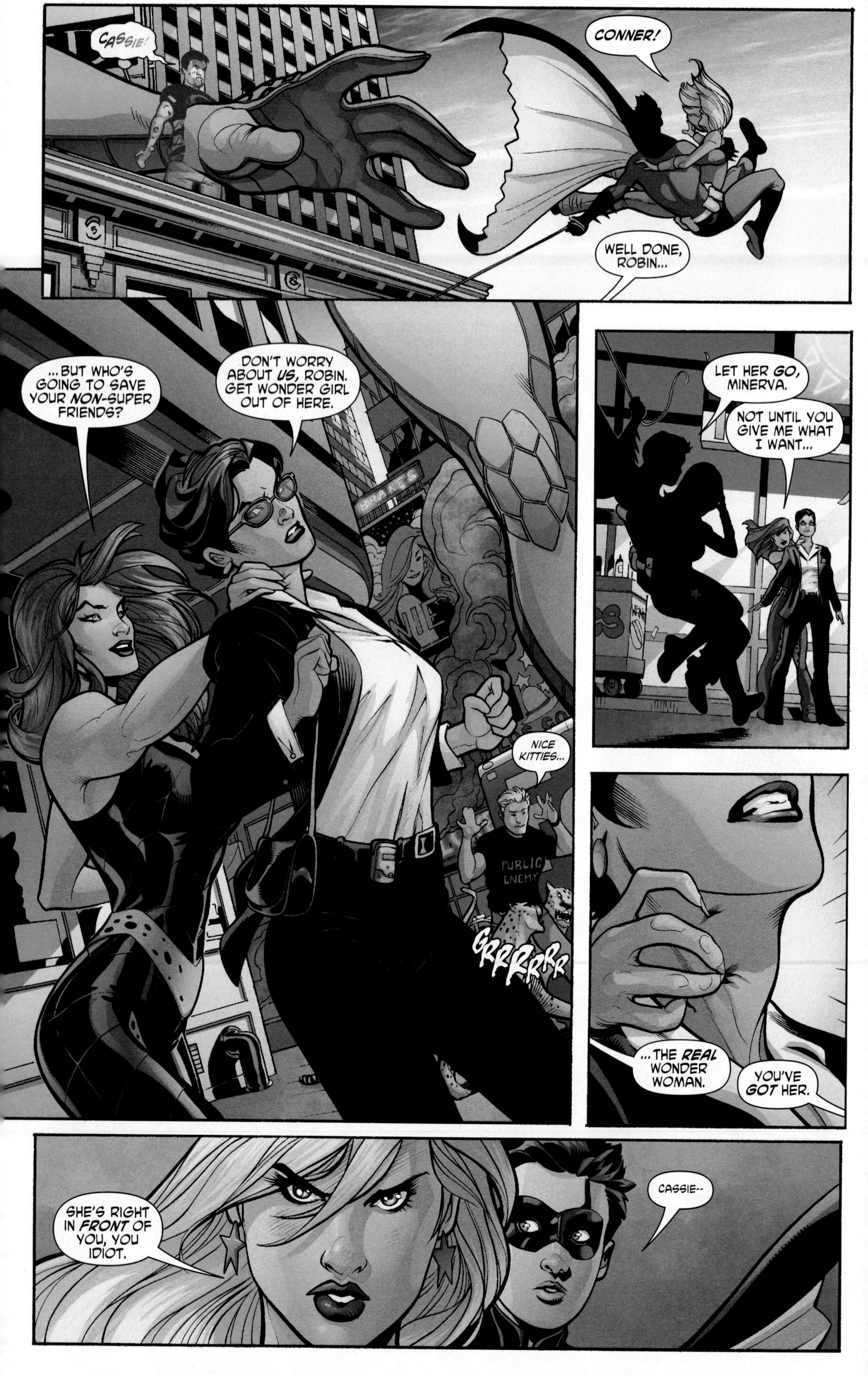
CASSIE!
CONNER!
WELL DONE, ROBIN...
...BUT WHO'S GOING TO SAVE YOUR NON-SUPER FRIENDS?
DON'T WORRY ABOUT US, ROBIN. GET WONDER GIRL OUT OF HERE.
BRAKES
NICE KITTIES...
PUBLIC ENEMY
GRRRRRR
LET HER GO, MINERVA.
NOT UNTIL YOU GIVE ME WHAT I WANT...
...THE REAL WONDER WOMAN.
YOU'VE GOT HER.
SHE'S RIGHT IN FRONT OF YOU, YOU IDIOT.
CASSIE--

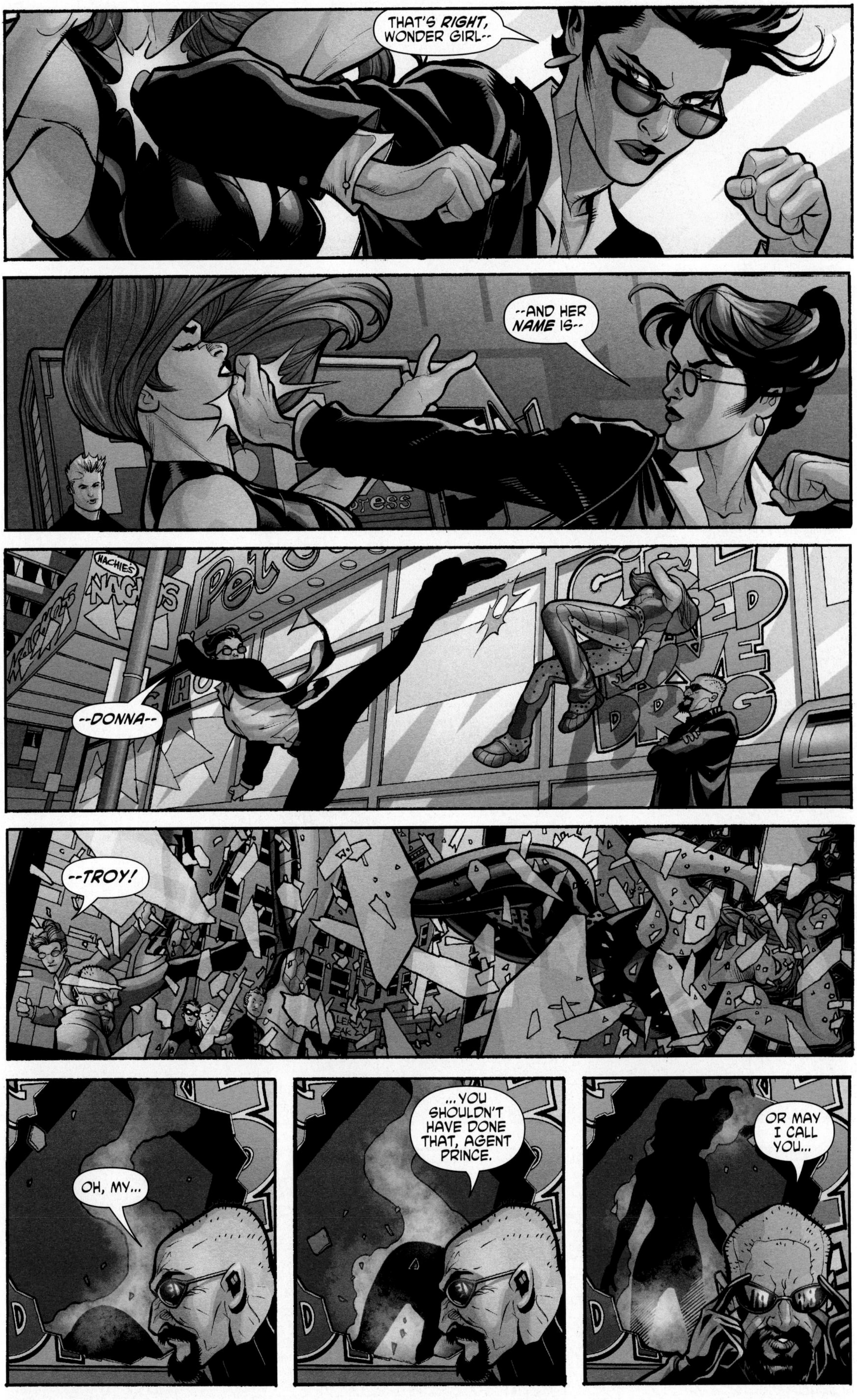
THAT'S *RIGHT*, WONDER GIRL--
--AND HER *NAME* IS--
NACHIES
--DONNA--
--TROY!
OH, MY...
...YOU SHOULDN'T HAVE DONE THAT, AGENT PRINCE.
OR MAY I CALL YOU...

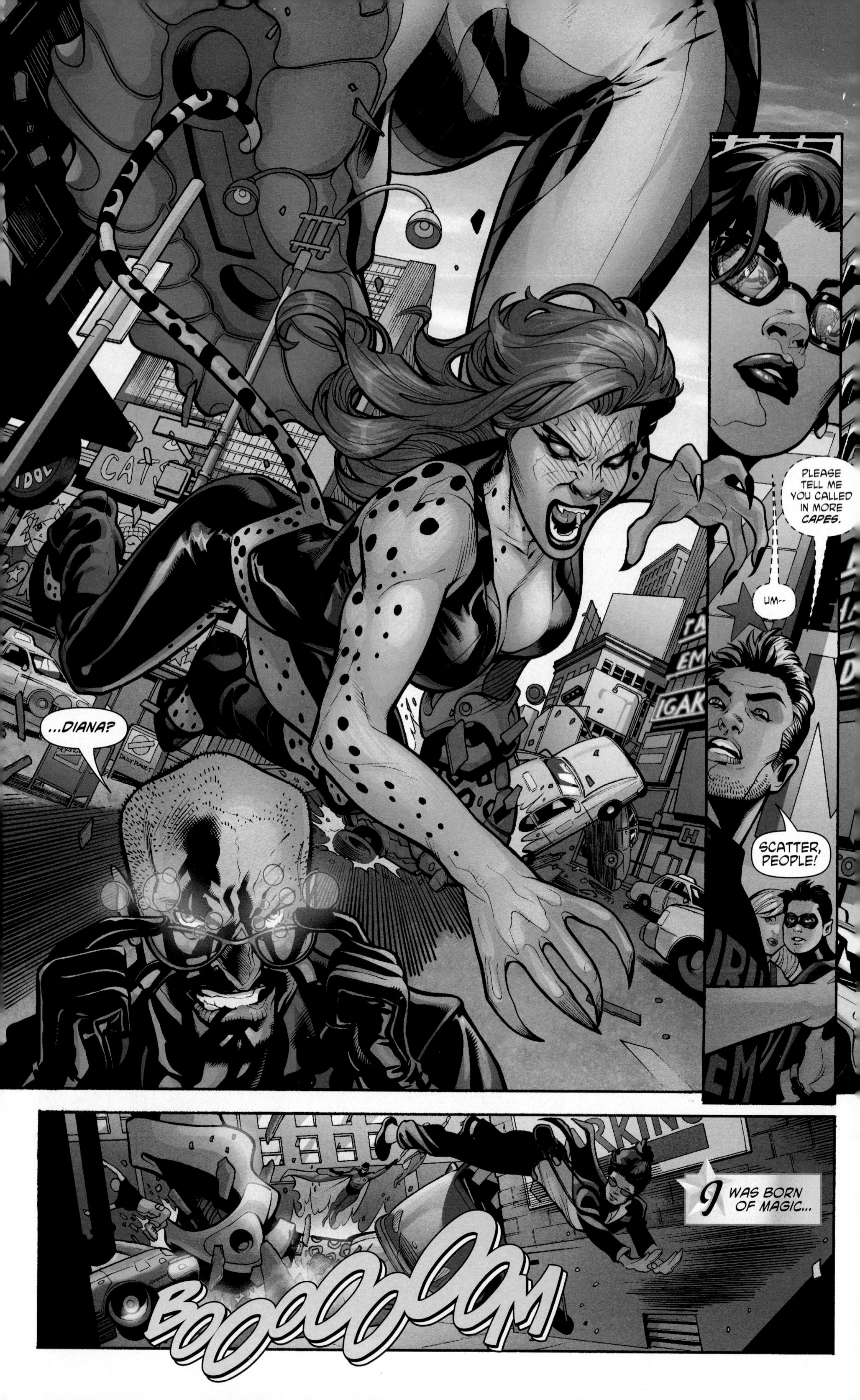

PLEASE TELL ME YOU CALLED IN MORE CAPES.
UM--
...DIANA?
SCATTER, PEOPLE!
I WAS BORN OF MAGIC...
BOOOOOOM

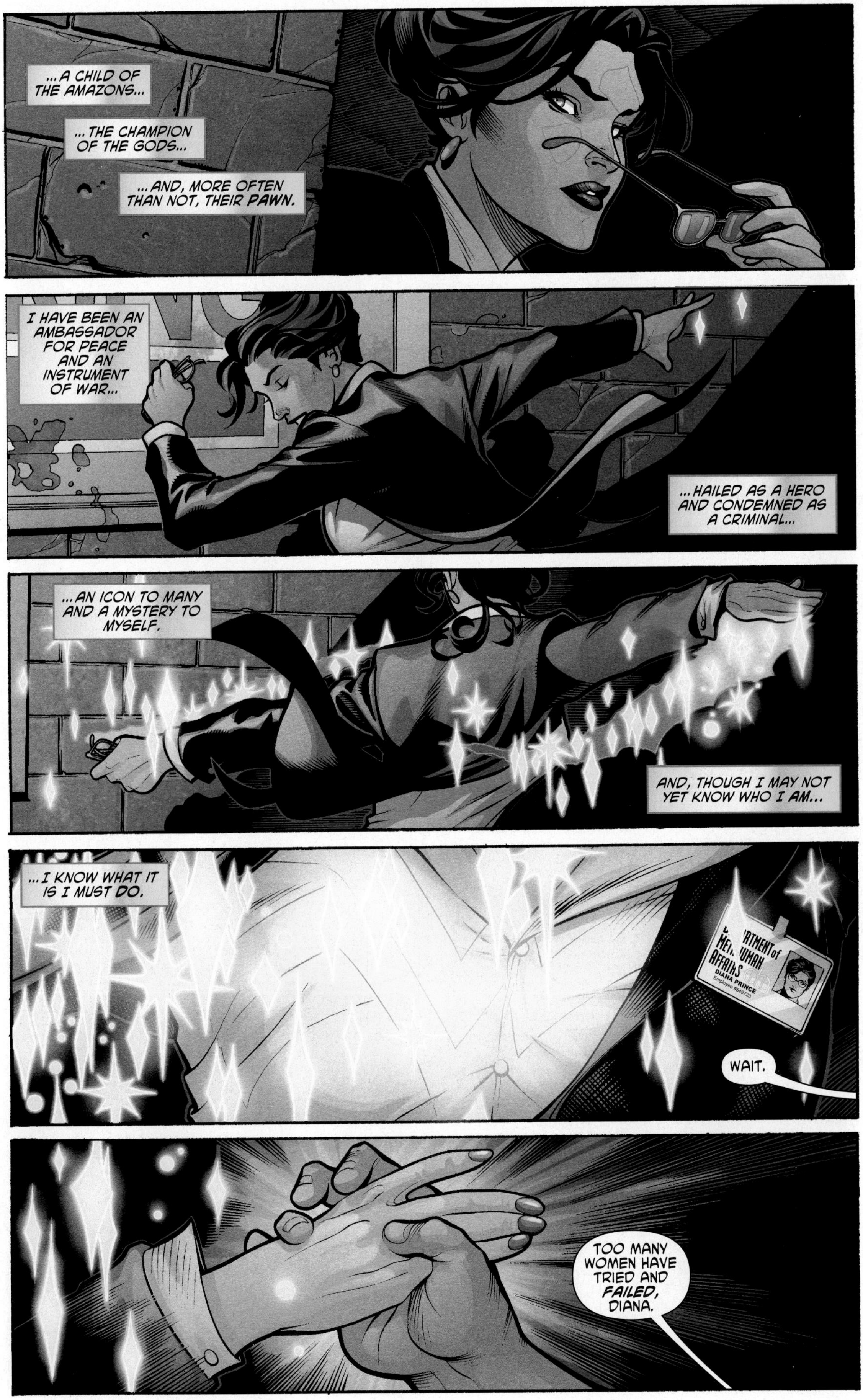
...A CHILD OF THE AMAZONS...
...THE CHAMPION OF THE GODS...
...AND, MORE OFTEN THAN NOT, THEIR PAWN.
I HAVE BEEN AN AMBASSADOR FOR PEACE AND AN INSTRUMENT OF WAR...
...HAILED AS A HERO AND CONDEMNED AS A CRIMINAL...
...AN ICON TO MANY AND A MYSTERY TO MYSELF.
AND, THOUGH I MAY NOT YET KNOW WHO I AM...
...I KNOW WHAT IT IS I MUST DO.
DIANA PRINCE
WAIT.
TOO MANY WOMEN HAVE TRIED AND FAILED, DIANA.

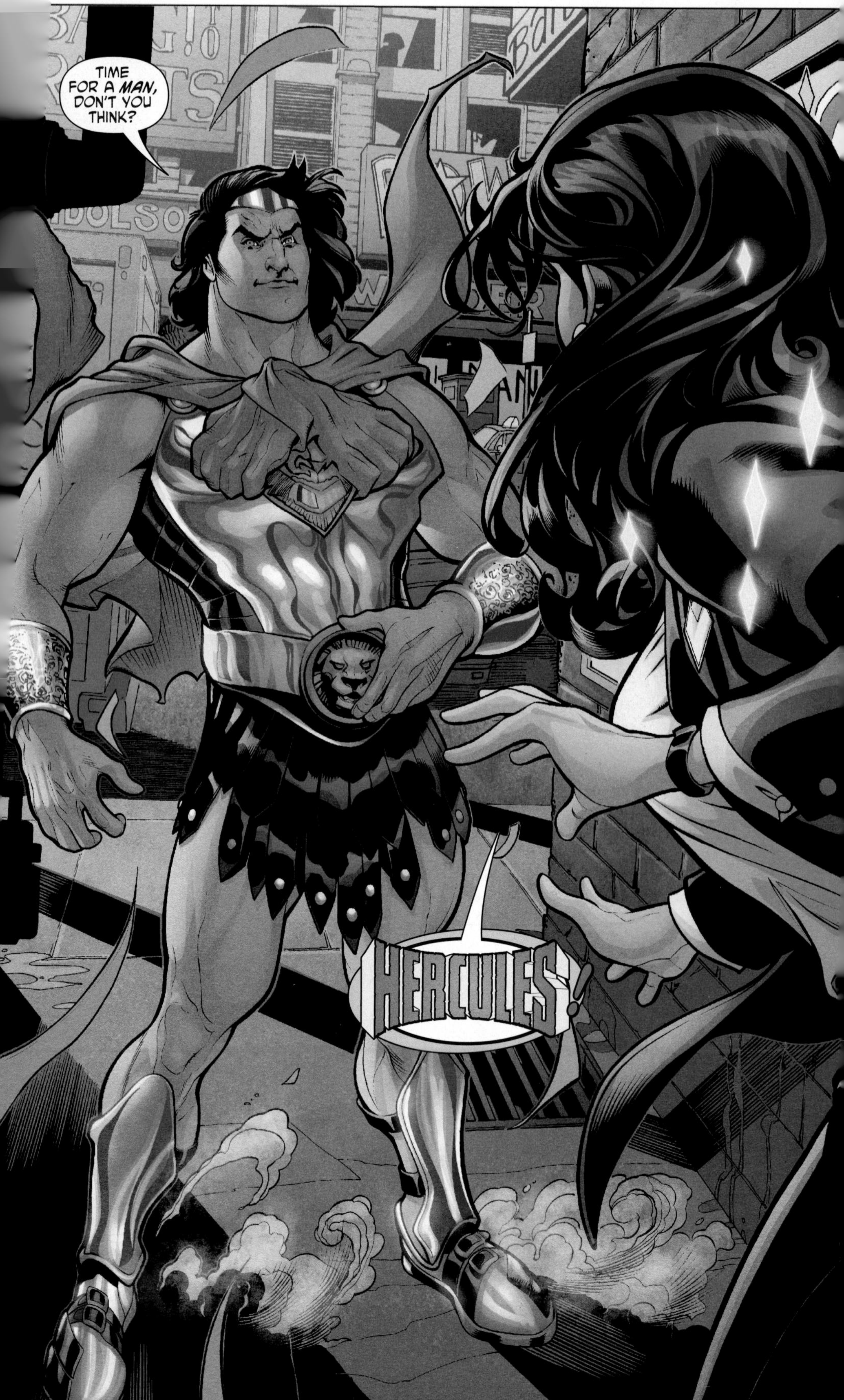
TIME FOR A MAN, DON'T YOU THINK?
HERCULES!

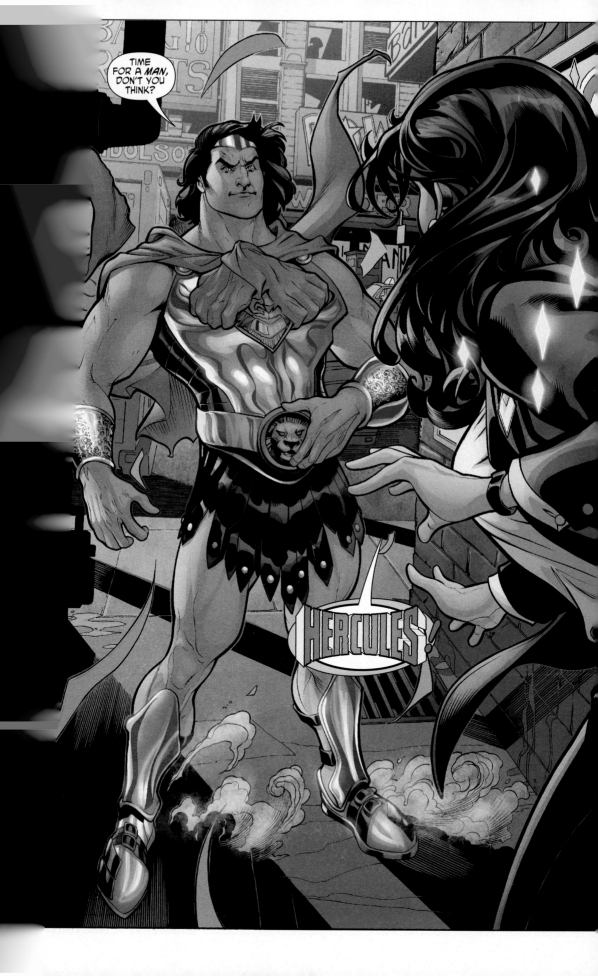

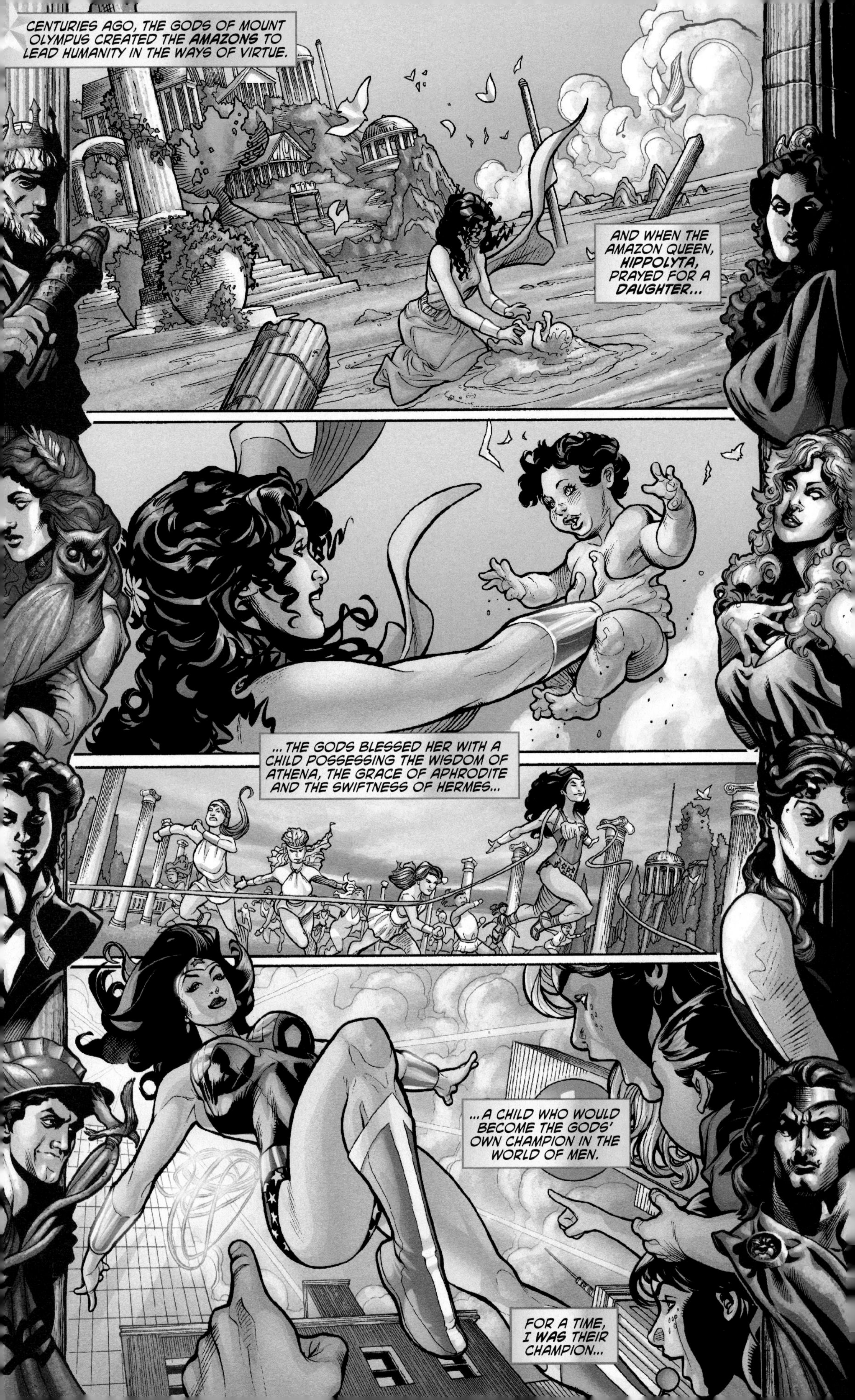
CENTURIES AGO, THE GODS OF MOUNT OLYMPUS CREATED THE AMAZONS TO LEAD HUMANITY IN THE WAYS OF VIRTUE.
AND WHEN THE AMAZON QUEEN, HIPPOLYTA, PRAYED FOR A DAUGHTER...
...THE GODS BLESSED HER WITH A CHILD POSSESSING THE WISDOM OF ATHENA, THE GRACE OF APHRODITE AND THE SWIFTNESS OF HERMES...
...A CHILD WHO WOULD BECOME THE GODS' OWN CHAMPION IN THE WORLD OF MEN.
FOR A TIME, I WAS THEIR CHAMPION...

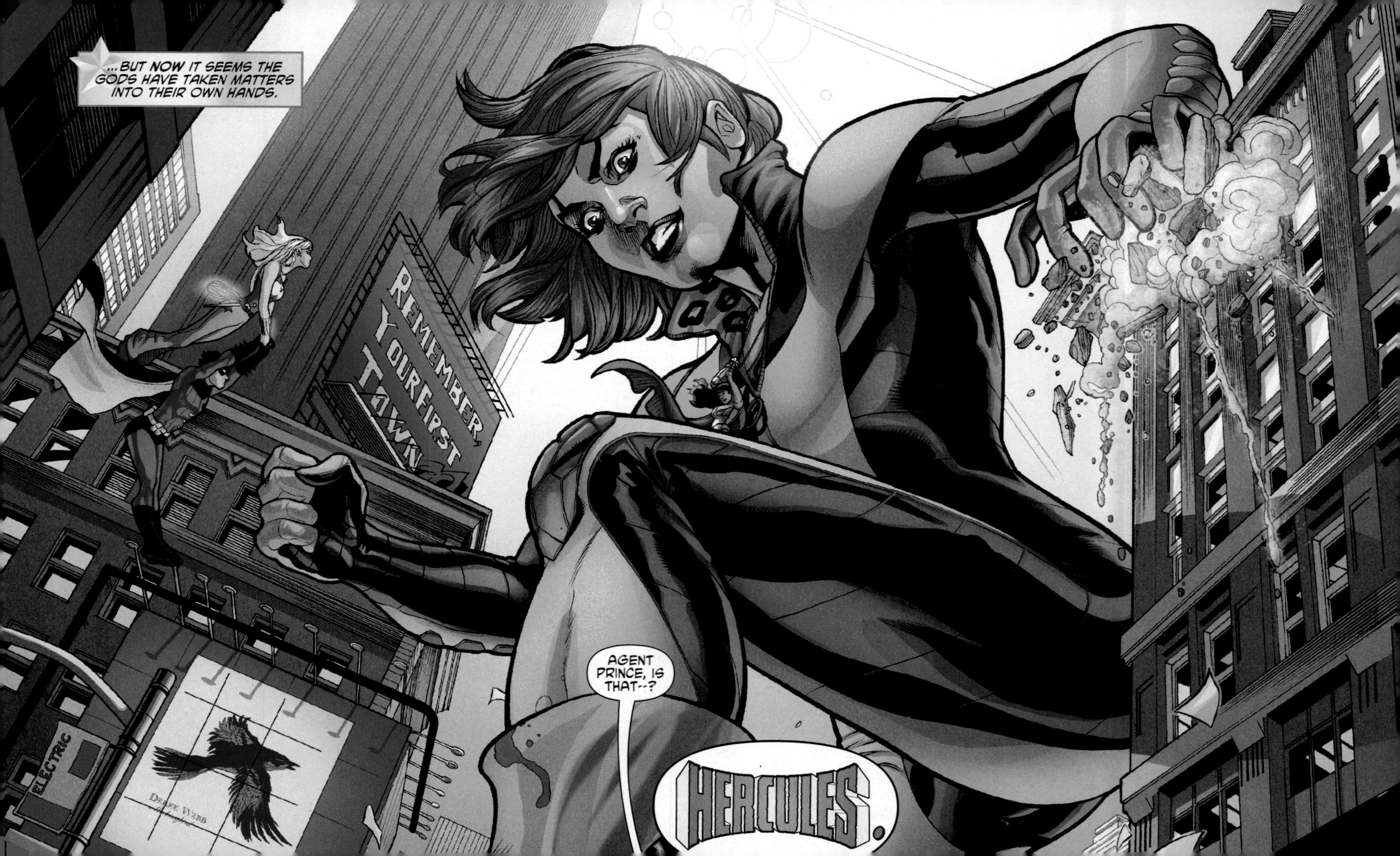
...BUT NOW IT SEEMS THE GODS HAVE TAKEN MATTERS INTO THEIR OWN HANDS.
REMEMBER YOUR FIRST TOWN
AGENT PRINCE, IS THAT--?
HERCULES.
ELECTRIC

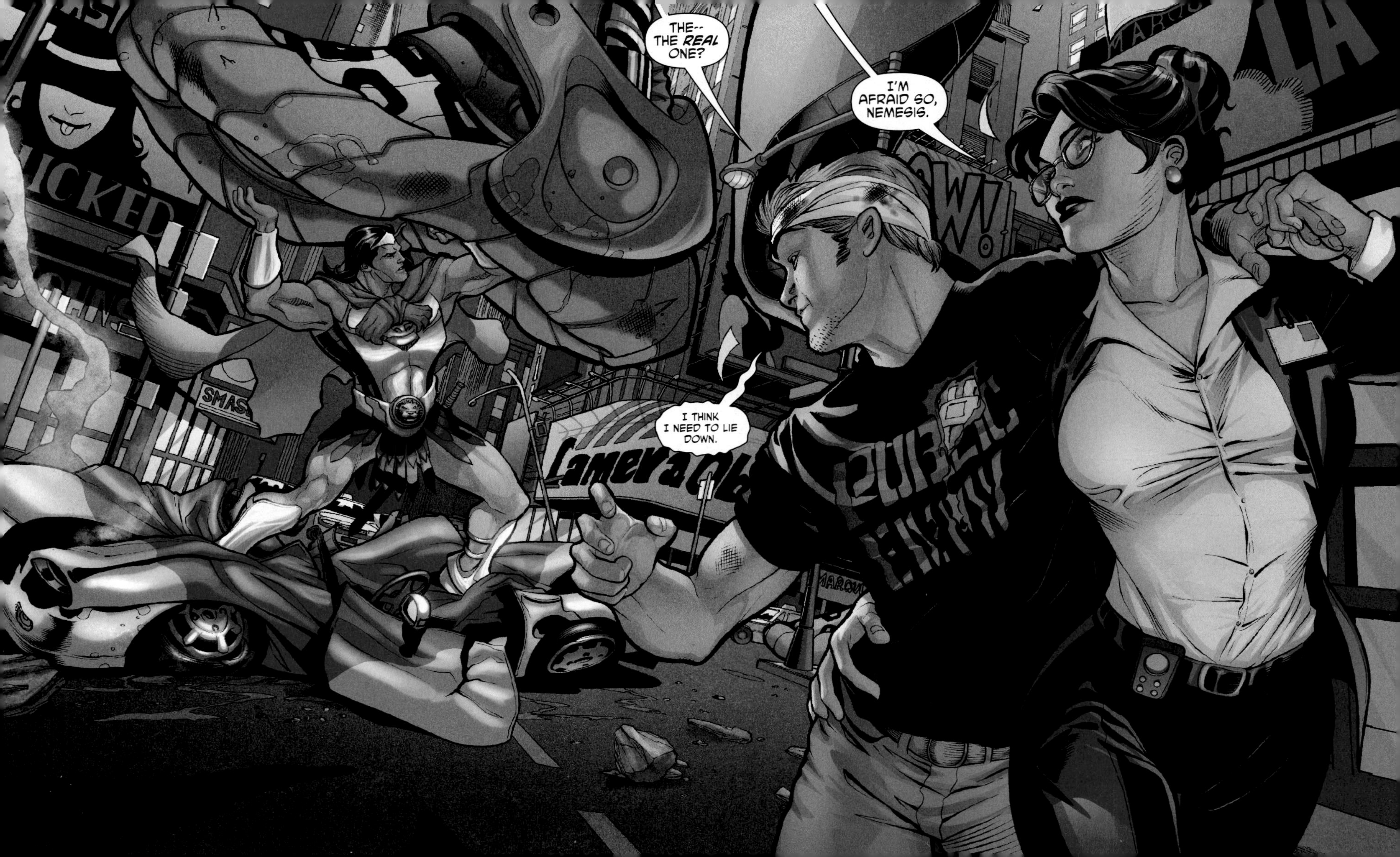
THE-- THE *REAL* ONE?
I'M AFRAID SO, NEMESIS.
I THINK I NEED TO LIE DOWN.
PUBLIC ENEMY

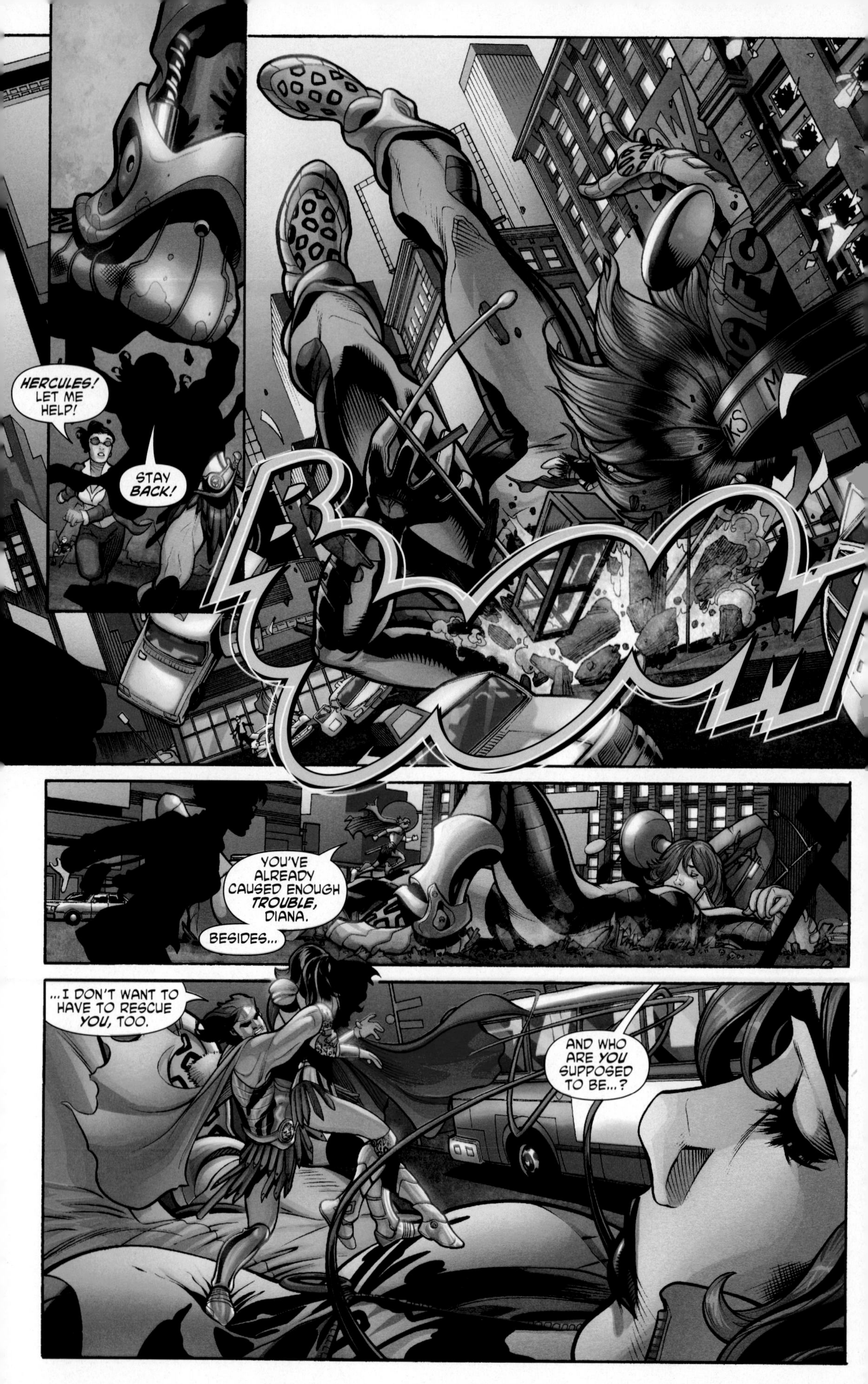
HERCULES! LET ME HELP!
STAY BACK!
BOOM
YOU'VE ALREADY CAUSED ENOUGH TROUBLE, DIANA.
BESIDES...
...I DON'T WANT TO HAVE TO RESCUE YOU, TOO.
AND WHO ARE YOU SUPPOSED TO BE...?

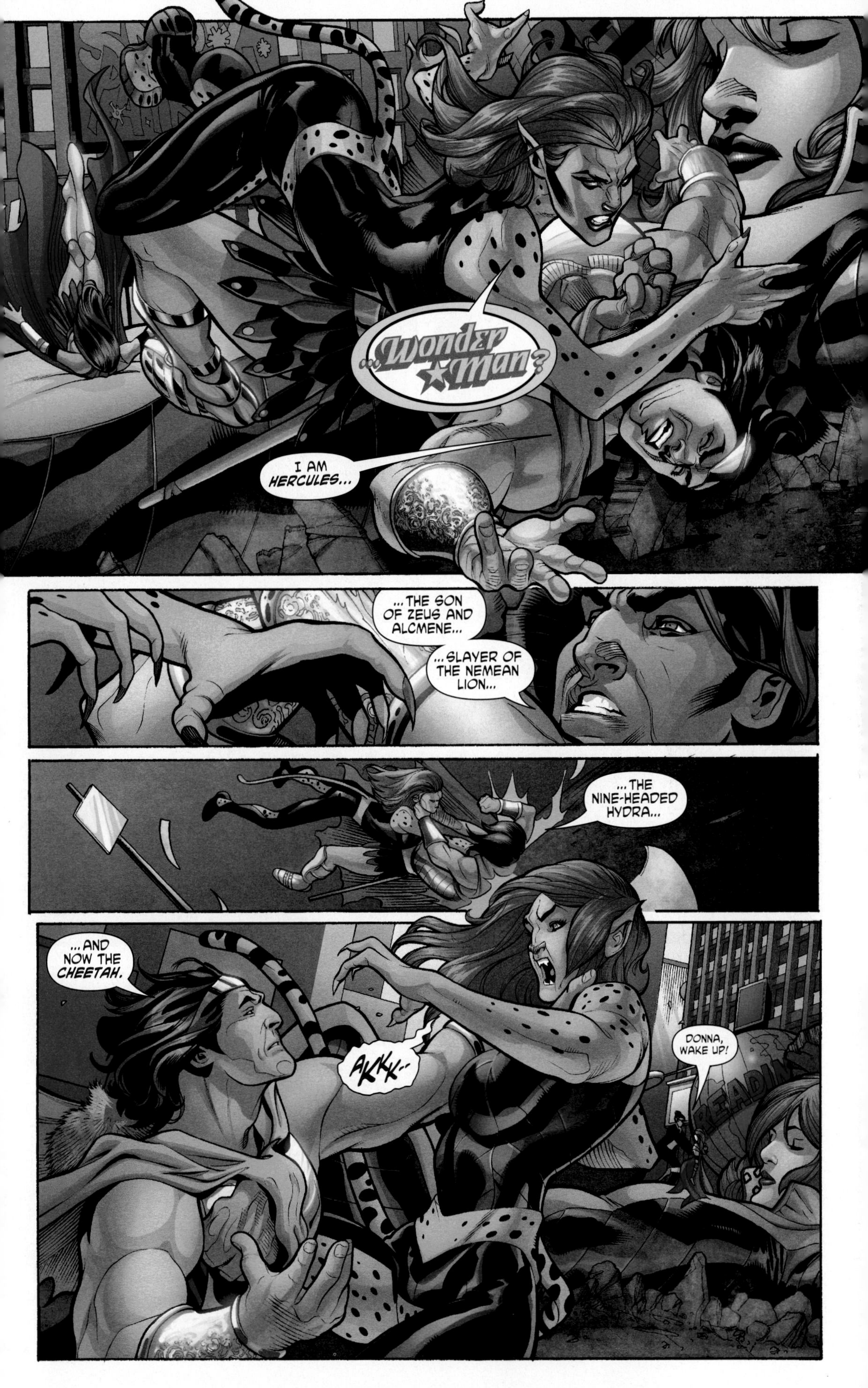
...Wonder Man?
I AM HERCULES...
...THE SON OF ZEUS AND ALCMENE...
...SLAYER OF THE NEMEAN LION...
...THE NINE-HEADED HYDRA...
...AND NOW THE CHEETAH.
AKKK--
DONNA, WAKE UP!

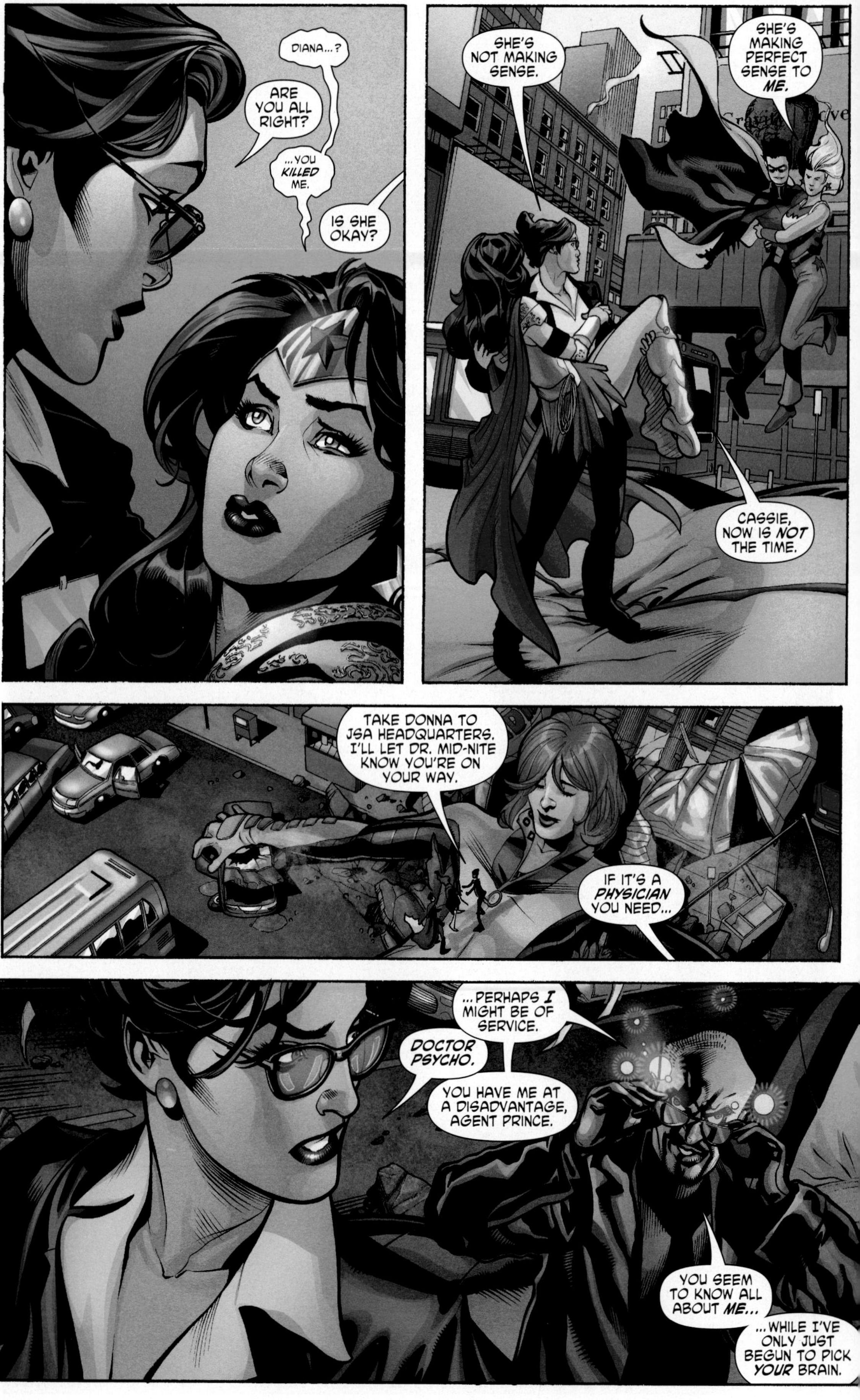
DIANA...?
ARE YOU ALL RIGHT?
...YOU *KILLED* ME.
IS SHE OKAY?
SHE'S NOT MAKING SENSE.
SHE'S MAKING PERFECT SENSE TO *ME.*
CASSIE, NOW IS *NOT* THE TIME.
TAKE DONNA TO JSA HEADQUARTERS. I'LL LET DR. MID-NITE KNOW YOU'RE ON YOUR WAY.
IF IT'S A *PHYSICIAN* YOU NEED...
...PERHAPS *I* MIGHT BE OF SERVICE.
DOCTOR PSYCHO.
YOU HAVE ME AT A DISADVANTAGE, AGENT PRINCE.
YOU SEEM TO KNOW ALL ABOUT *ME...*
...WHILE I'VE ONLY JUST BEGUN TO PICK *YOUR* BRAIN.

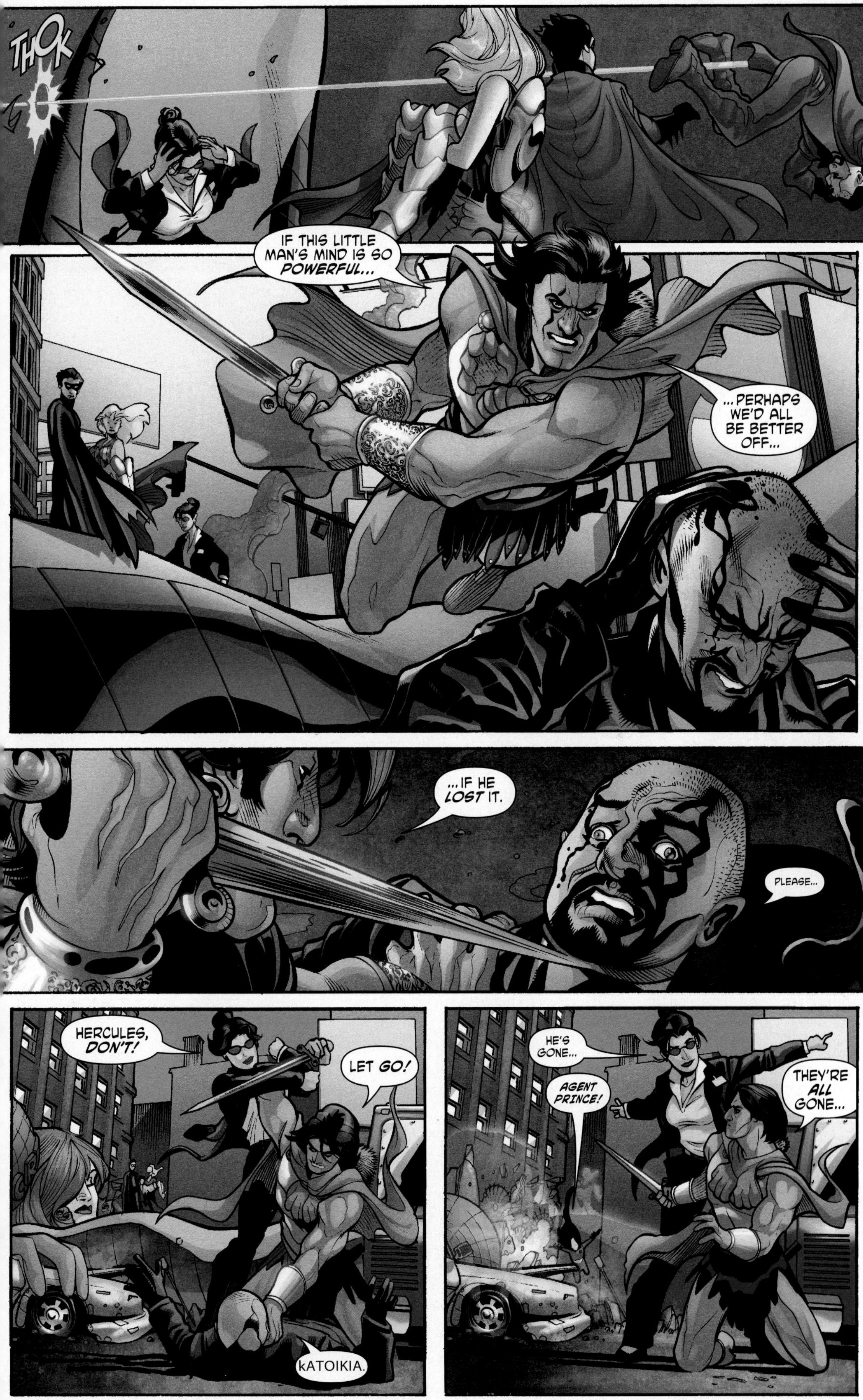
THOK
IF THIS LITTLE MAN'S MIND IS SO POWERFUL...
...PERHAPS WE'D ALL BE BETTER OFF...
...IF HE LOST IT.
PLEASE...
HERCULES, DON'T!
LET GO!
kATOIKIA.
HE'S GONE...
AGENT PRINCE!
THEY'RE ALL GONE...

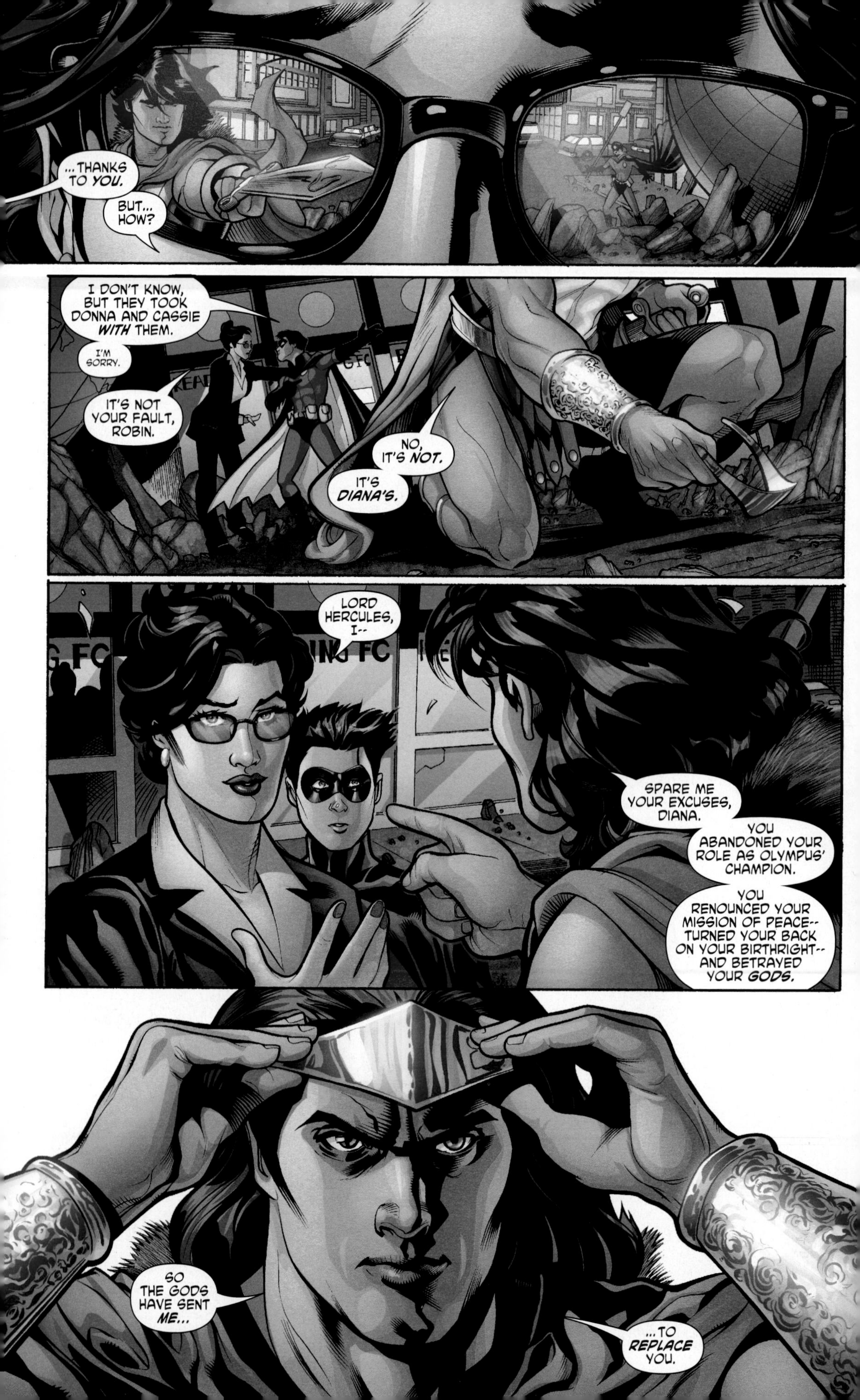
...THANKS TO YOU.
BUT... HOW?
I DON'T KNOW, BUT THEY TOOK DONNA AND CASSIE WITH THEM.
I'M SORRY.
IT'S NOT YOUR FAULT, ROBIN.
NO, IT'S NOT.
IT'S DIANA'S.
LORD HERCULES, I--
SPARE ME YOUR EXCUSES, DIANA.
YOU ABANDONED YOUR ROLE AS OLYMPUS' CHAMPION.
YOU RENOUNCED YOUR MISSION OF PEACE-- TURNED YOUR BACK ON YOUR BIRTHRIGHT-- AND BETRAYED YOUR GODS.
SO THE GODS HAVE SENT ME...
...TO REPLACE YOU.

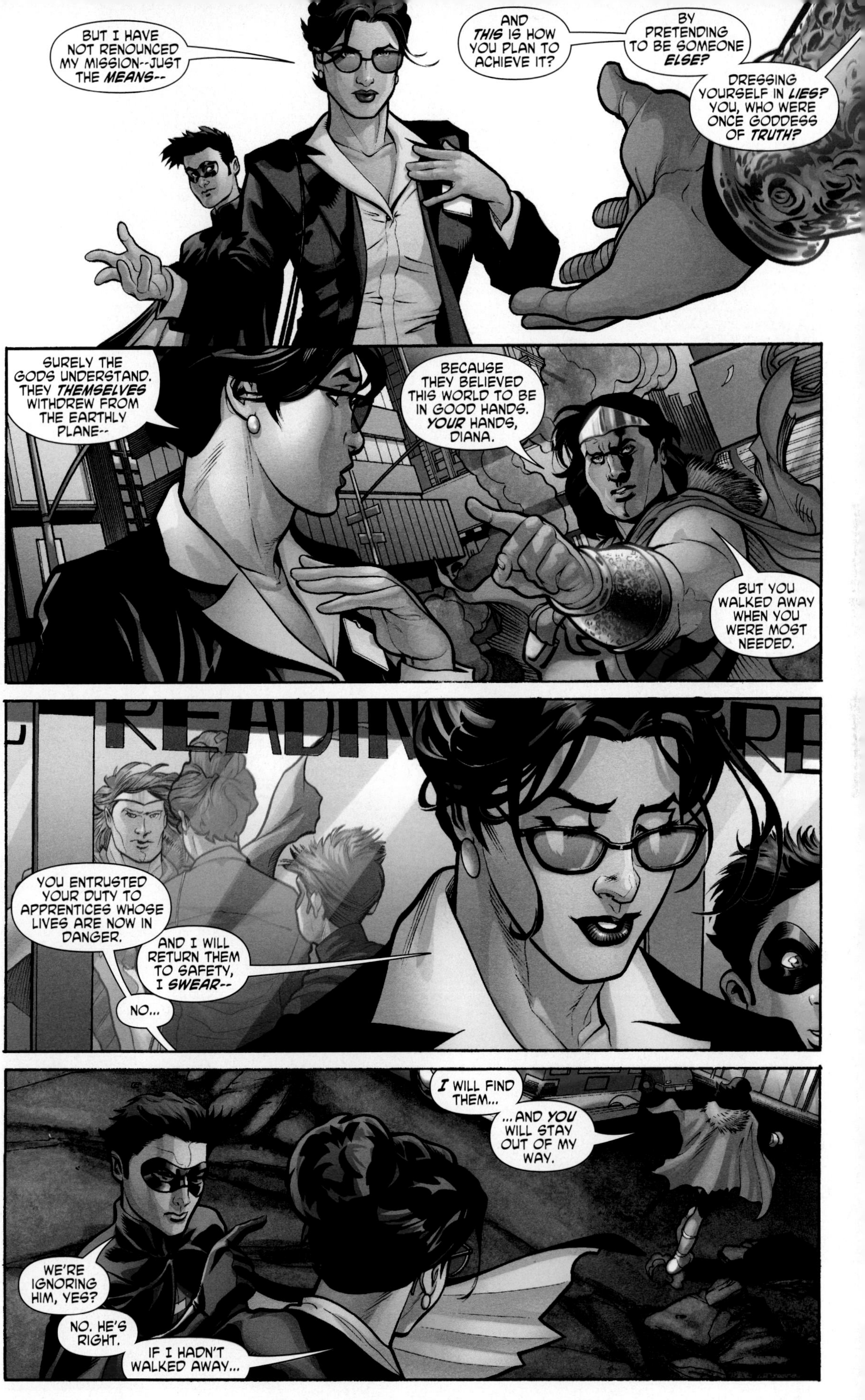
BUT I HAVE NOT RENOUNCED MY MISSION--JUST THE *MEANS*--
AND *THIS* IS HOW YOU PLAN TO ACHIEVE IT?
BY PRETENDING TO BE SOMEONE *ELSE?*
DRESSING YOURSELF IN *LIES?* YOU, WHO WERE ONCE GODDESS OF *TRUTH?*
SURELY THE GODS UNDERSTAND. THEY *THEMSELVES* WITHDREW FROM THE EARTHLY PLANE--
BECAUSE THEY BELIEVED THIS WORLD TO BE IN GOOD HANDS. *YOUR* HANDS, DIANA.
BUT YOU WALKED AWAY WHEN YOU WERE MOST NEEDED.
READIN
RE
YOU ENTRUSTED YOUR DUTY TO APPRENTICES WHOSE LIVES ARE NOW IN DANGER.
AND I WILL RETURN THEM TO SAFETY, I *SWEAR*--
NO...
I WILL FIND THEM...
...AND *YOU* WILL STAY OUT OF MY WAY.
WE'RE IGNORING HIM, YES?
NO. HE'S RIGHT.
IF I HADN'T WALKED AWAY...

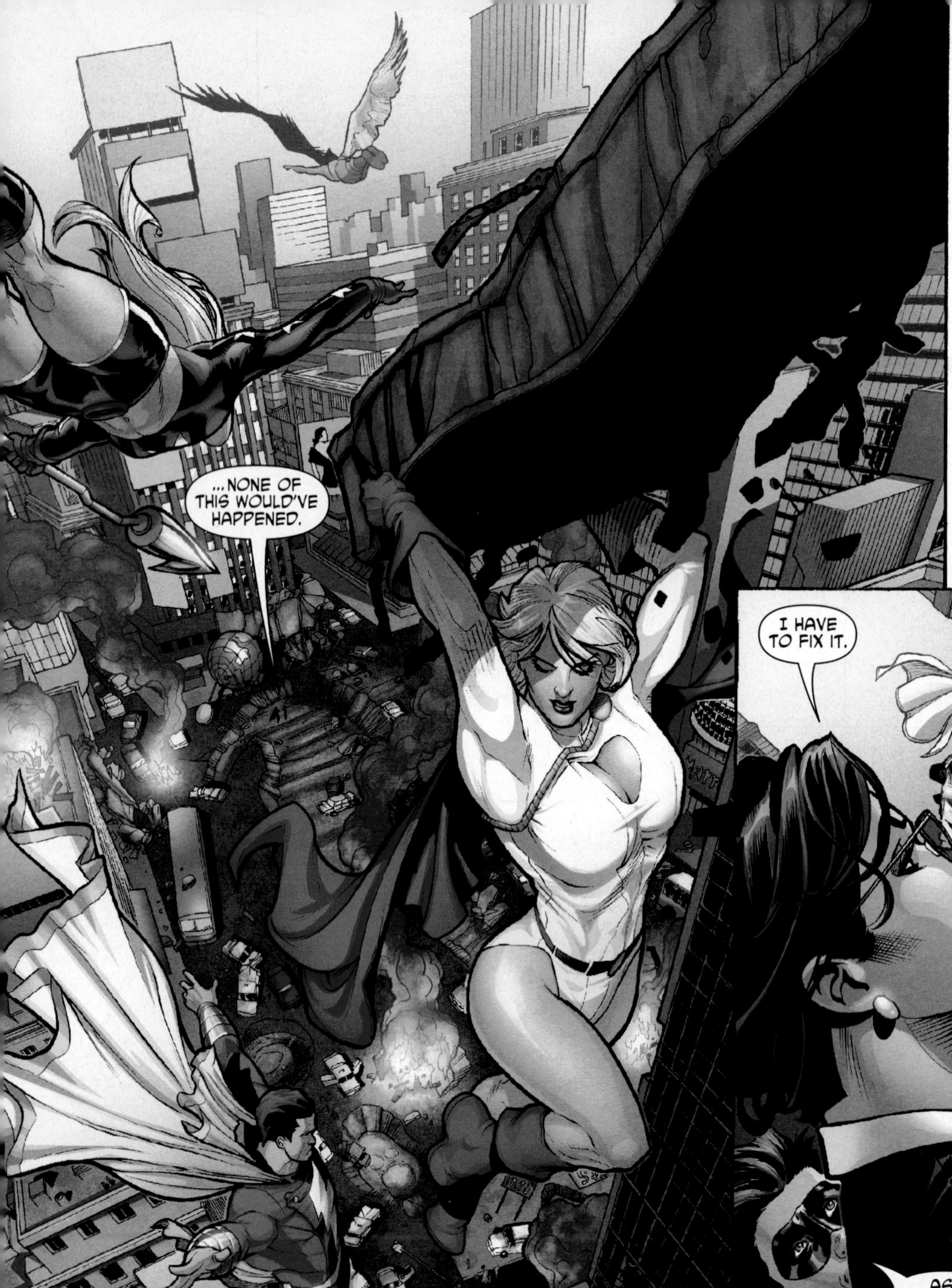
...NONE OF THIS WOULD'VE HAPPENED.

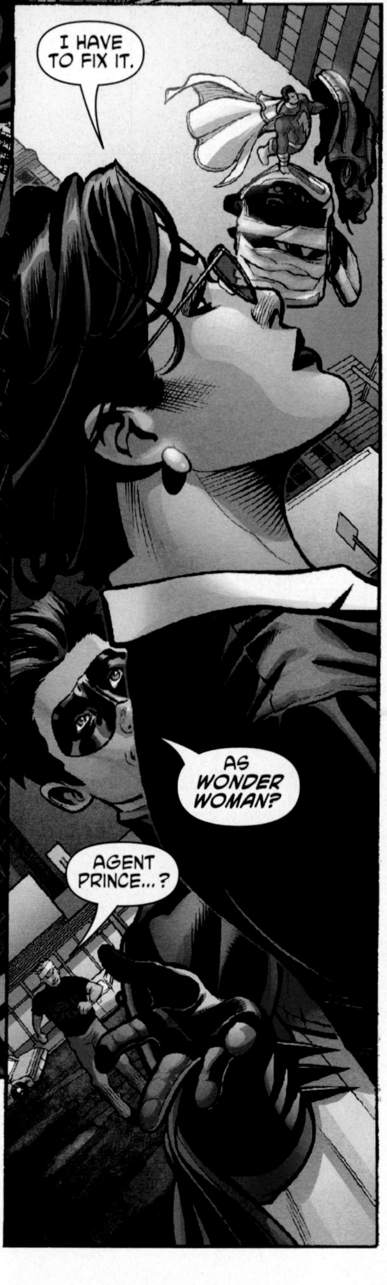
I HAVE TO FIX IT.
AS WONDER WOMAN?
AGENT PRINCE...?

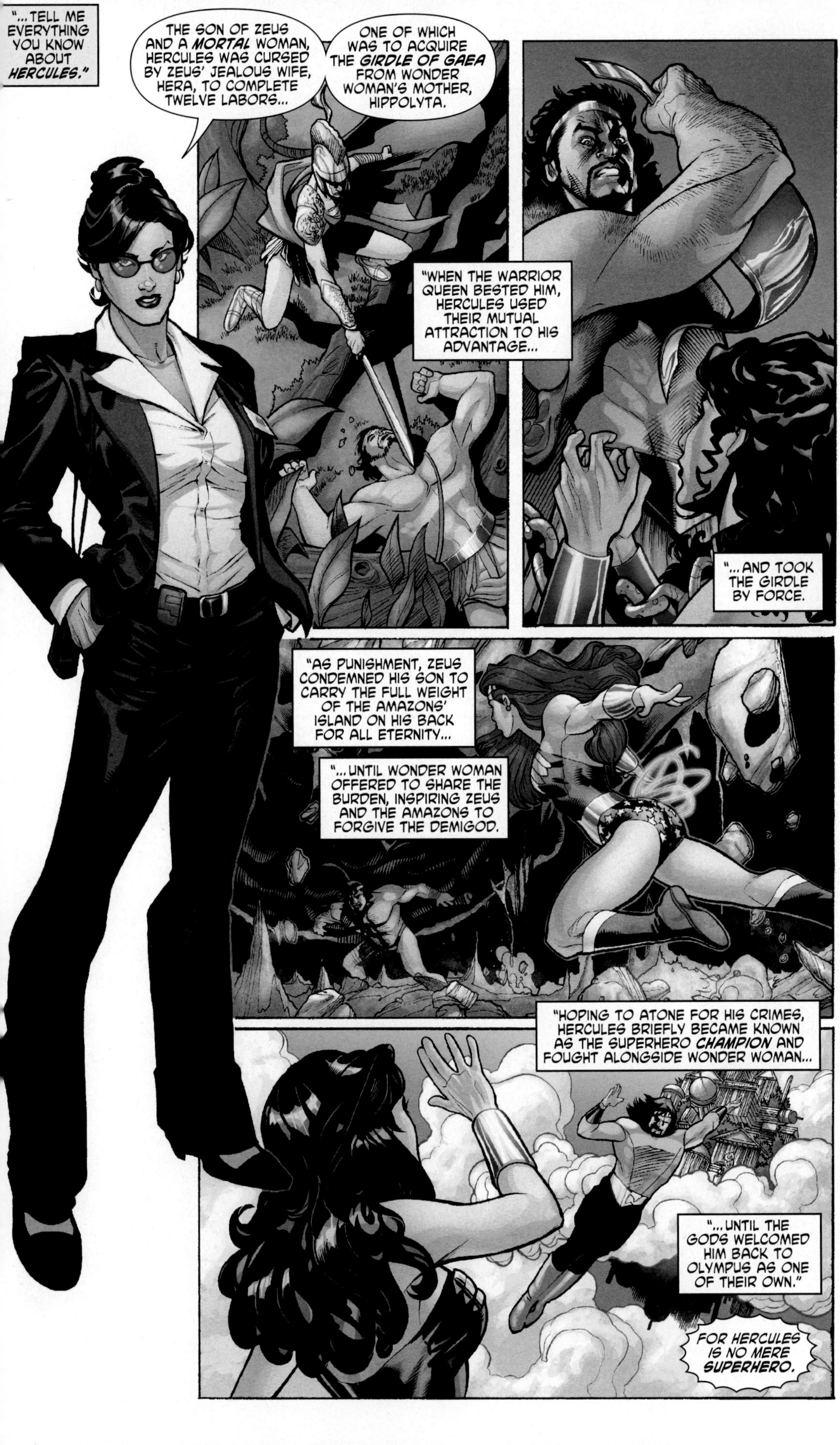
"...TELL ME EVERYTHING YOU KNOW ABOUT HERCULES."
THE SON OF ZEUS AND A MORTAL WOMAN, HERCULES WAS CURSED BY ZEUS' JEALOUS WIFE, HERA, TO COMPLETE TWELVE LABORS...
ONE OF WHICH WAS TO ACQUIRE THE GIRDLE OF GAEA FROM WONDER WOMAN'S MOTHER, HIPPOLYTA.
"WHEN THE WARRIOR QUEEN BESTED HIM, HERCULES USED THEIR MUTUAL ATTRACTION TO HIS ADVANTAGE...
"...AND TOOK THE GIRDLE BY FORCE.
"AS PUNISHMENT, ZEUS CONDEMNED HIS SON TO CARRY THE FULL WEIGHT OF THE AMAZONS' ISLAND ON HIS BACK FOR ALL ETERNITY...
"...UNTIL WONDER WOMAN OFFERED TO SHARE THE BURDEN, INSPIRING ZEUS AND THE AMAZONS TO FORGIVE THE DEMIGOD.
"HOPING TO ATONE FOR HIS CRIMES, HERCULES BRIEFLY BECAME KNOWN AS THE SUPERHERO CHAMPION AND FOUGHT ALONGSIDE WONDER WOMAN...
"...UNTIL THE GODS WELCOMED HIM BACK TO OLYMPUS AS ONE OF THEIR OWN."
FOR HERCULES IS NO MERE SUPERHERO.

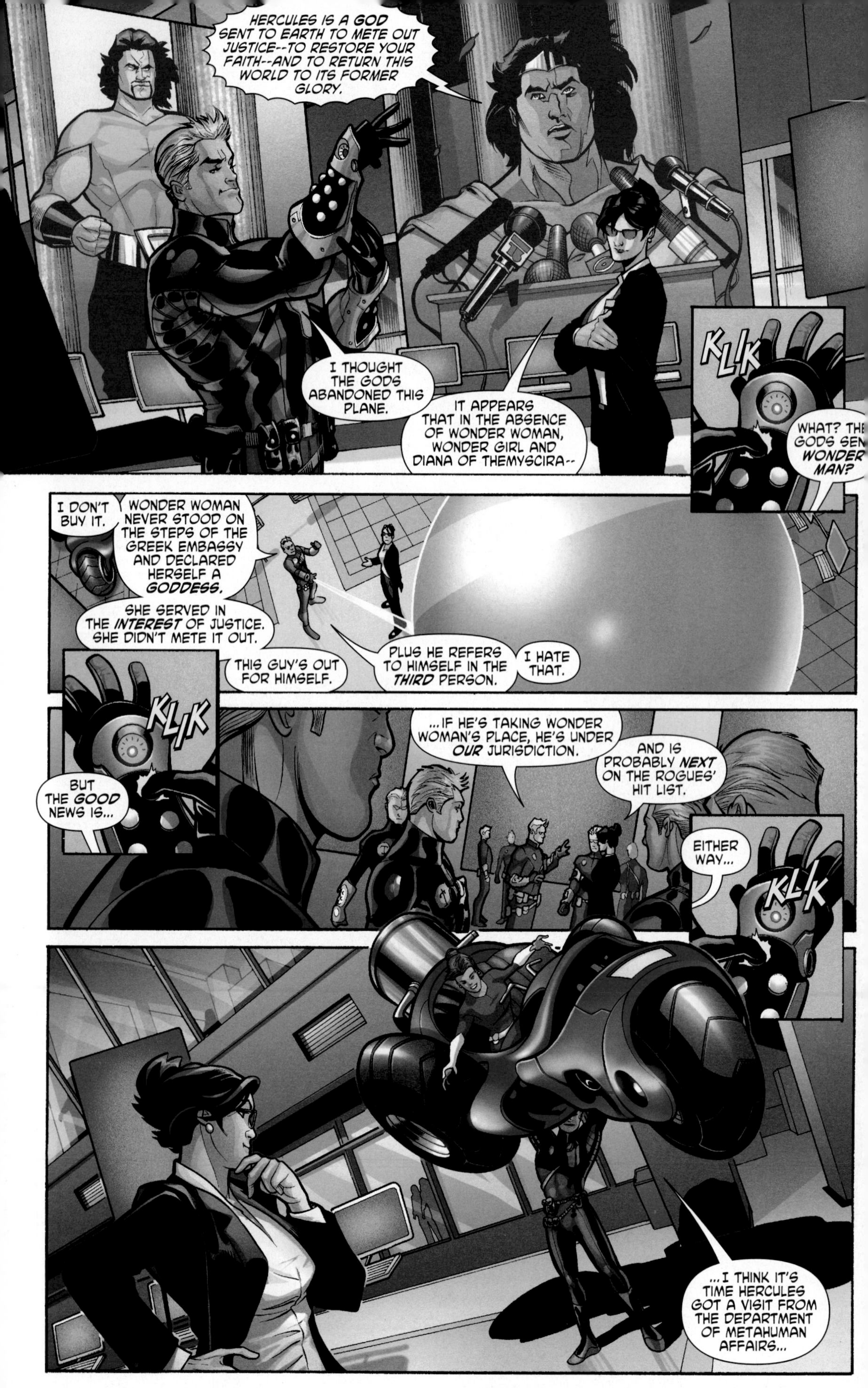

HERCULES IS A GOD SENT TO EARTH TO METE OUT JUSTICE--TO RESTORE YOUR FAITH--AND TO RETURN THIS WORLD TO ITS FORMER GLORY.
I THOUGHT THE GODS ABANDONED THIS PLANE.
IT APPEARS THAT IN THE ABSENCE OF WONDER WOMAN, WONDER GIRL AND DIANA OF THEMYSCIRA--
KLIK
WHAT? THE GODS SEN WONDER MAN?
I DON'T BUY IT.
WONDER WOMAN NEVER STOOD ON THE STEPS OF THE GREEK EMBASSY AND DECLARED HERSELF A GODDESS.
SHE SERVED IN THE INTEREST OF JUSTICE. SHE DIDN'T METE IT OUT.
THIS GUY'S OUT FOR HIMSELF.
PLUS HE REFERS TO HIMSELF IN THE THIRD PERSON.
I HATE THAT.
KLIK
BUT THE GOOD NEWS IS...
...IF HE'S TAKING WONDER WOMAN'S PLACE, HE'S UNDER OUR JURISDICTION.
AND IS PROBABLY NEXT ON THE ROGUES' HIT LIST.
EITHER WAY...
KLIK
...I THINK IT'S TIME HERCULES GOT A VISIT FROM THE DEPARTMENT OF METAHUMAN AFFAIRS...

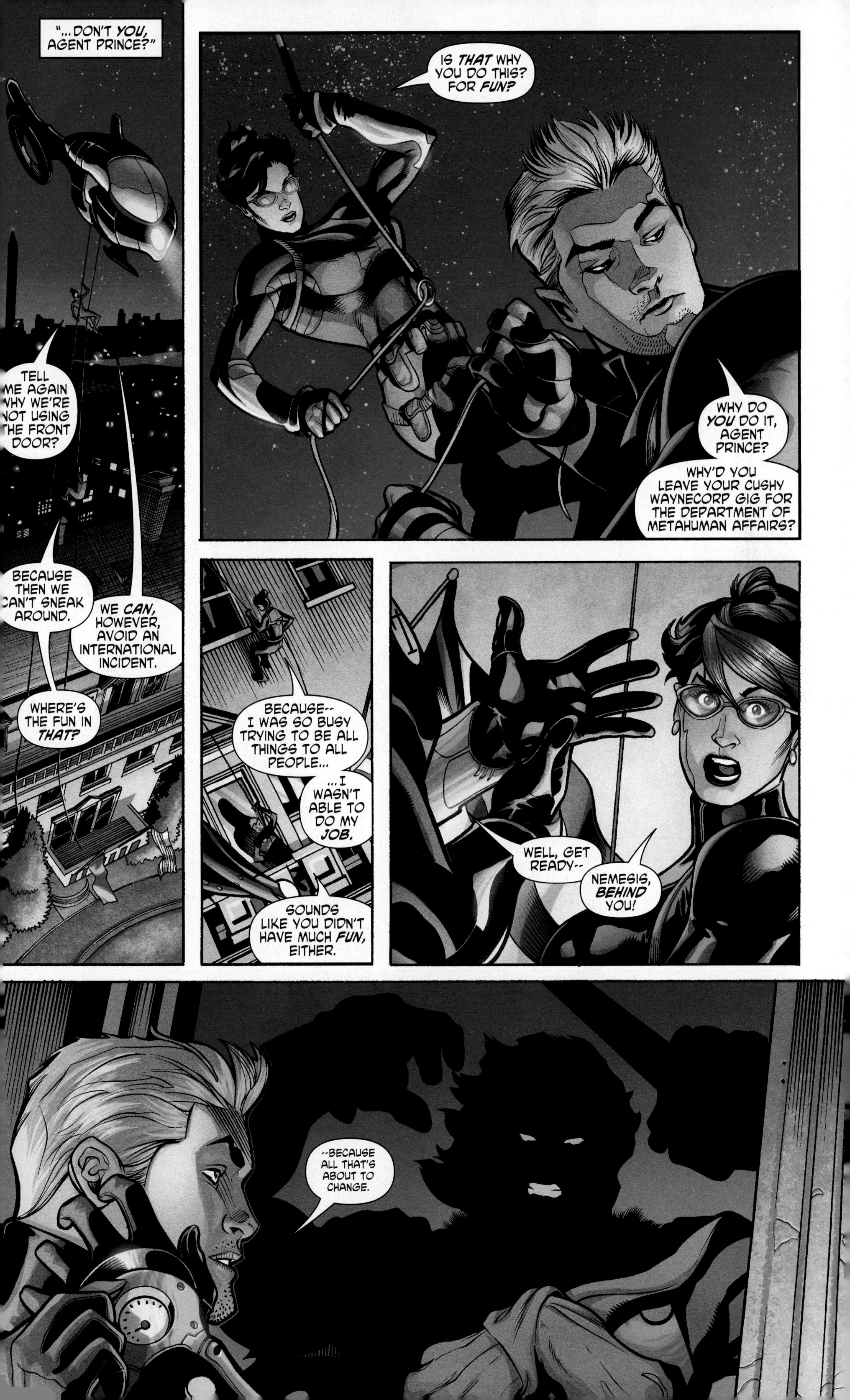
"...DON'T YOU, AGENT PRINCE?"
IS THAT WHY YOU DO THIS? FOR FUN?
WHY DO YOU DO IT, AGENT PRINCE?
WHY'D YOU LEAVE YOUR CUSHY WAYNECORP GIG FOR THE DEPARTMENT OF METAHUMAN AFFAIRS?
TELL ME AGAIN WHY WE'RE NOT USING THE FRONT DOOR?
BECAUSE THEN WE CAN'T SNEAK AROUND.
WE CAN, HOWEVER, AVOID AN INTERNATIONAL INCIDENT.
WHERE'S THE FUN IN THAT?
BECAUSE-- I WAS SO BUSY TRYING TO BE ALL THINGS TO ALL PEOPLE...
...I WASN'T ABLE TO DO MY JOB.
SOUNDS LIKE YOU DIDN'T HAVE MUCH FUN, EITHER.
WELL, GET READY--
NEMESIS, BEHIND YOU!
--BECAUSE ALL THAT'S ABOUT TO CHANGE.

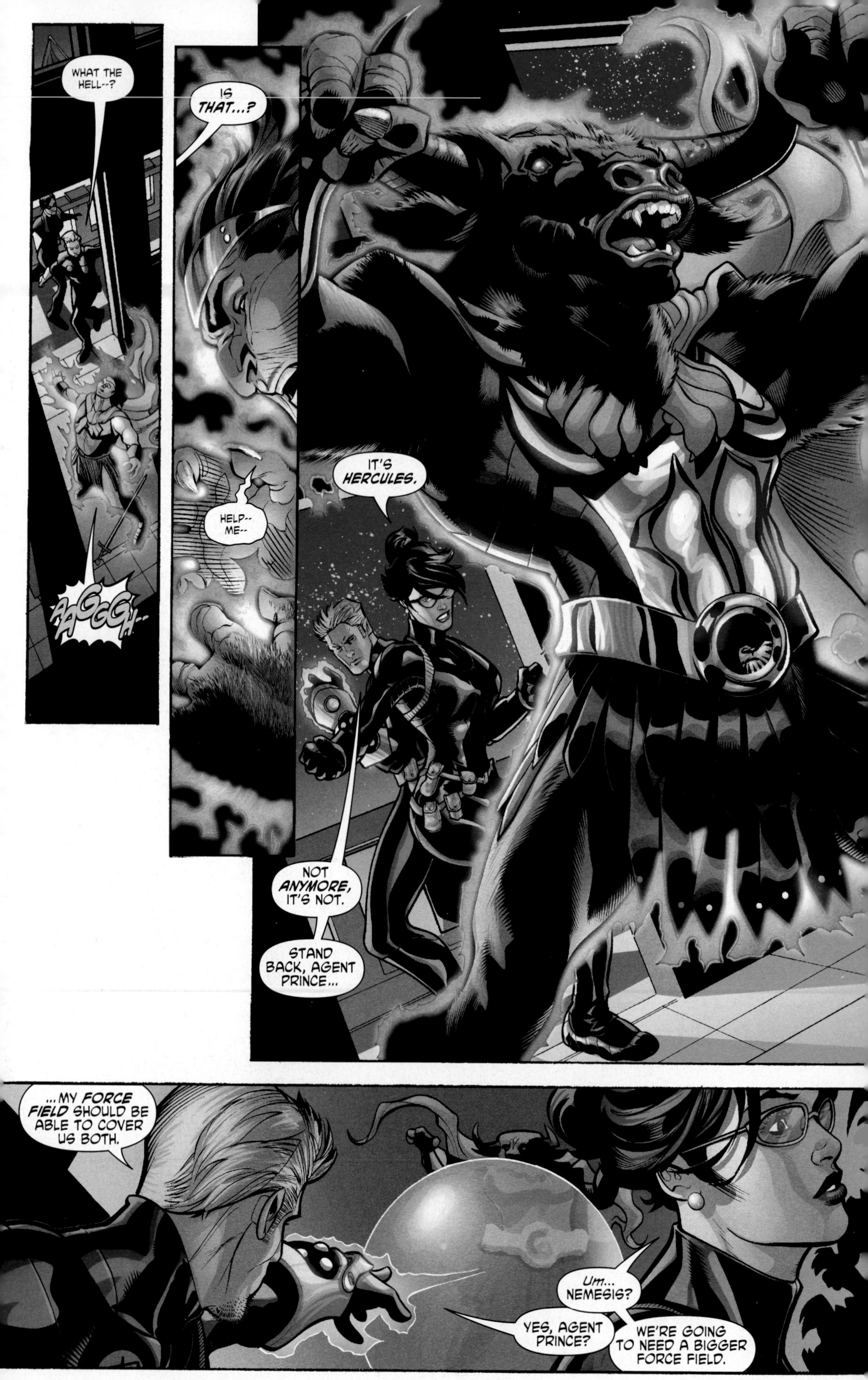
WHAT THE HELL--?
IS *THAT*...?
HELP-- ME--
AAGGGH--
IT'S *HERCULES.*
NOT *ANYMORE,* IT'S NOT.
STAND BACK, AGENT PRINCE...
...MY *FORCE FIELD* SHOULD BE ABLE TO COVER US BOTH.
Um... NEMESIS?
YES, AGENT PRINCE?
WE'RE GOING TO NEED A BIGGER FORCE FIELD.

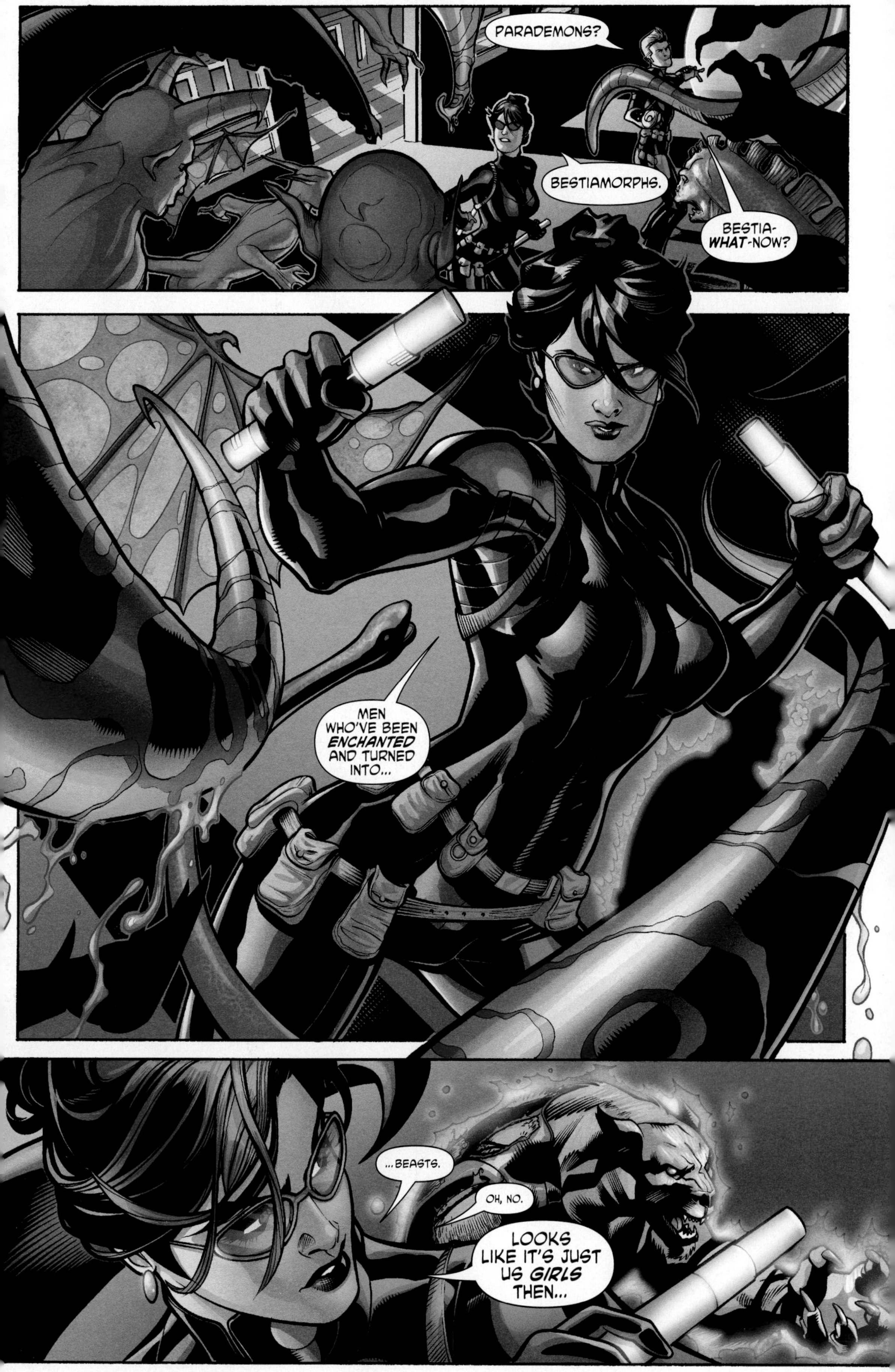
PARADEMONS?
BESTIAMORPHS.
BESTIA-*WHAT*-NOW?
MEN WHO'VE BEEN *ENCHANTED* AND TURNED INTO...
...BEASTS.
OH, NO.
LOOKS LIKE IT'S JUST US *GIRLS* THEN...

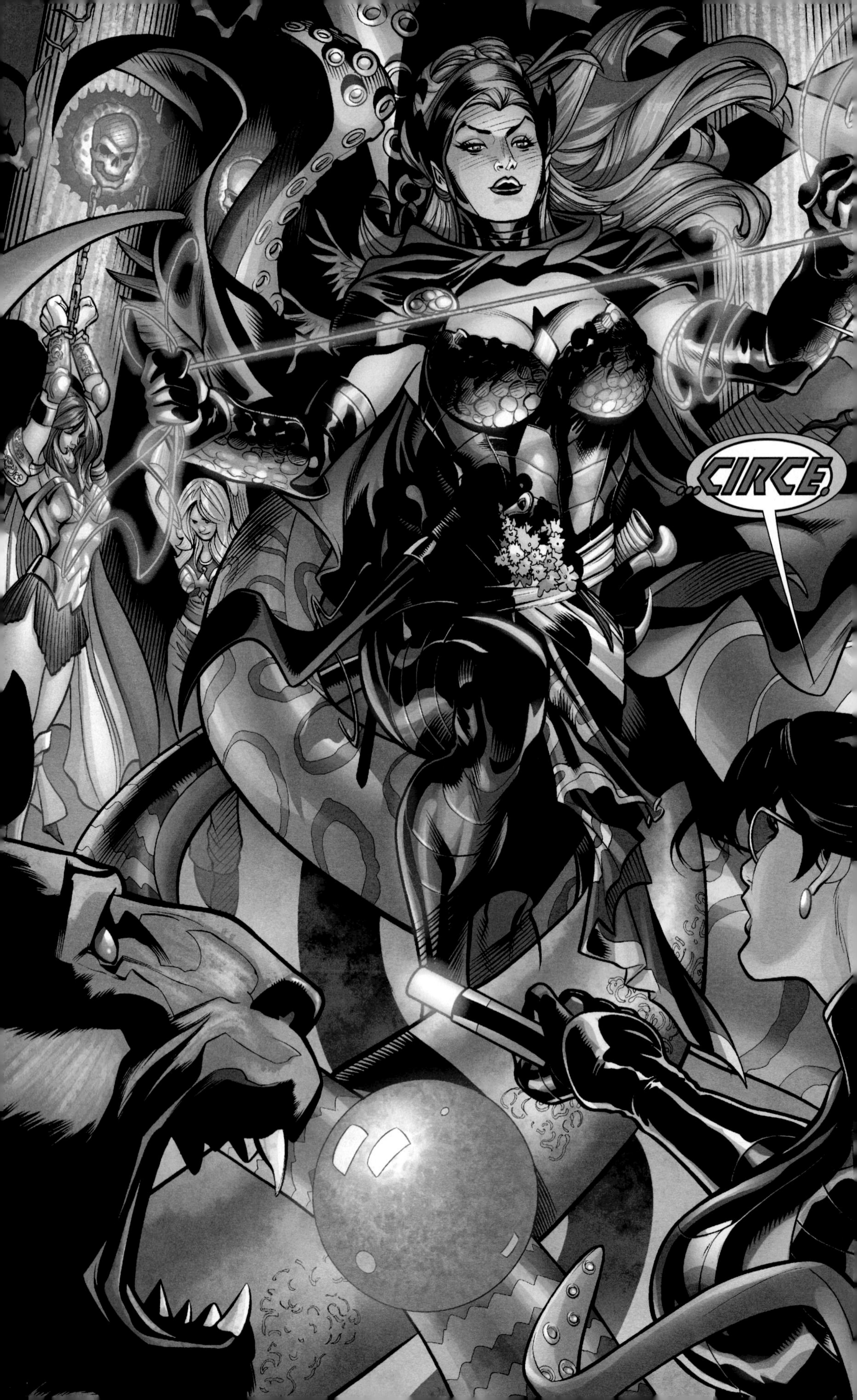
...CIRCE.

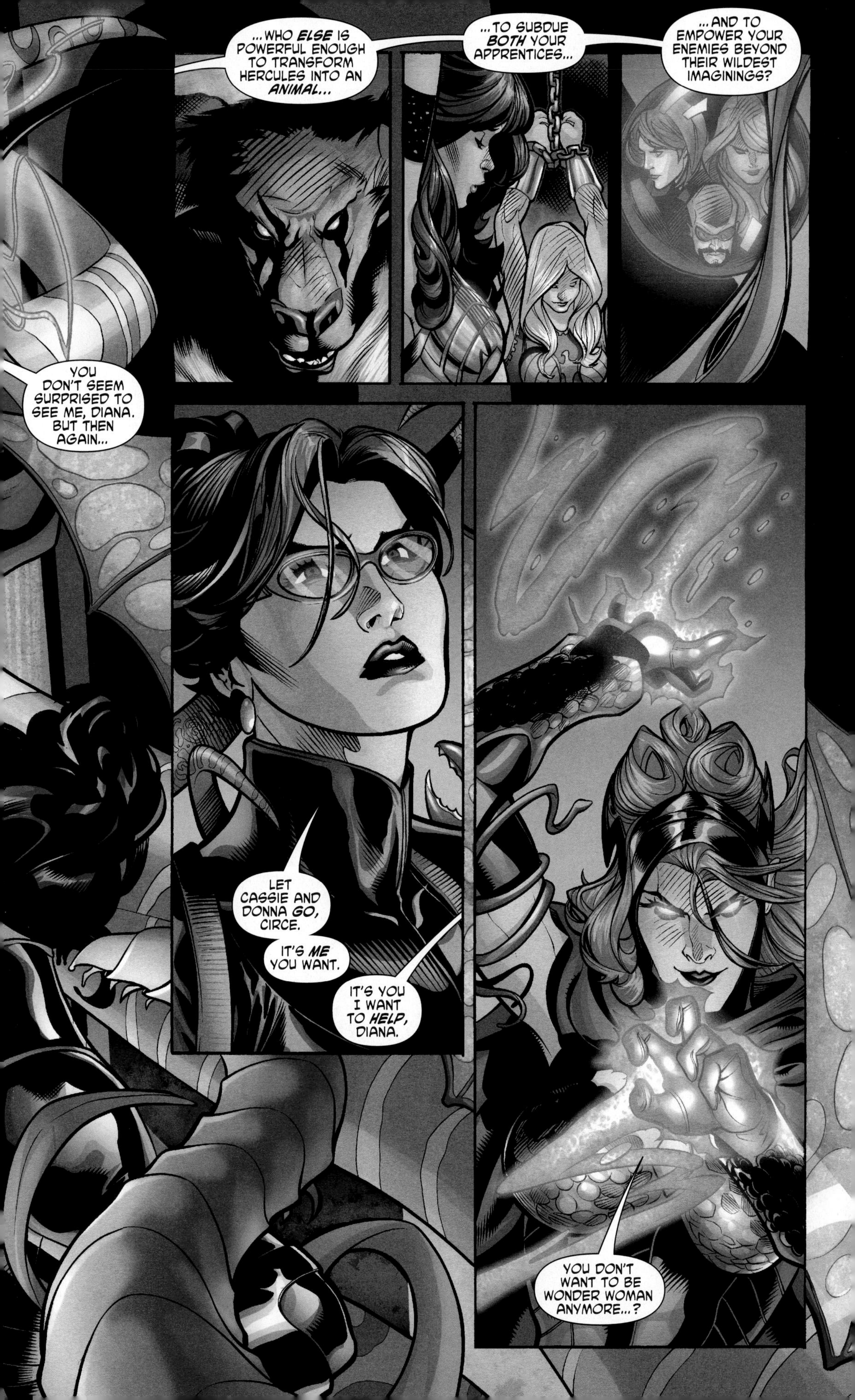
...WHO *ELSE* IS POWERFUL ENOUGH TO TRANSFORM HERCULES INTO AN *ANIMAL*...
...TO SUBDUE *BOTH* YOUR APPRENTICES...
...AND TO EMPOWER YOUR ENEMIES BEYOND THEIR WILDEST IMAGININGS?
YOU DON'T SEEM SURPRISED TO SEE ME, DIANA. BUT THEN AGAIN...
LET CASSIE AND DONNA *GO*, CIRCE.
IT'S *ME* YOU WANT.
IT'S YOU I WANT TO *HELP*, DIANA.
YOU DON'T WANT TO BE WONDER WOMAN ANYMORE...?

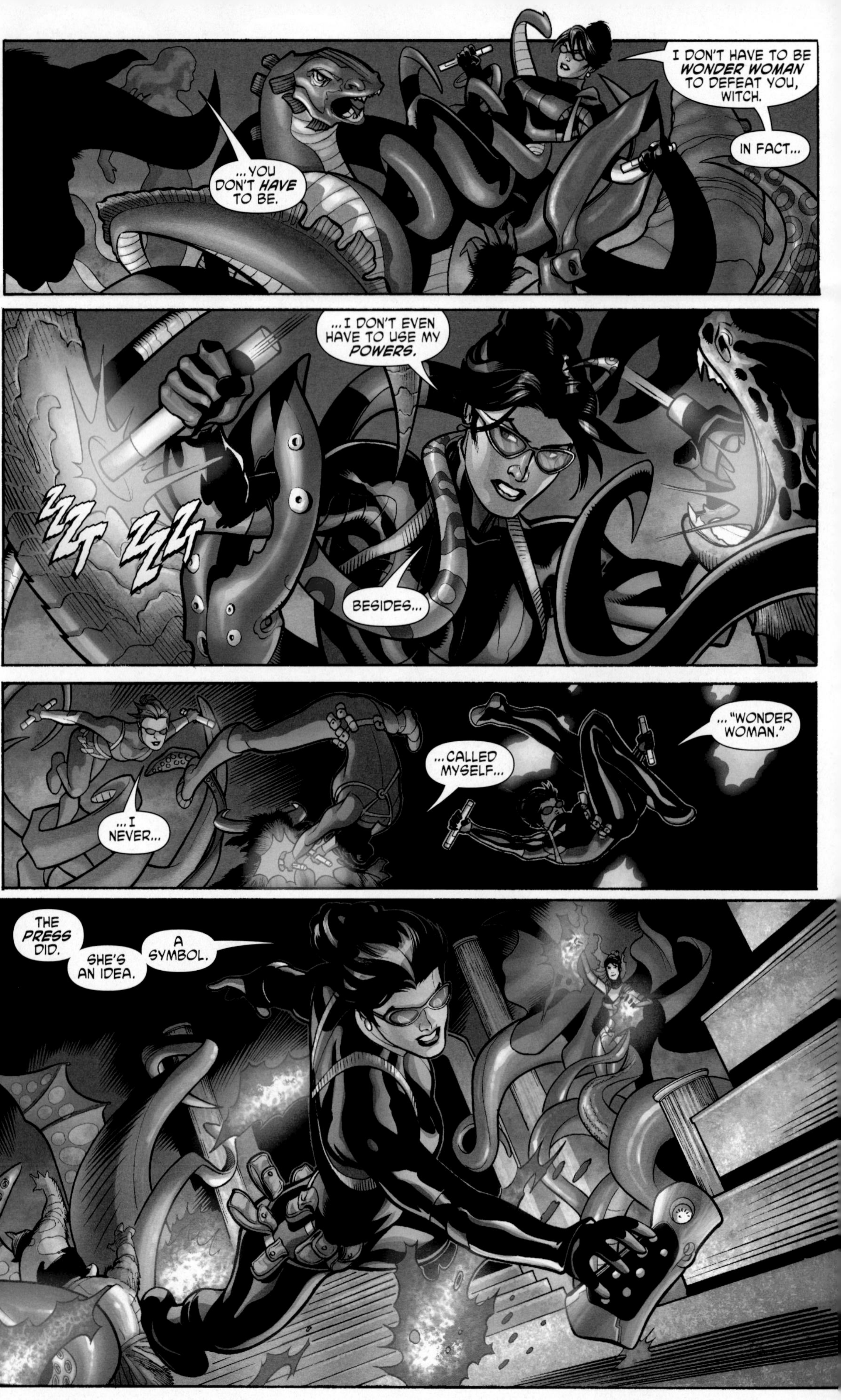
I DON'T HAVE TO BE *WONDER WOMAN* TO DEFEAT YOU, WITCH.
IN FACT...
...YOU DON'T *HAVE* TO BE.
...I DON'T EVEN HAVE TO USE MY *POWERS.*
ZZZT ZZZT
BESIDES...
...I NEVER...
...CALLED MYSELF...
..."WONDER WOMAN."
THE *PRESS* DID.
SHE'S AN IDEA.
A SYMBOL.

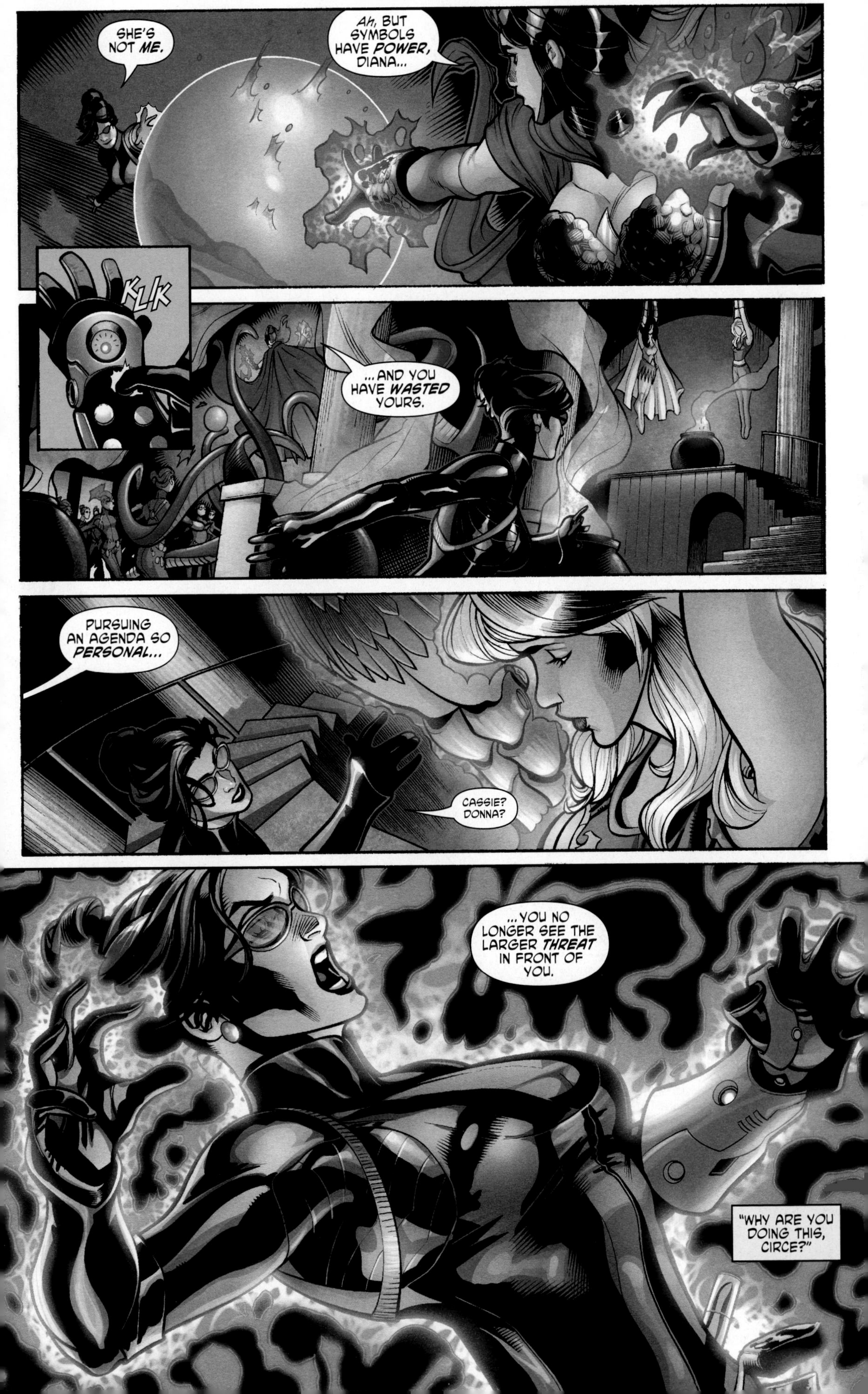

SHE'S NOT ME.
Ah, BUT SYMBOLS HAVE POWER, DIANA...
KLIK
...AND YOU HAVE WASTED YOURS.
PURSUING AN AGENDA SO PERSONAL...
CASSIE? DONNA?
...YOU NO LONGER SEE THE LARGER THREAT IN FRONT OF YOU.
"WHY ARE YOU DOING THIS, CIRCE?"

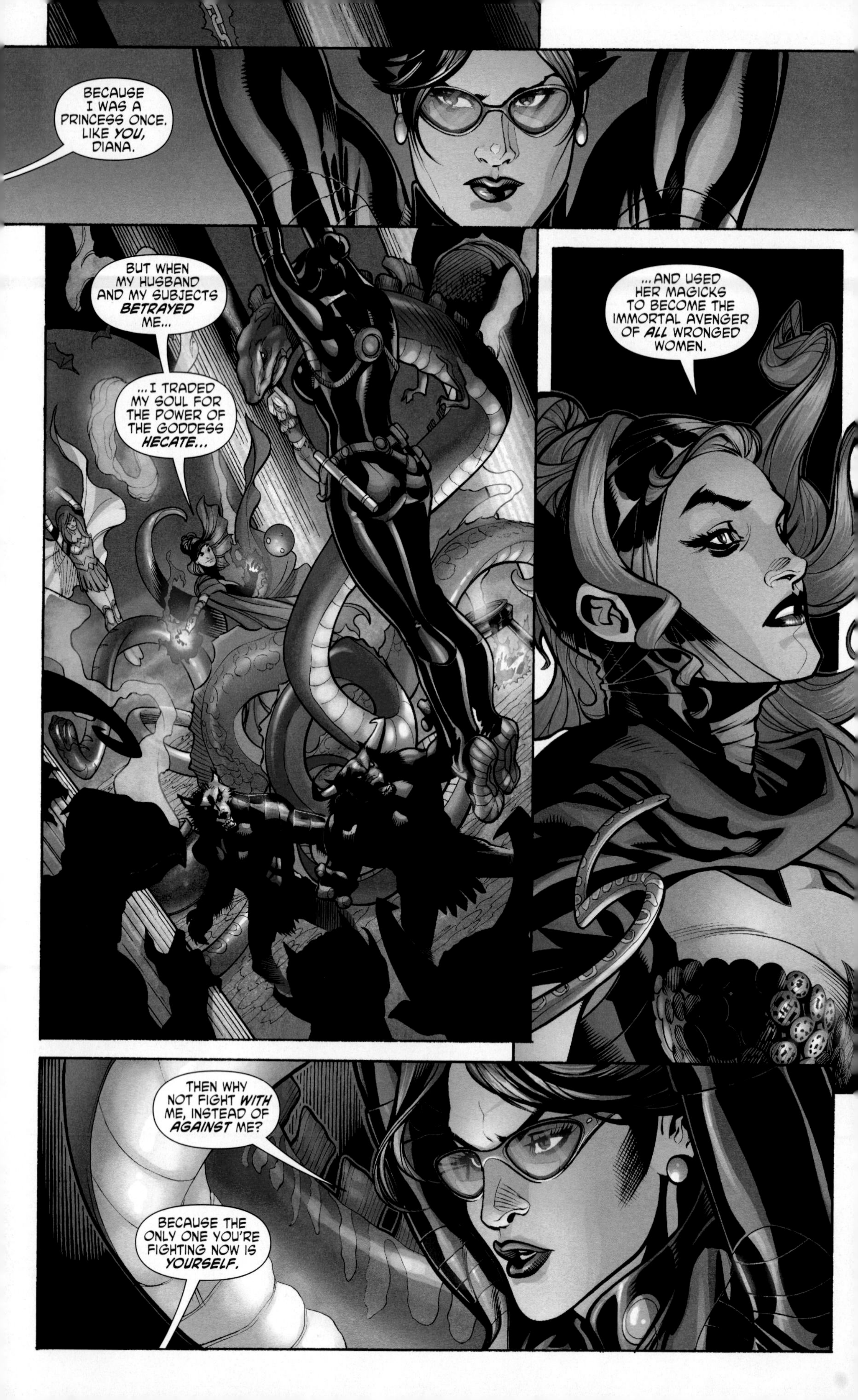
BECAUSE I WAS A PRINCESS ONCE. LIKE *YOU,* DIANA.
BUT WHEN MY HUSBAND AND MY SUBJECTS ***BETRAYED*** ME...
...I TRADED MY SOUL FOR THE POWER OF THE GODDESS ***HECATE...***
...AND USED HER MAGICKS TO BECOME THE IMMORTAL AVENGER OF ***ALL*** WRONGED WOMEN.
THEN WHY NOT FIGHT ***WITH*** ME, INSTEAD OF ***AGAINST*** ME?
BECAUSE THE ONLY ONE YOU'RE FIGHTING NOW IS ***YOURSELF.***

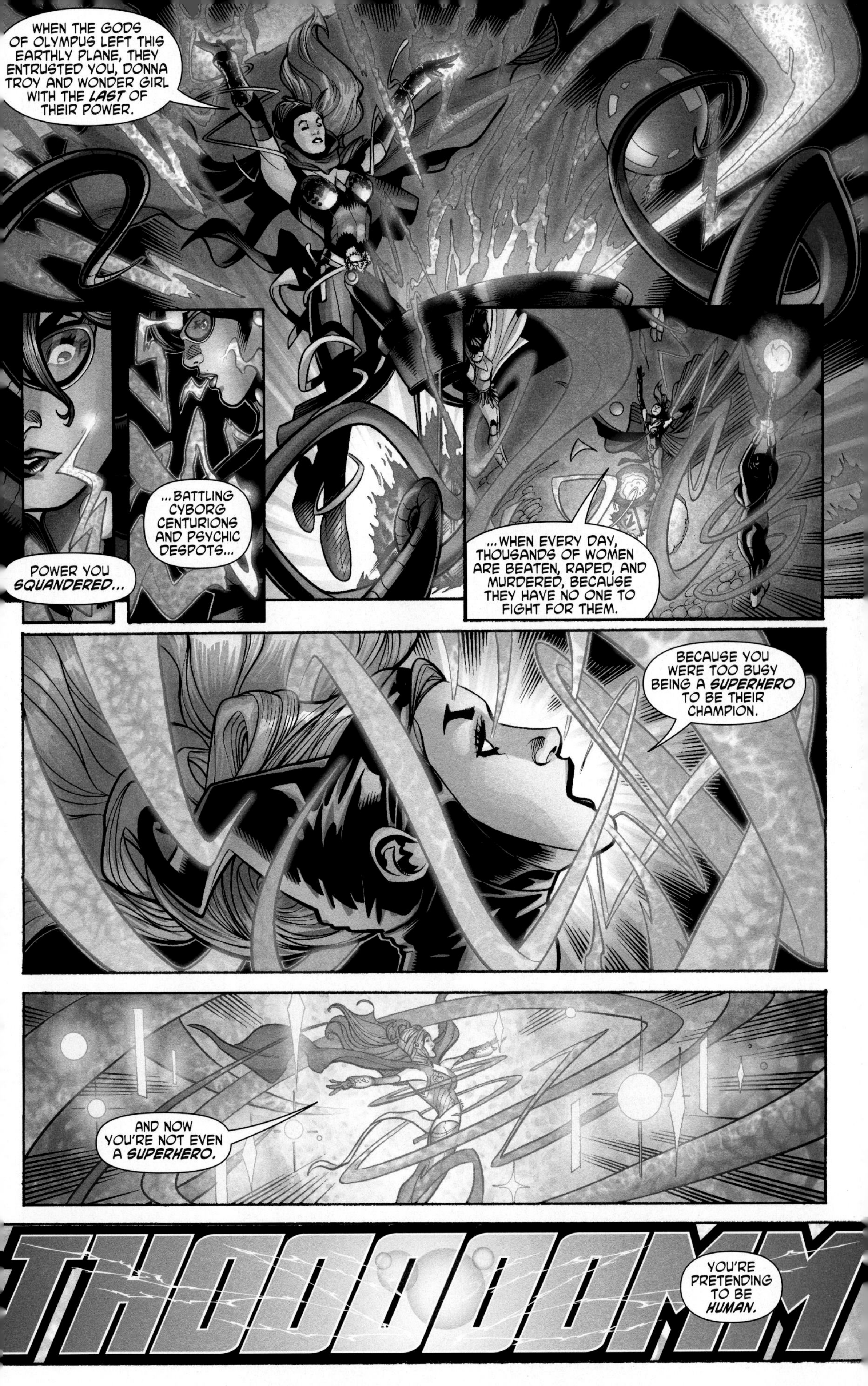
WHEN THE GODS OF OLYMPUS LEFT THIS EARTHLY PLANE, THEY ENTRUSTED YOU, DONNA TROY AND WONDER GIRL WITH THE *LAST* OF THEIR POWER.
POWER YOU *SQUANDERED*...
...BATTLING CYBORG CENTURIONS AND PSYCHIC DESPOTS...
...WHEN EVERY DAY, THOUSANDS OF WOMEN ARE BEATEN, RAPED, AND MURDERED, BECAUSE THEY HAVE NO ONE TO FIGHT FOR THEM.
BECAUSE YOU WERE TOO BUSY BEING A *SUPERHERO* TO BE THEIR CHAMPION.
AND NOW YOU'RE NOT EVEN A *SUPERHERO.*
THOOOOOMM
YOU'RE PRETENDING TO BE *HUMAN.*

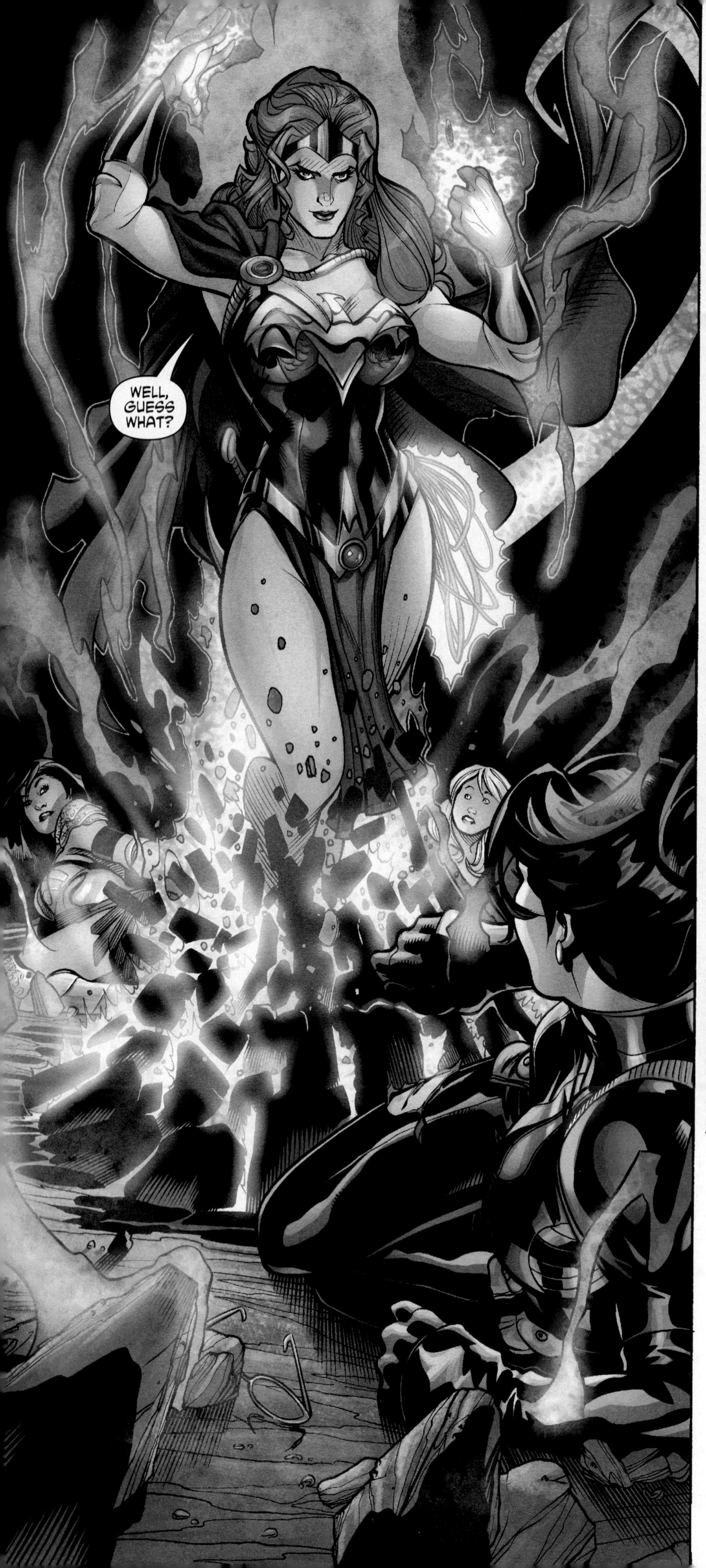
WELL, GUESS WHAT?

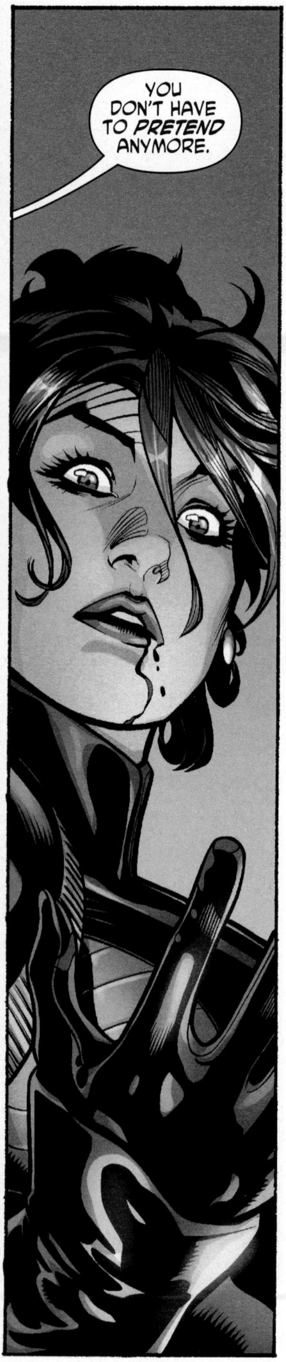
YOU DON'T HAVE TO *PRETEND* ANYMORE.

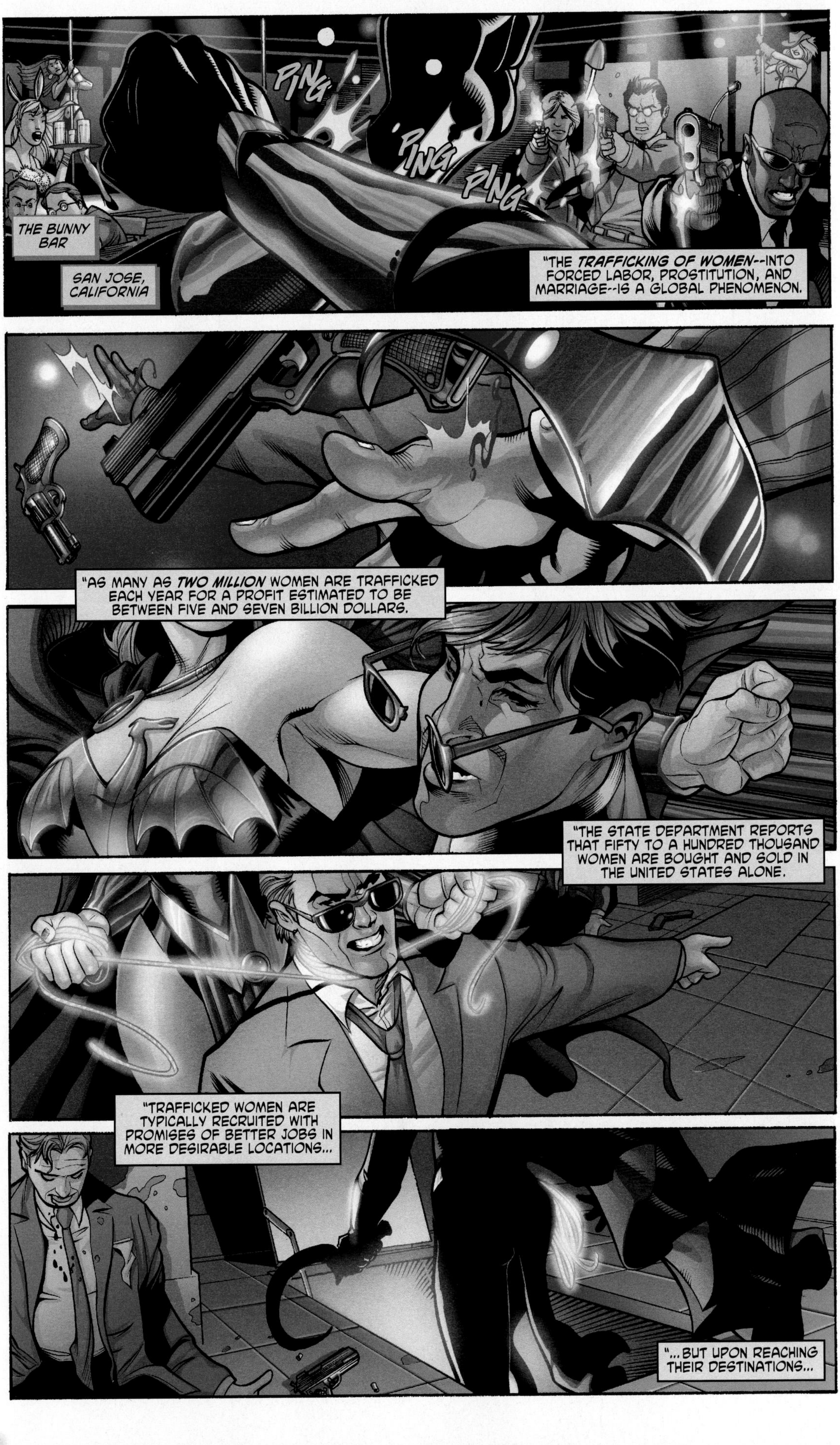

PING
PING
PING
THE BUNNY BAR
SAN JOSE, CALIFORNIA
"THE TRAFFICKING OF WOMEN--INTO FORCED LABOR, PROSTITUTION, AND MARRIAGE--IS A GLOBAL PHENOMENON.
"AS MANY AS TWO MILLION WOMEN ARE TRAFFICKED EACH YEAR FOR A PROFIT ESTIMATED TO BE BETWEEN FIVE AND SEVEN BILLION DOLLARS.
"THE STATE DEPARTMENT REPORTS THAT FIFTY TO A HUNDRED THOUSAND WOMEN ARE BOUGHT AND SOLD IN THE UNITED STATES ALONE.
"TRAFFICKED WOMEN ARE TYPICALLY RECRUITED WITH PROMISES OF BETTER JOBS IN MORE DESIRABLE LOCATIONS...
"...BUT UPON REACHING THEIR DESTINATIONS...

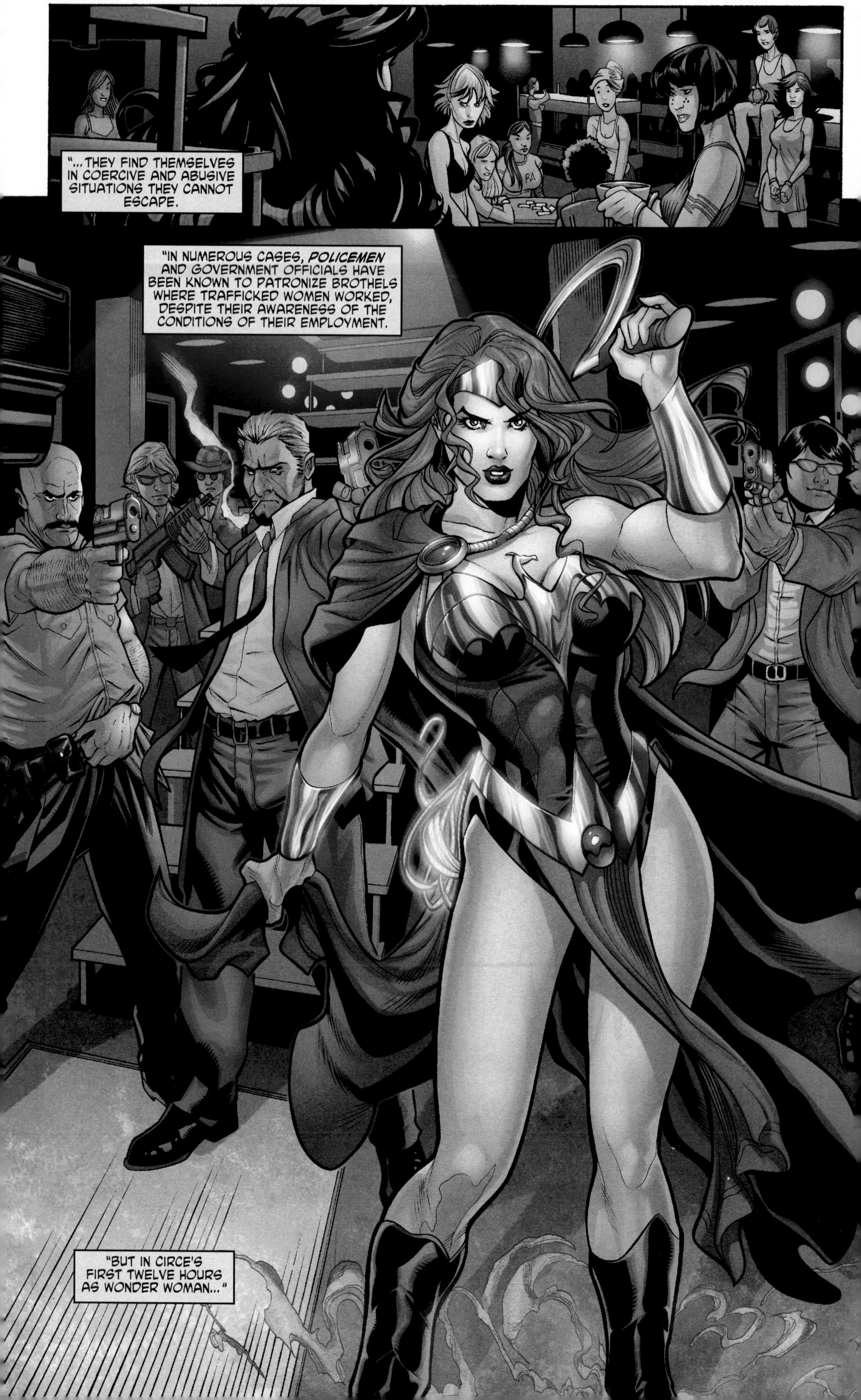
"...THEY FIND THEMSELVES IN COERCIVE AND ABUSIVE SITUATIONS THEY CANNOT ESCAPE.
"IN NUMEROUS CASES, POLICEMEN AND GOVERNMENT OFFICIALS HAVE BEEN KNOWN TO PATRONIZE BROTHELS WHERE TRAFFICKED WOMEN WORKED, DESPITE THEIR AWARENESS OF THE CONDITIONS OF THEIR EMPLOYMENT.
"BUT IN CIRCE'S FIRST TWELVE HOURS AS WONDER WOMAN..."

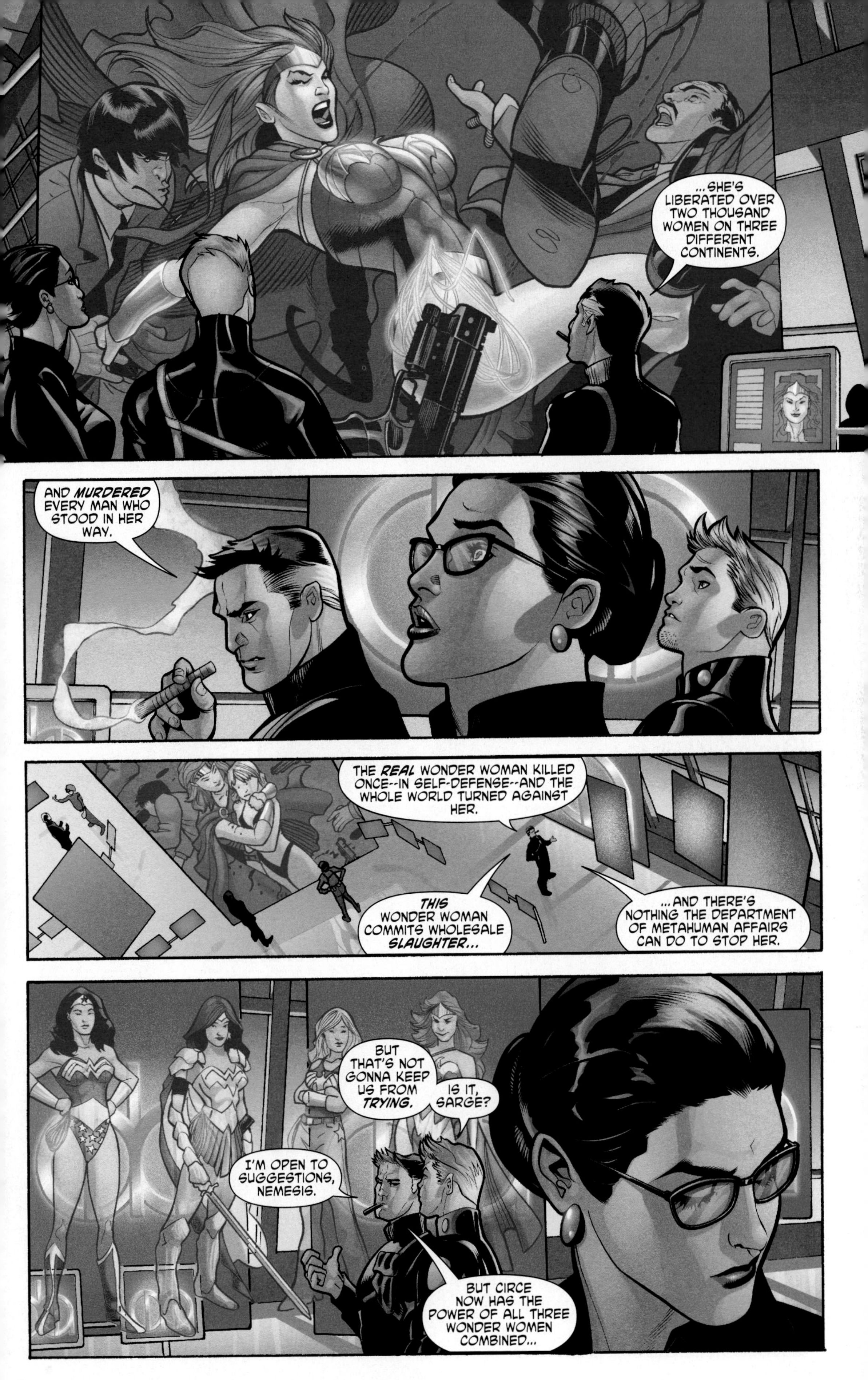
...SHE'S LIBERATED OVER TWO THOUSAND WOMEN ON THREE DIFFERENT CONTINENTS.
AND *MURDERED* EVERY MAN WHO STOOD IN HER WAY.
THE *REAL* WONDER WOMAN KILLED ONCE--IN SELF-DEFENSE--AND THE WHOLE WORLD TURNED AGAINST HER.
THIS WONDER WOMAN COMMITS WHOLESALE *SLAUGHTER*...
...AND THERE'S NOTHING THE DEPARTMENT OF METAHUMAN AFFAIRS CAN DO TO STOP HER.
BUT THAT'S NOT GONNA KEEP US FROM *TRYING.*
IS IT, SARGE?
I'M OPEN TO SUGGESTIONS, NEMESIS.
BUT CIRCE NOW HAS THE POWER OF ALL THREE WONDER WOMEN COMBINED...

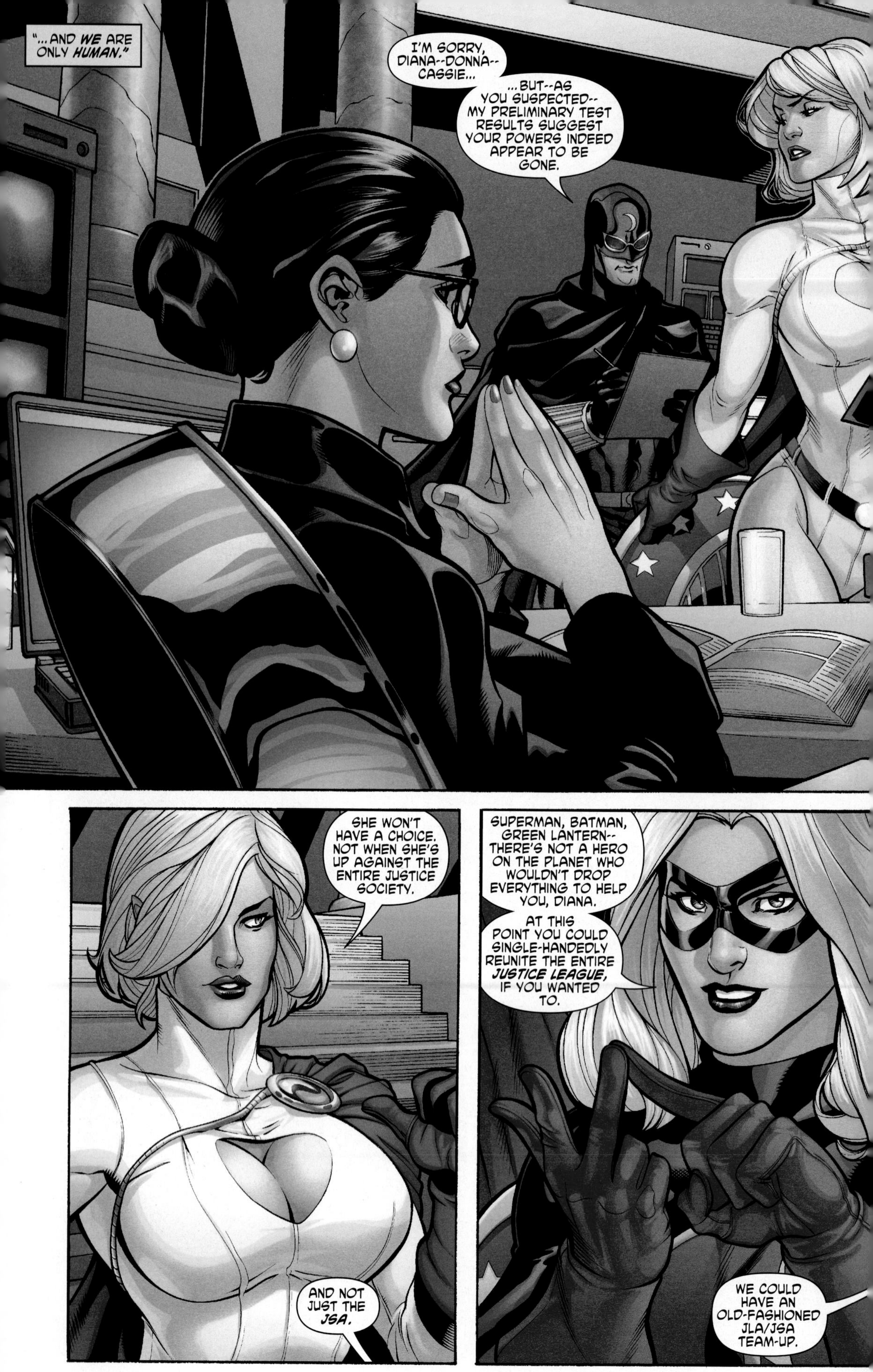
"...AND *WE* ARE ONLY *HUMAN.*"
I'M SORRY, DIANA--DONNA--CASSIE...
...BUT--AS YOU SUSPECTED--MY PRELIMINARY TEST RESULTS SUGGEST YOUR POWERS INDEED APPEAR TO BE GONE.
SHE WON'T HAVE A CHOICE. NOT WHEN SHE'S UP AGAINST THE ENTIRE JUSTICE SOCIETY.
AND NOT JUST THE *JSA.*
SUPERMAN, BATMAN, GREEN LANTERN--THERE'S NOT A HERO ON THE PLANET WHO WOULDN'T DROP EVERYTHING TO HELP YOU, DIANA.
AT THIS POINT YOU COULD SINGLE-HANDEDLY REUNITE THE ENTIRE *JUSTICE LEAGUE,* IF YOU WANTED TO.
WE COULD HAVE AN OLD-FASHIONED JLA/JSA TEAM-UP.

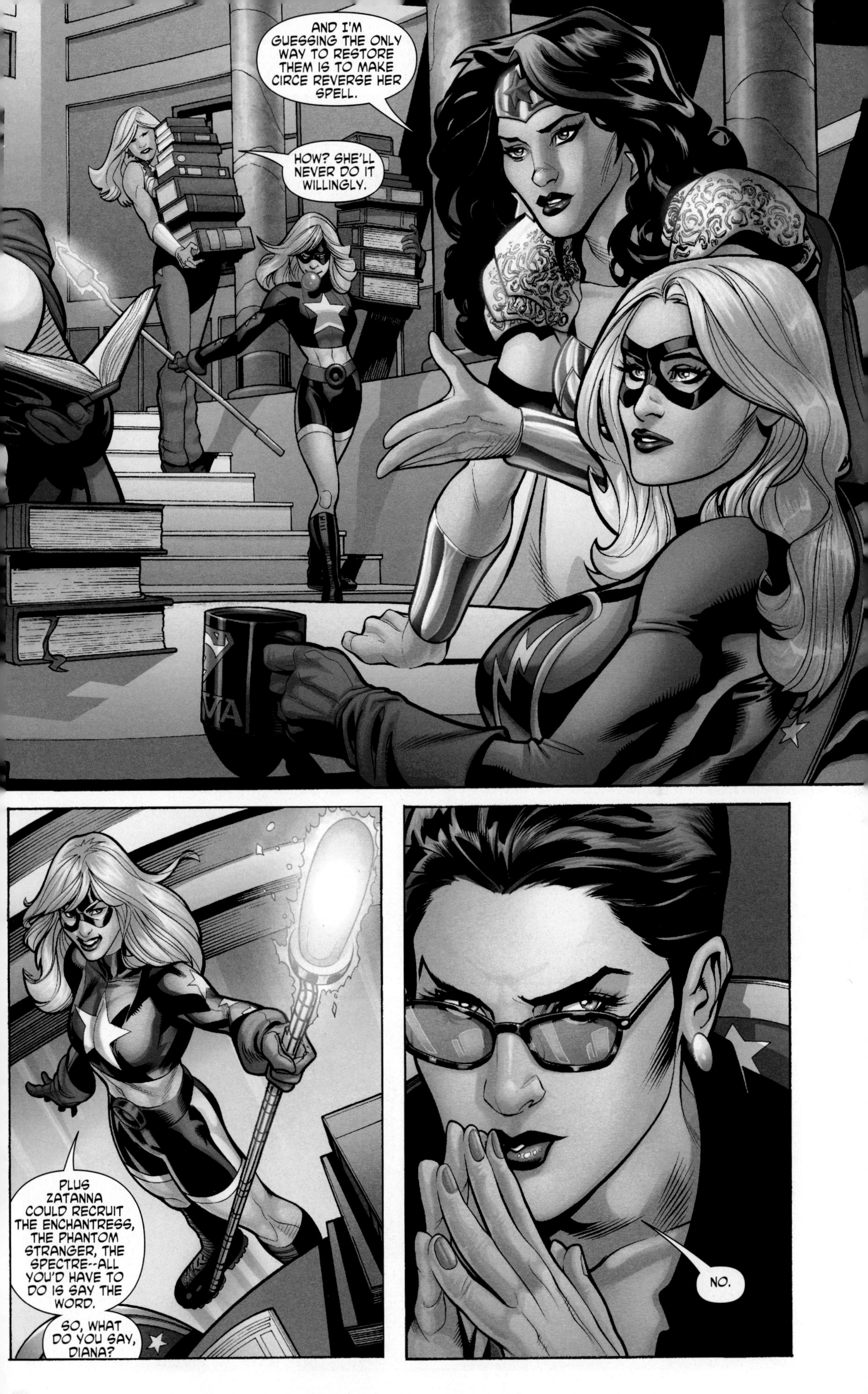
AND I'M GUESSING THE ONLY WAY TO RESTORE THEM IS TO MAKE CIRCE REVERSE HER SPELL.
HOW? SHE'LL NEVER DO IT WILLINGLY.
PLUS ZATANNA COULD RECRUIT THE ENCHANTRESS, THE PHANTOM STRANGER, THE SPECTRE--ALL YOU'D HAVE TO DO IS SAY THE WORD.
SO, WHAT DO YOU SAY, DIANA?
NO.

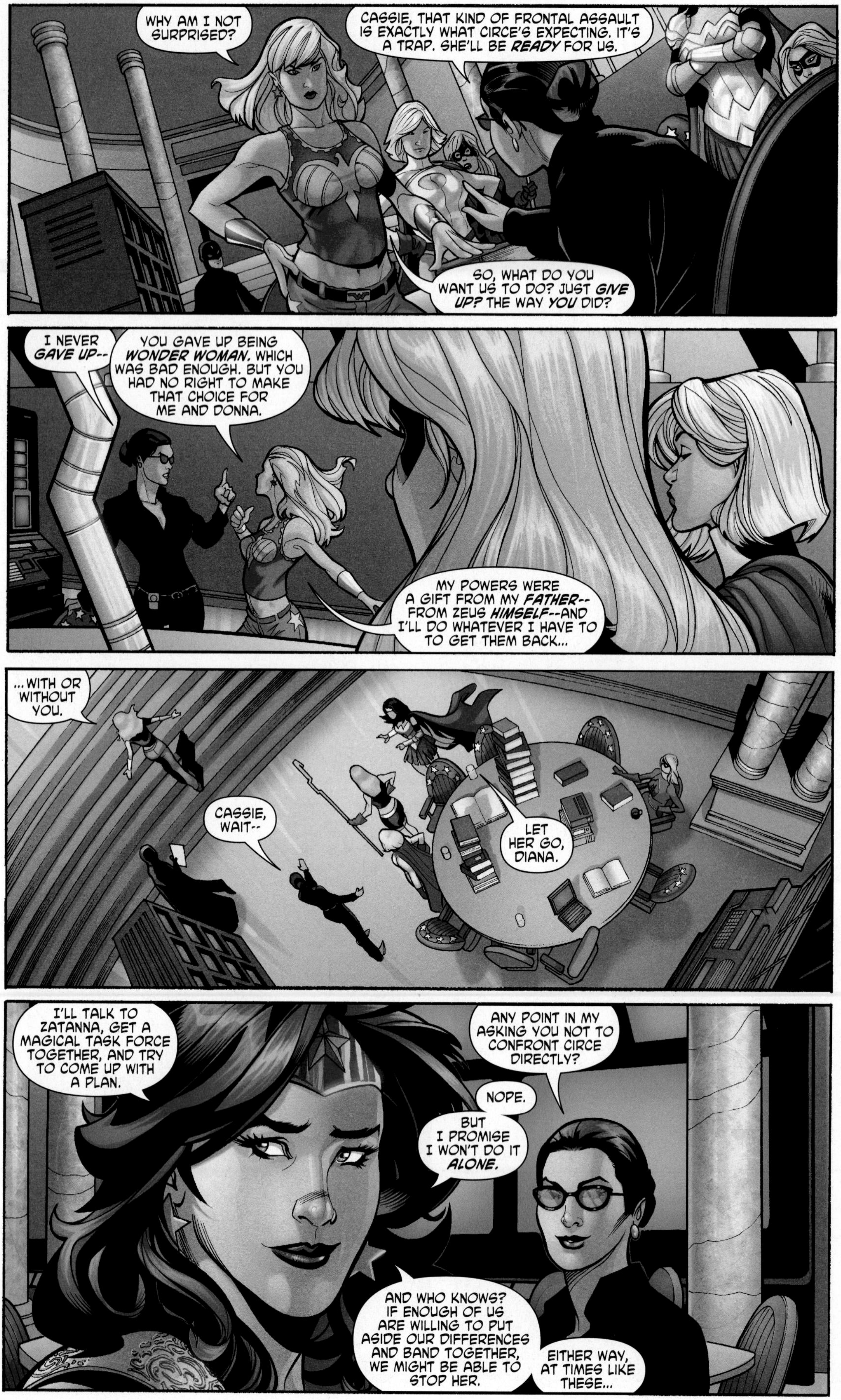
WHY AM I NOT SURPRISED?
CASSIE, THAT KIND OF FRONTAL ASSAULT IS EXACTLY WHAT CIRCE'S EXPECTING. IT'S A TRAP. SHE'LL BE READY FOR US.
SO, WHAT DO YOU WANT US TO DO? JUST GIVE UP? THE WAY YOU DID?
I NEVER GAVE UP--
YOU GAVE UP BEING WONDER WOMAN. WHICH WAS BAD ENOUGH. BUT YOU HAD NO RIGHT TO MAKE THAT CHOICE FOR ME AND DONNA.
MY POWERS WERE A GIFT FROM MY FATHER-- FROM ZEUS HIMSELF--AND I'LL DO WHATEVER I HAVE TO TO GET THEM BACK...
...WITH OR WITHOUT YOU.
CASSIE, WAIT--
LET HER GO, DIANA.
I'LL TALK TO ZATANNA, GET A MAGICAL TASK FORCE TOGETHER, AND TRY TO COME UP WITH A PLAN.
ANY POINT IN MY ASKING YOU NOT TO CONFRONT CIRCE DIRECTLY?
NOPE.
BUT I PROMISE I WON'T DO IT ALONE.
AND WHO KNOWS? IF ENOUGH OF US ARE WILLING TO PUT ASIDE OUR DIFFERENCES AND BAND TOGETHER, WE MIGHT BE ABLE TO STOP HER.
EITHER WAY, AT TIMES LIKE THESE...

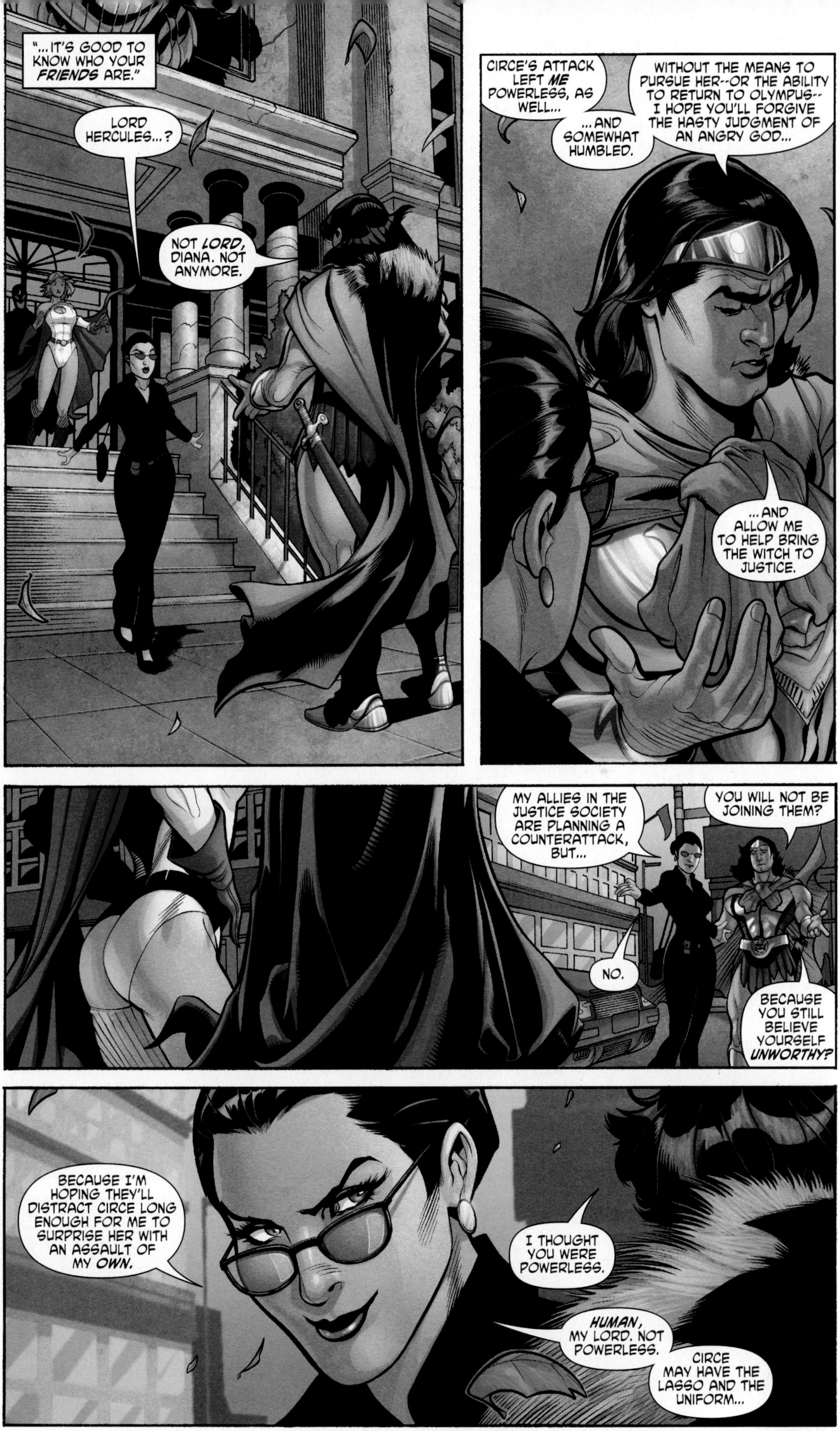
"...IT'S GOOD TO KNOW WHO YOUR *FRIENDS* ARE."
LORD HERCULES...?
NOT *LORD*, DIANA. NOT ANYMORE.
CIRCE'S ATTACK LEFT *ME* POWERLESS, AS WELL...
...AND SOMEWHAT HUMBLED.
WITHOUT THE MEANS TO PURSUE HER--OR THE ABILITY TO RETURN TO OLYMPUS--I HOPE YOU'LL FORGIVE THE HASTY JUDGMENT OF AN ANGRY GOD...
...AND ALLOW ME TO HELP BRING THE WITCH TO JUSTICE.
MY ALLIES IN THE JUSTICE SOCIETY ARE PLANNING A COUNTERATTACK, BUT...
YOU WILL NOT BE JOINING THEM?
NO.
BECAUSE YOU STILL BELIEVE YOURSELF *UNWORTHY?*
BECAUSE I'M HOPING THEY'LL DISTRACT CIRCE LONG ENOUGH FOR ME TO SURPRISE HER WITH AN ASSAULT OF MY *OWN.*
I THOUGHT YOU WERE POWERLESS.
HUMAN, MY LORD. NOT POWERLESS.
CIRCE MAY HAVE THE LASSO AND THE UNIFORM...

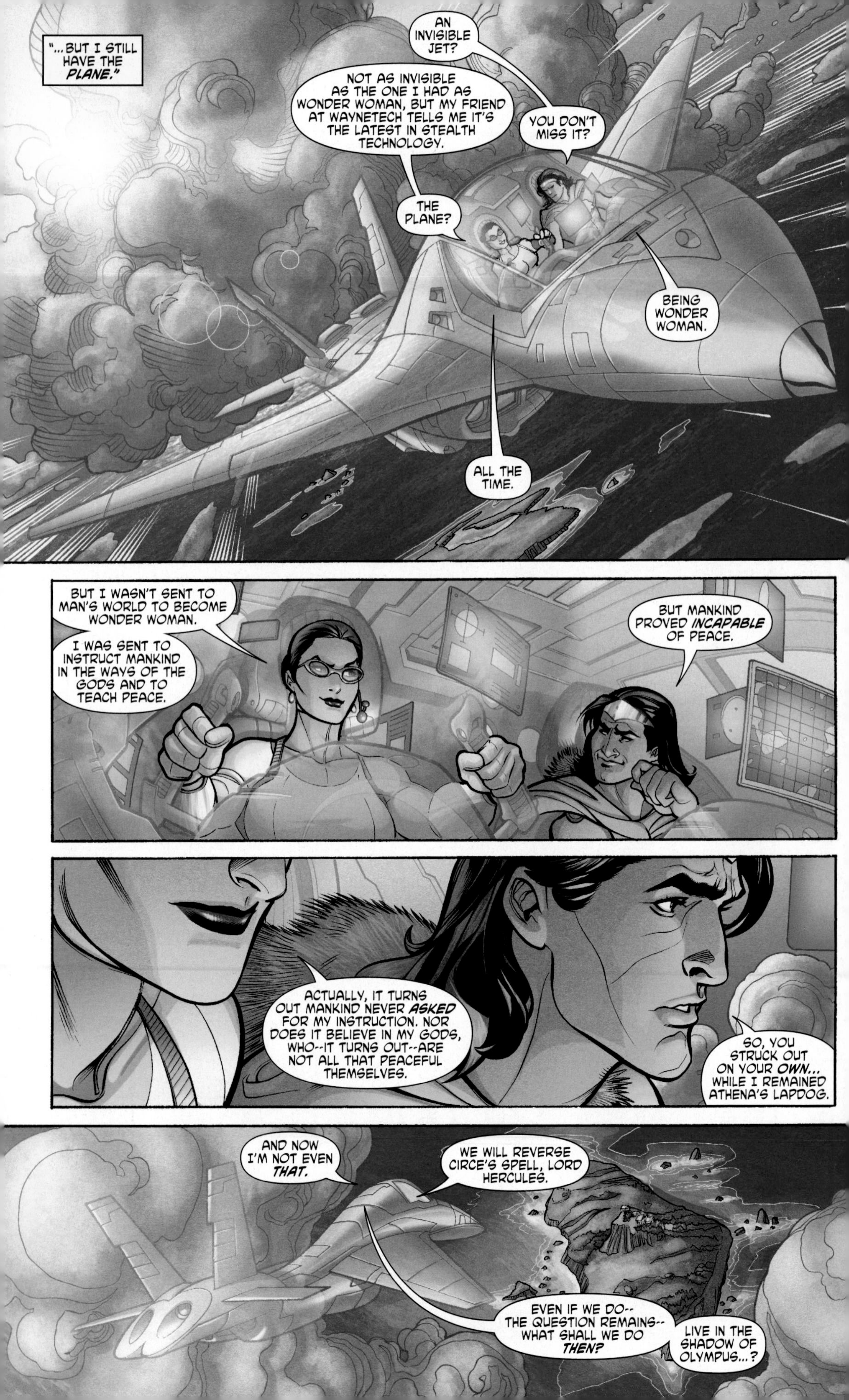
"...BUT I STILL HAVE THE *PLANE.*"
AN INVISIBLE JET?
NOT AS INVISIBLE AS THE ONE I HAD AS WONDER WOMAN, BUT MY FRIEND AT WAYNETECH TELLS ME IT'S THE LATEST IN STEALTH TECHNOLOGY.
YOU DON'T MISS IT?
THE PLANE?
BEING WONDER WOMAN.
ALL THE TIME.
BUT I WASN'T SENT TO MAN'S WORLD TO BECOME WONDER WOMAN.
I WAS SENT TO INSTRUCT MANKIND IN THE WAYS OF THE GODS AND TO TEACH PEACE.
BUT MANKIND PROVED *INCAPABLE* OF PEACE.
ACTUALLY, IT TURNS OUT MANKIND NEVER *ASKED* FOR MY INSTRUCTION. NOR DOES IT BELIEVE IN MY GODS, WHO--IT TURNS OUT--ARE NOT ALL THAT PEACEFUL THEMSELVES.
SO, YOU STRUCK OUT ON YOUR *OWN*... WHILE I REMAINED ATHENA'S LAPDOG.
AND NOW I'M NOT EVEN *THAT.*
WE WILL REVERSE CIRCE'S SPELL, LORD HERCULES.
EVEN IF WE DO-- THE QUESTION REMAINS-- WHAT SHALL WE DO *THEN?*
LIVE IN THE SHADOW OF OLYMPUS...?

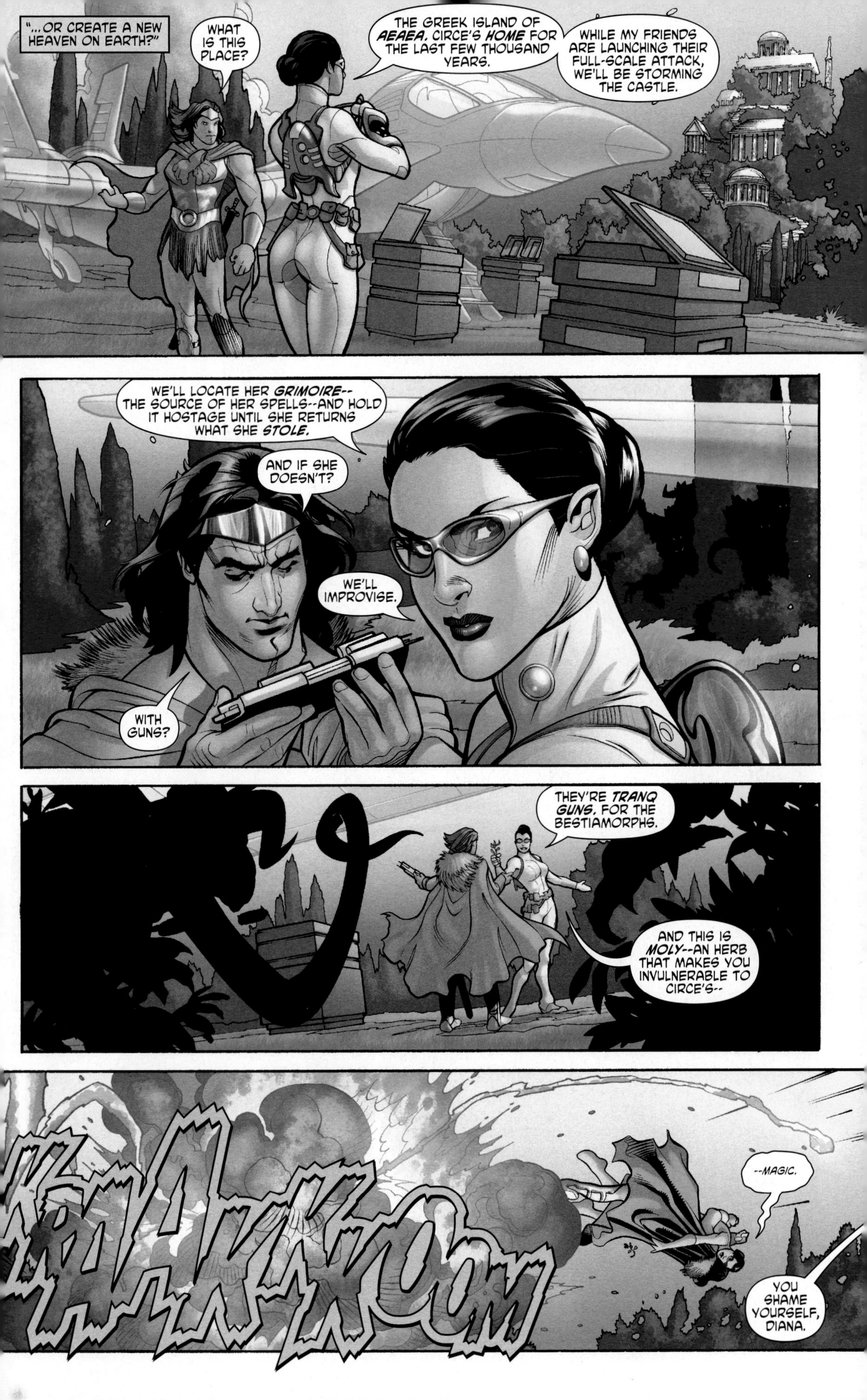
"...OR CREATE A NEW HEAVEN ON EARTH?"
WHAT IS THIS PLACE?
THE GREEK ISLAND OF AEAEA. CIRCE'S HOME FOR THE LAST FEW THOUSAND YEARS.
WHILE MY FRIENDS ARE LAUNCHING THEIR FULL-SCALE ATTACK, WE'LL BE STORMING THE CASTLE.
WE'LL LOCATE HER GRIMOIRE-- THE SOURCE OF HER SPELLS--AND HOLD IT HOSTAGE UNTIL SHE RETURNS WHAT SHE STOLE.
AND IF SHE DOESN'T?
WE'LL IMPROVISE.
WITH GUNS?
THEY'RE TRANQ GUNS. FOR THE BESTIAMORPHS.
AND THIS IS MOLY--AN HERB THAT MAKES YOU INVULNERABLE TO CIRCE'S--
KRAKKKOOM
--MAGIC.
YOU SHAME YOURSELF, DIANA.

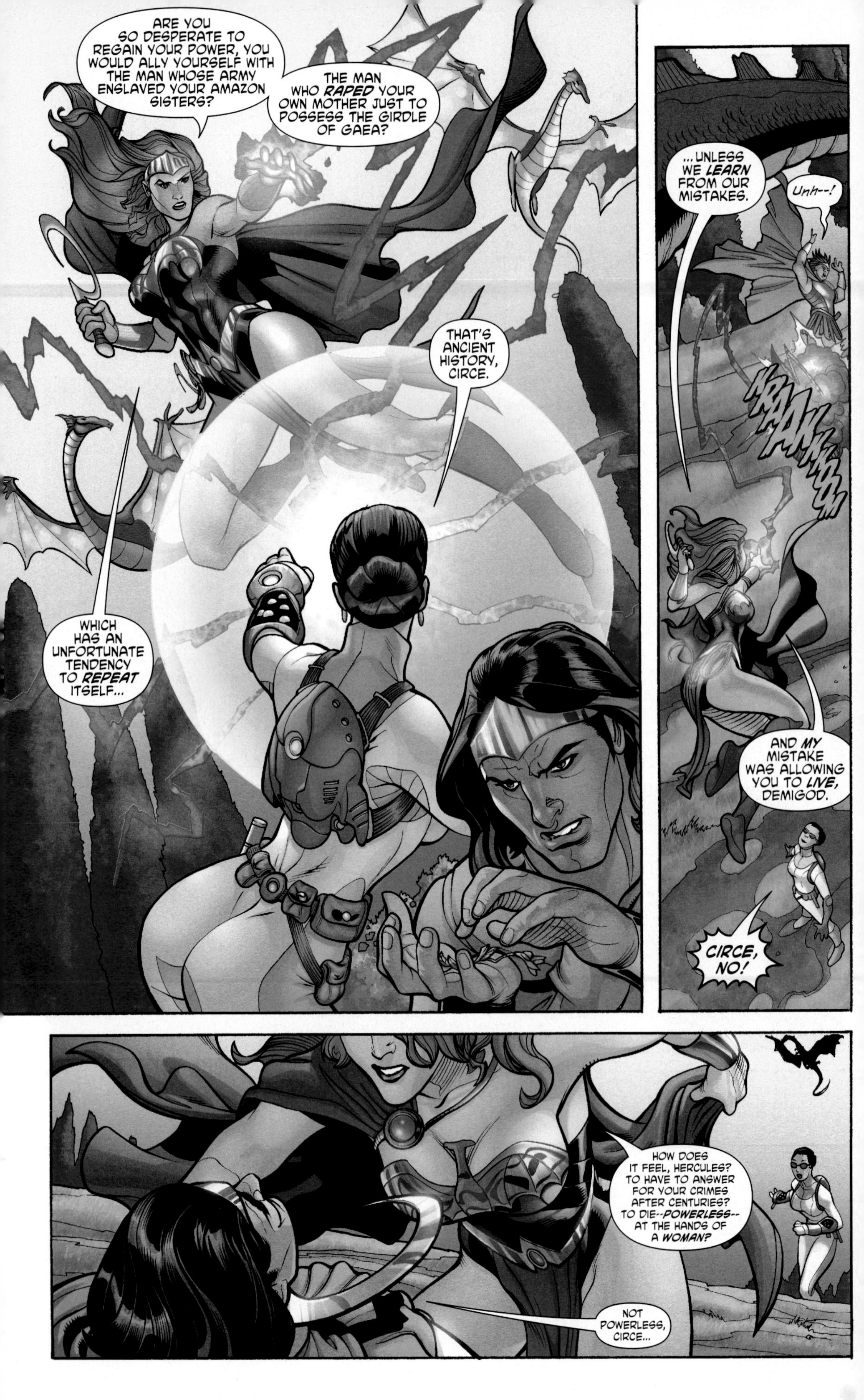

ARE YOU SO DESPERATE TO REGAIN YOUR POWER, YOU WOULD ALLY YOURSELF WITH THE MAN WHOSE ARMY ENSLAVED YOUR AMAZON SISTERS?
THE MAN WHO *RAPED* YOUR OWN MOTHER JUST TO POSSESS THE GIRDLE OF GAEA?
THAT'S ANCIENT HISTORY, CIRCE.
WHICH HAS AN UNFORTUNATE TENDENCY TO *REPEAT* ITSELF...
...UNLESS WE *LEARN* FROM OUR MISTAKES.
Unh--!
KRAKKOOM
AND *MY* MISTAKE WAS ALLOWING YOU TO *LIVE*, DEMIGOD.
CIRCE, NO!
HOW DOES IT FEEL, HERCULES? TO HAVE TO ANSWER FOR YOUR CRIMES AFTER CENTURIES? TO DIE--*POWERLESS*--AT THE HANDS OF A *WOMAN?*
NOT POWERLESS, CIRCE...

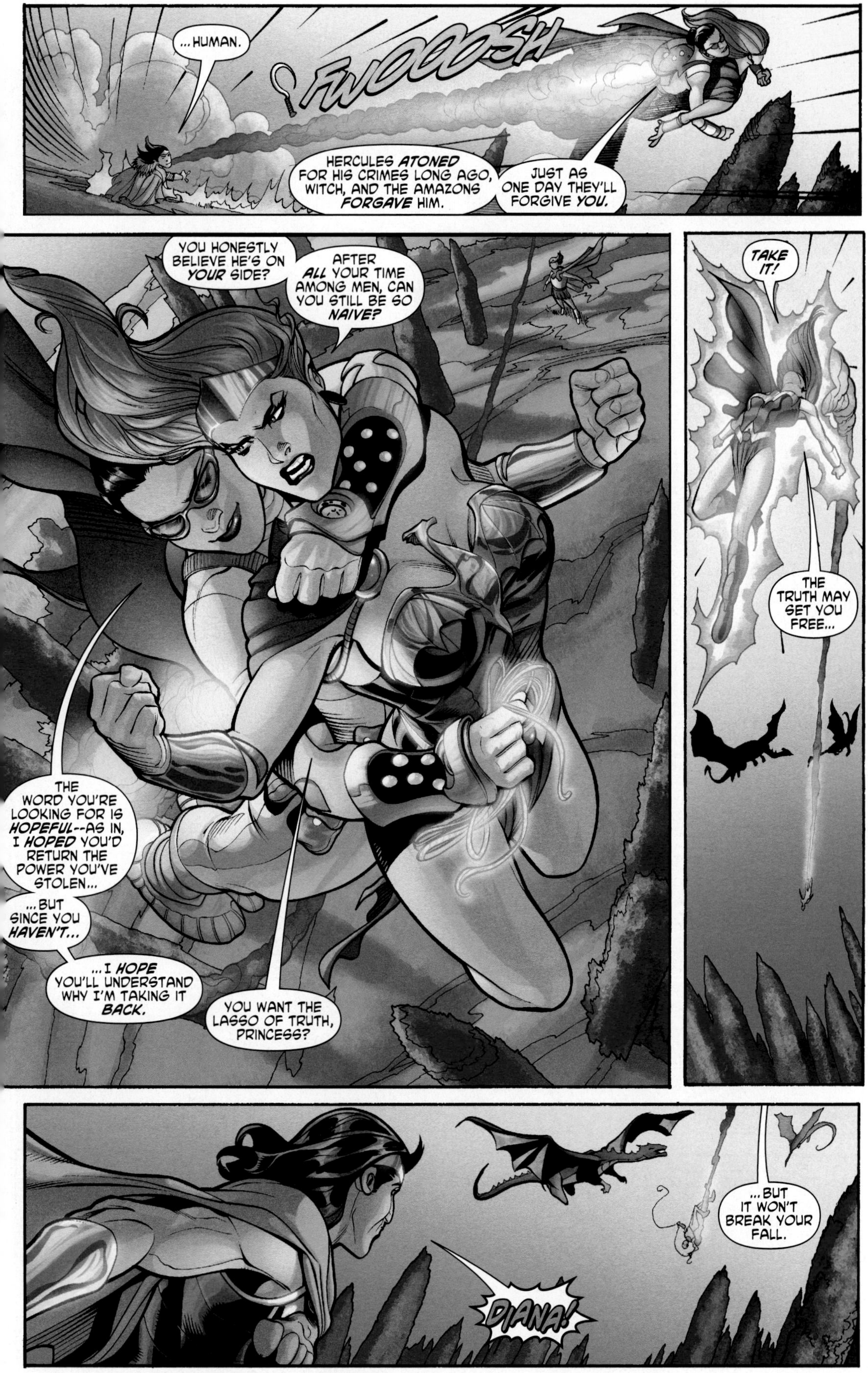
...HUMAN.
FWOOOSH
HERCULES ATONED FOR HIS CRIMES LONG AGO, WITCH, AND THE AMAZONS FORGAVE HIM.
JUST AS ONE DAY THEY'LL FORGIVE YOU.
YOU HONESTLY BELIEVE HE'S ON YOUR SIDE?
AFTER ALL YOUR TIME AMONG MEN, CAN YOU STILL BE SO NAIVE?
THE WORD YOU'RE LOOKING FOR IS HOPEFUL--AS IN, I HOPED YOU'D RETURN THE POWER YOU'VE STOLEN...
...BUT SINCE YOU HAVEN'T...
...I HOPE YOU'LL UNDERSTAND WHY I'M TAKING IT BACK.
YOU WANT THE LASSO OF TRUTH, PRINCESS?
TAKE IT!
THE TRUTH MAY SET YOU FREE...
...BUT IT WON'T BREAK YOUR FALL.
DIANA!

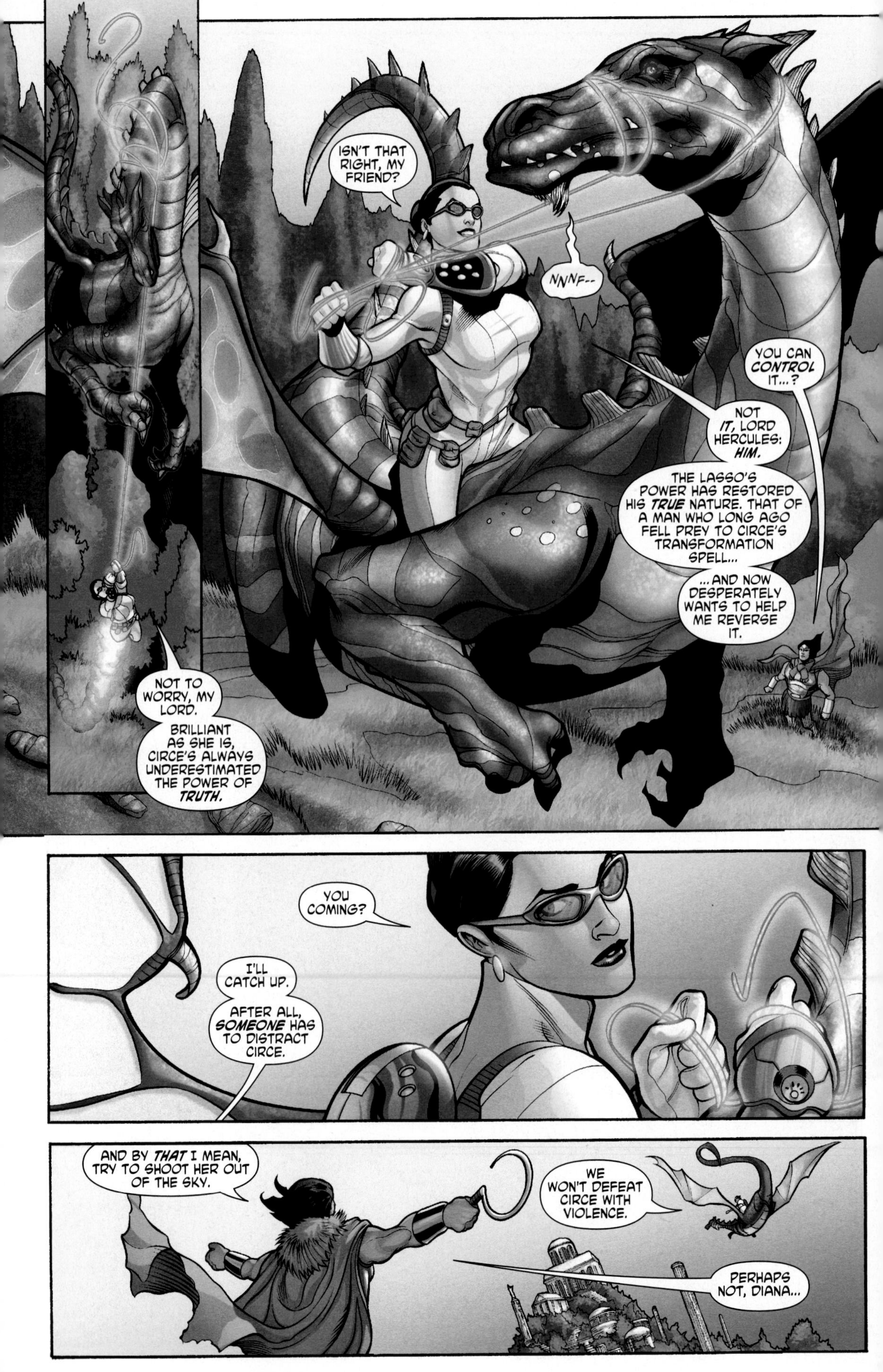
ISN'T THAT RIGHT, MY FRIEND?
NNNF--
YOU CAN CONTROL IT...?
NOT IT, LORD HERCULES: HIM.
THE LASSO'S POWER HAS RESTORED HIS TRUE NATURE. THAT OF A MAN WHO LONG AGO FELL PREY TO CIRCE'S TRANSFORMATION SPELL...
...AND NOW DESPERATELY WANTS TO HELP ME REVERSE IT.
NOT TO WORRY, MY LORD.
BRILLIANT AS SHE IS, CIRCE'S ALWAYS UNDERESTIMATED THE POWER OF TRUTH.
YOU COMING?
I'LL CATCH UP.
AFTER ALL, SOMEONE HAS TO DISTRACT CIRCE.
AND BY THAT I MEAN, TRY TO SHOOT HER OUT OF THE SKY.
WE WON'T DEFEAT CIRCE WITH VIOLENCE.
PERHAPS NOT, DIANA...

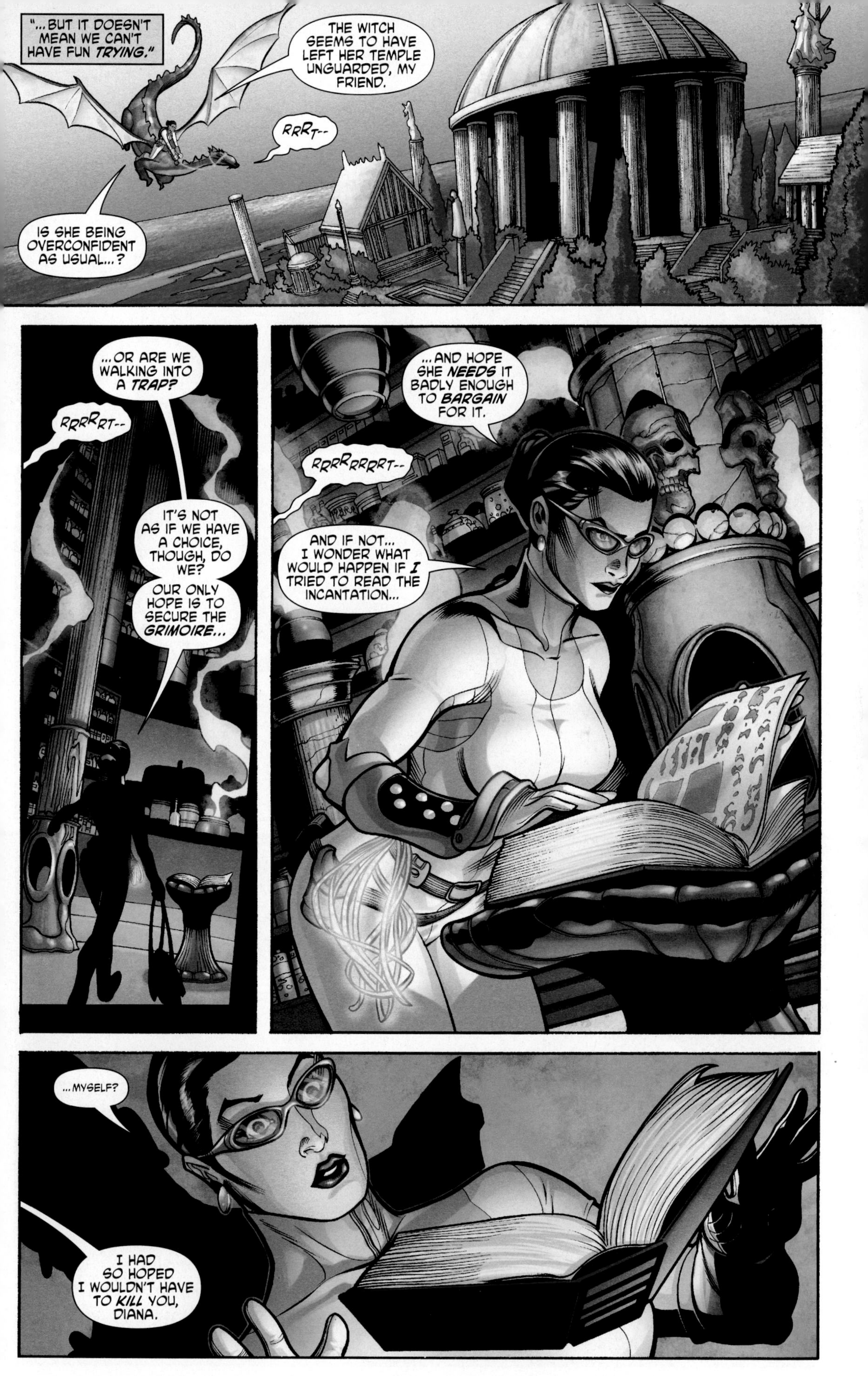
"...BUT IT DOESN'T MEAN WE CAN'T HAVE FUN *TRYING*."
THE WITCH SEEMS TO HAVE LEFT HER TEMPLE UNGUARDED, MY FRIEND.
RRRT--
IS SHE BEING OVERCONFIDENT AS USUAL...?
...OR ARE WE WALKING INTO A *TRAP?*
RRRRRT--
IT'S NOT AS IF WE HAVE A CHOICE, THOUGH, DO WE?
OUR ONLY HOPE IS TO SECURE THE *GRIMOIRE*...
...AND HOPE SHE *NEEDS* IT BADLY ENOUGH TO *BARGAIN* FOR IT.
RRRRRRRRT--
AND IF NOT... I WONDER WHAT WOULD HAPPEN IF *I* TRIED TO READ THE INCANTATION...
...MYSELF?
I HAD SO HOPED I WOULDN'T HAVE TO *KILL* YOU, DIANA.

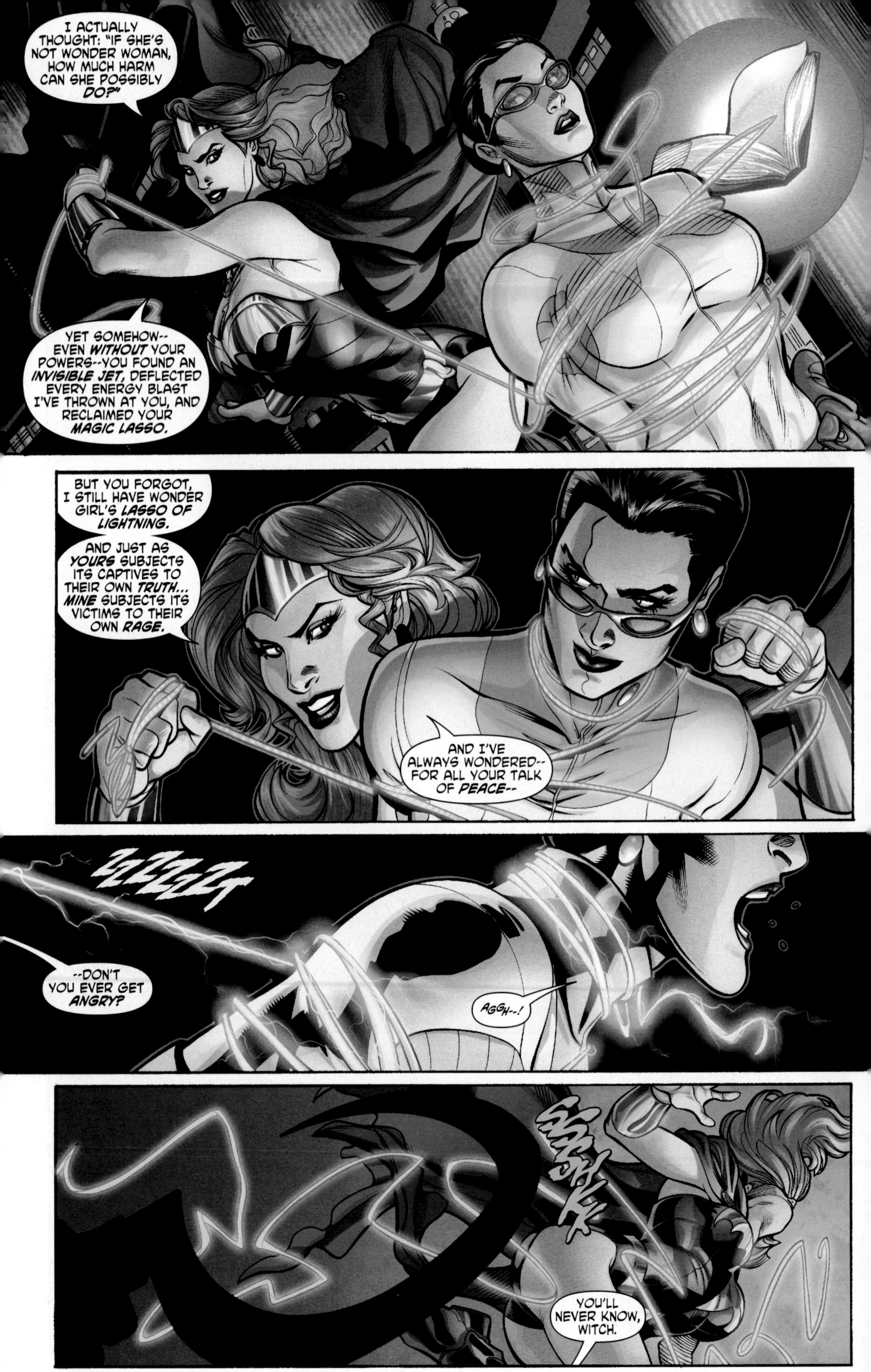
I ACTUALLY THOUGHT: "IF SHE'S NOT WONDER WOMAN, HOW MUCH HARM CAN SHE POSSIBLY DO?"
YET SOMEHOW-- EVEN WITHOUT YOUR POWERS--YOU FOUND AN INVISIBLE JET, DEFLECTED EVERY ENERGY BLAST I'VE THROWN AT YOU, AND RECLAIMED YOUR MAGIC LASSO.
BUT YOU FORGOT, I STILL HAVE WONDER GIRL'S LASSO OF LIGHTNING.
AND JUST AS YOURS SUBJECTS ITS CAPTIVES TO THEIR OWN TRUTH... MINE SUBJECTS ITS VICTIMS TO THEIR OWN RAGE.
AND I'VE ALWAYS WONDERED-- FOR ALL YOUR TALK OF PEACE--
ZZZZZZZT
--DON'T YOU EVER GET ANGRY?
AGGH--!
SHSHSHKK
YOU'LL NEVER KNOW, WITCH.

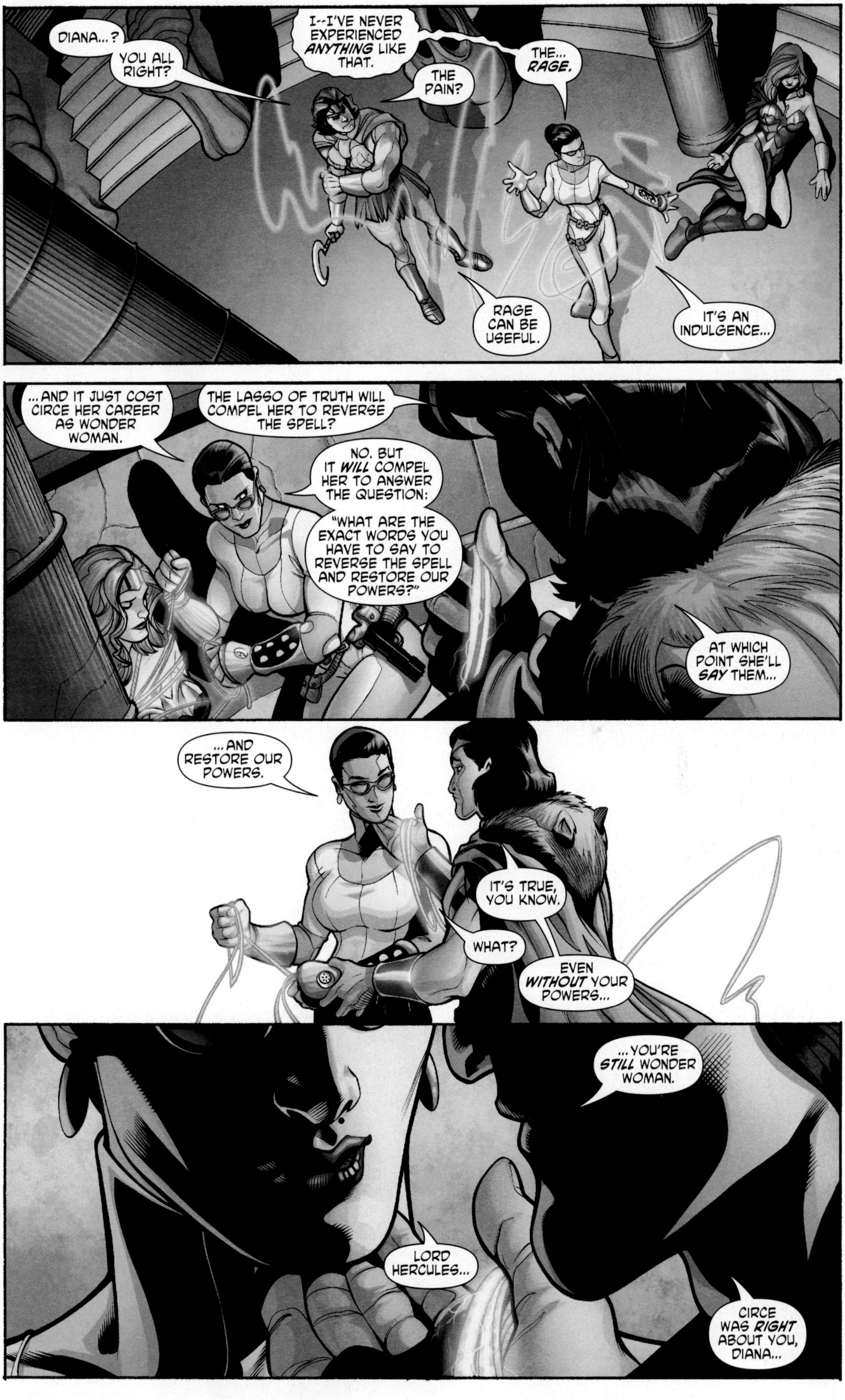
DIANA...?
YOU ALL RIGHT?
I--I'VE NEVER EXPERIENCED ANYTHING LIKE THAT.
THE PAIN?
THE... RAGE.
RAGE CAN BE USEFUL.
IT'S AN INDULGENCE...
...AND IT JUST COST CIRCE HER CAREER AS WONDER WOMAN.
THE LASSO OF TRUTH WILL COMPEL HER TO REVERSE THE SPELL?
NO. BUT IT WILL COMPEL HER TO ANSWER THE QUESTION:
"WHAT ARE THE EXACT WORDS YOU HAVE TO SAY TO REVERSE THE SPELL AND RESTORE OUR POWERS?"
AT WHICH POINT SHE'LL SAY THEM...
...AND RESTORE OUR POWERS.
IT'S TRUE, YOU KNOW.
WHAT?
EVEN WITHOUT YOUR POWERS...
...YOU'RE STILL WONDER WOMAN.
LORD HERCULES...
CIRCE WAS RIGHT ABOUT YOU, DIANA...

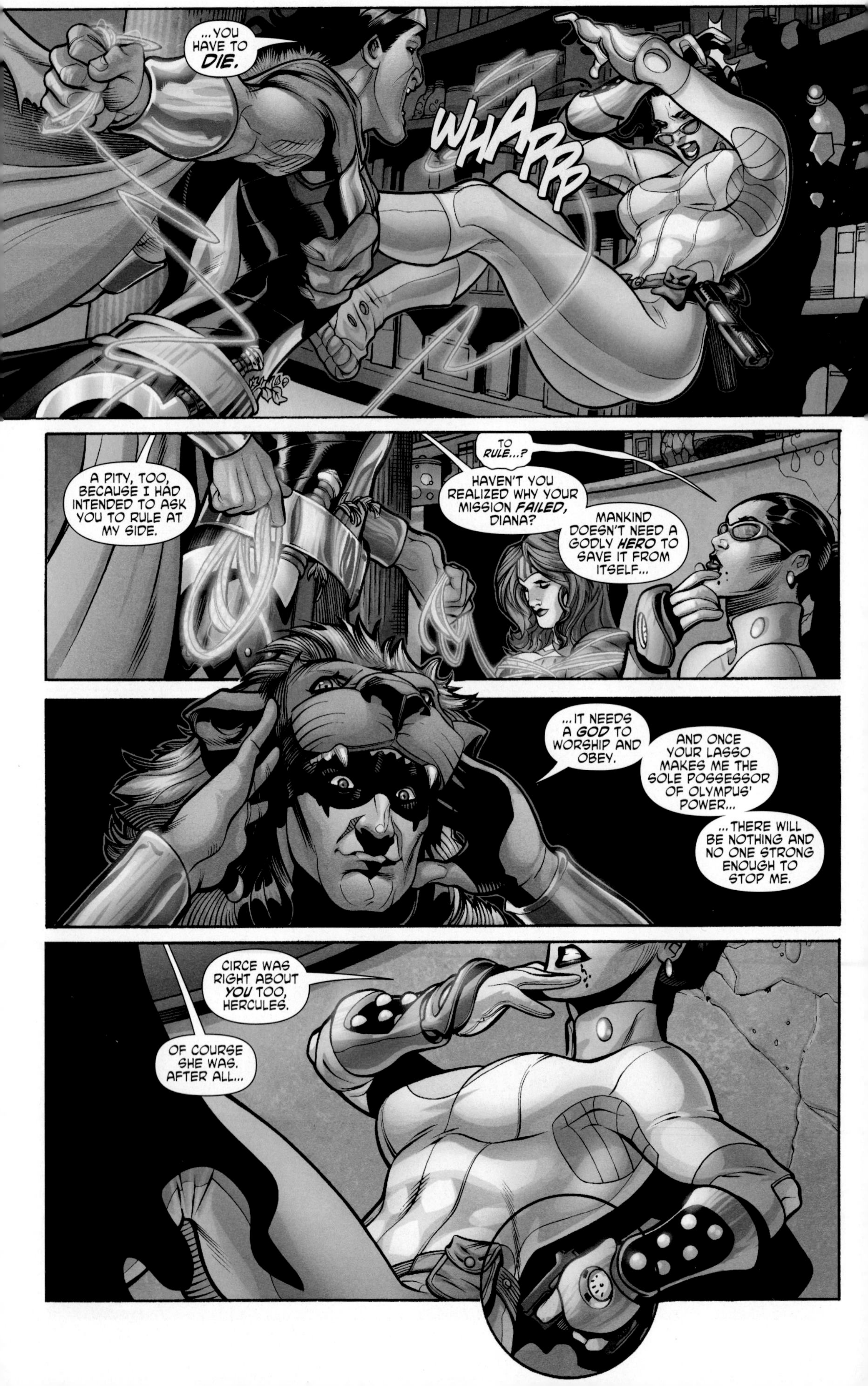
...YOU HAVE TO DIE.
WHAPP
A PITY, TOO, BECAUSE I HAD INTENDED TO ASK YOU TO RULE AT MY SIDE.
TO RULE...?
HAVEN'T YOU REALIZED WHY YOUR MISSION FAILED, DIANA?
MANKIND DOESN'T NEED A GODLY HERO TO SAVE IT FROM ITSELF...
...IT NEEDS A GOD TO WORSHIP AND OBEY.
AND ONCE YOUR LASSO MAKES ME THE SOLE POSSESSOR OF OLYMPUS' POWER...
...THERE WILL BE NOTHING AND NO ONE STRONG ENOUGH TO STOP ME.
CIRCE WAS RIGHT ABOUT YOU TOO, HERCULES.
OF COURSE SHE WAS. AFTER ALL...

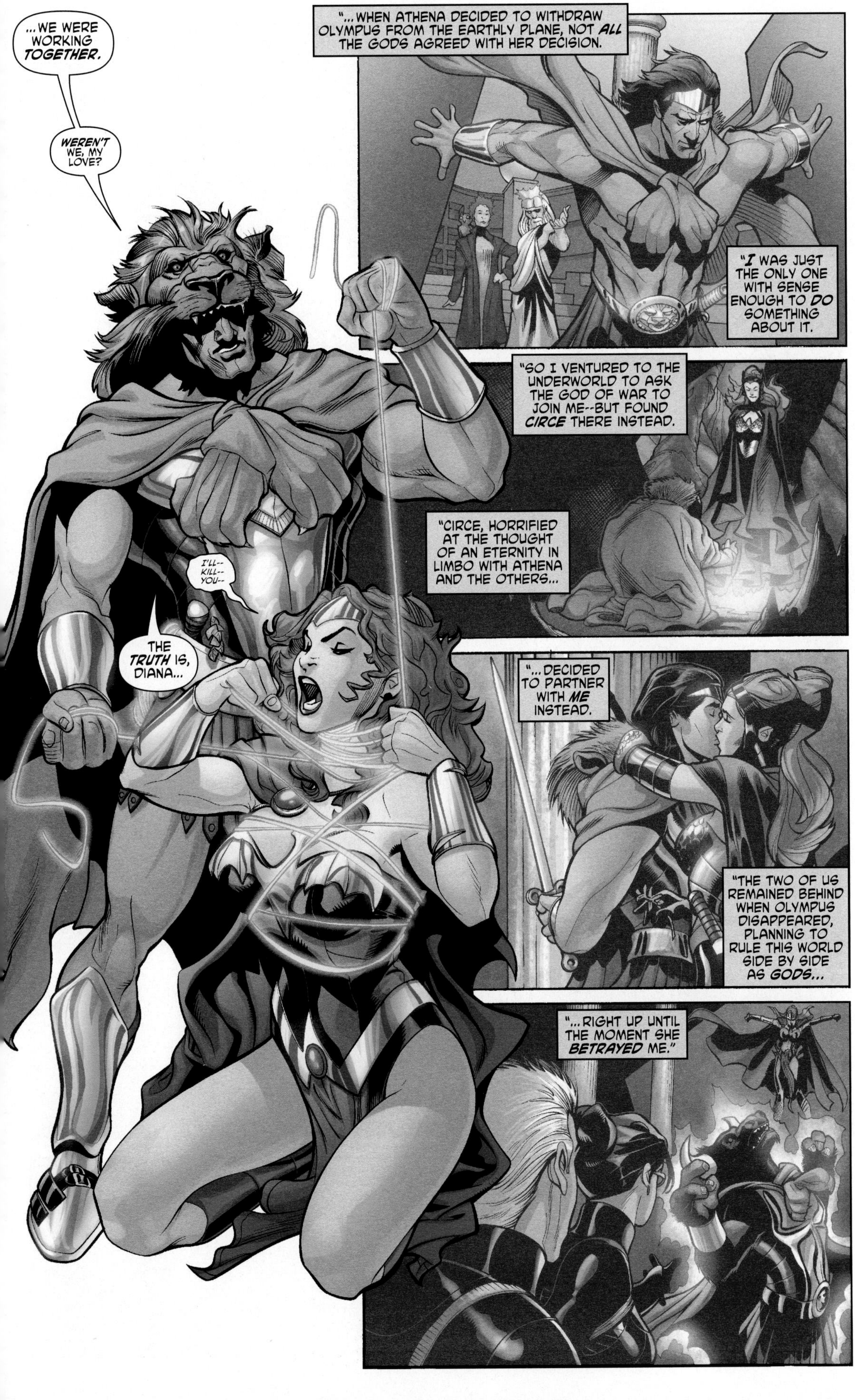

...WE WERE WORKING TOGETHER.
WEREN'T WE, MY LOVE?
"...WHEN ATHENA DECIDED TO WITHDRAW OLYMPUS FROM THE EARTHLY PLANE, NOT ALL THE GODS AGREED WITH HER DECISION.
"I WAS JUST THE ONLY ONE WITH SENSE ENOUGH TO DO SOMETHING ABOUT IT.
"SO I VENTURED TO THE UNDERWORLD TO ASK THE GOD OF WAR TO JOIN ME--BUT FOUND CIRCE THERE INSTEAD.
"CIRCE, HORRIFIED AT THE THOUGHT OF AN ETERNITY IN LIMBO WITH ATHENA AND THE OTHERS...
I'LL-- KILL-- YOU--
THE TRUTH IS, DIANA...
"...DECIDED TO PARTNER WITH ME INSTEAD.
"THE TWO OF US REMAINED BEHIND WHEN OLYMPUS DISAPPEARED, PLANNING TO RULE THIS WORLD SIDE BY SIDE AS GODS...
"...RIGHT UP UNTIL THE MOMENT SHE BETRAYED ME."

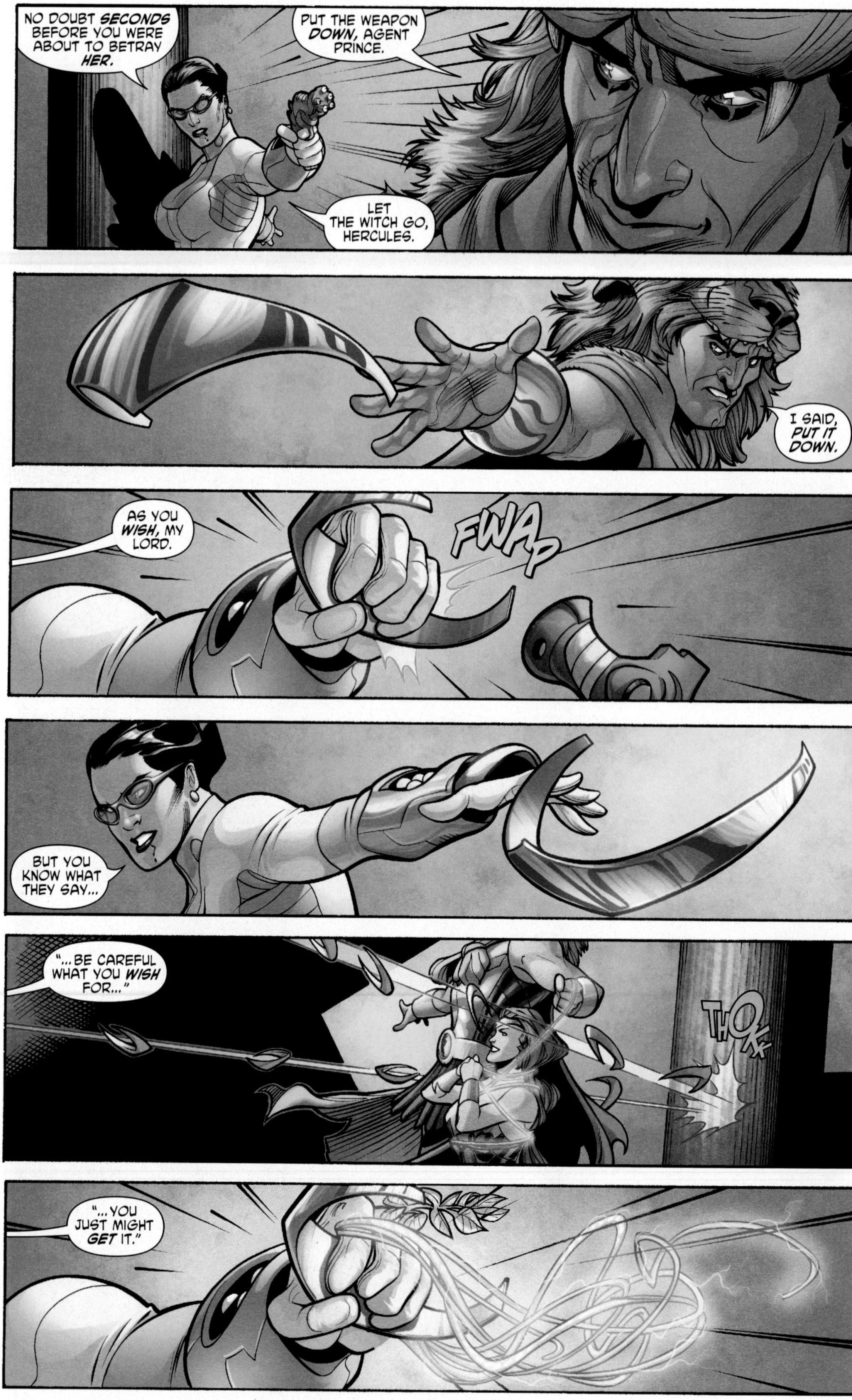
NO DOUBT *SECONDS* BEFORE YOU WERE ABOUT TO BETRAY *HER.*
PUT THE WEAPON *DOWN,* AGENT PRINCE.
LET THE WITCH GO, HERCULES.
I SAID, *PUT IT DOWN.*
AS YOU *WISH,* MY LORD.
FWAP
BUT YOU KNOW WHAT THEY SAY...
"...BE CAREFUL WHAT YOU *WISH* FOR..."
THOKK
"...YOU JUST MIGHT *GET* IT."

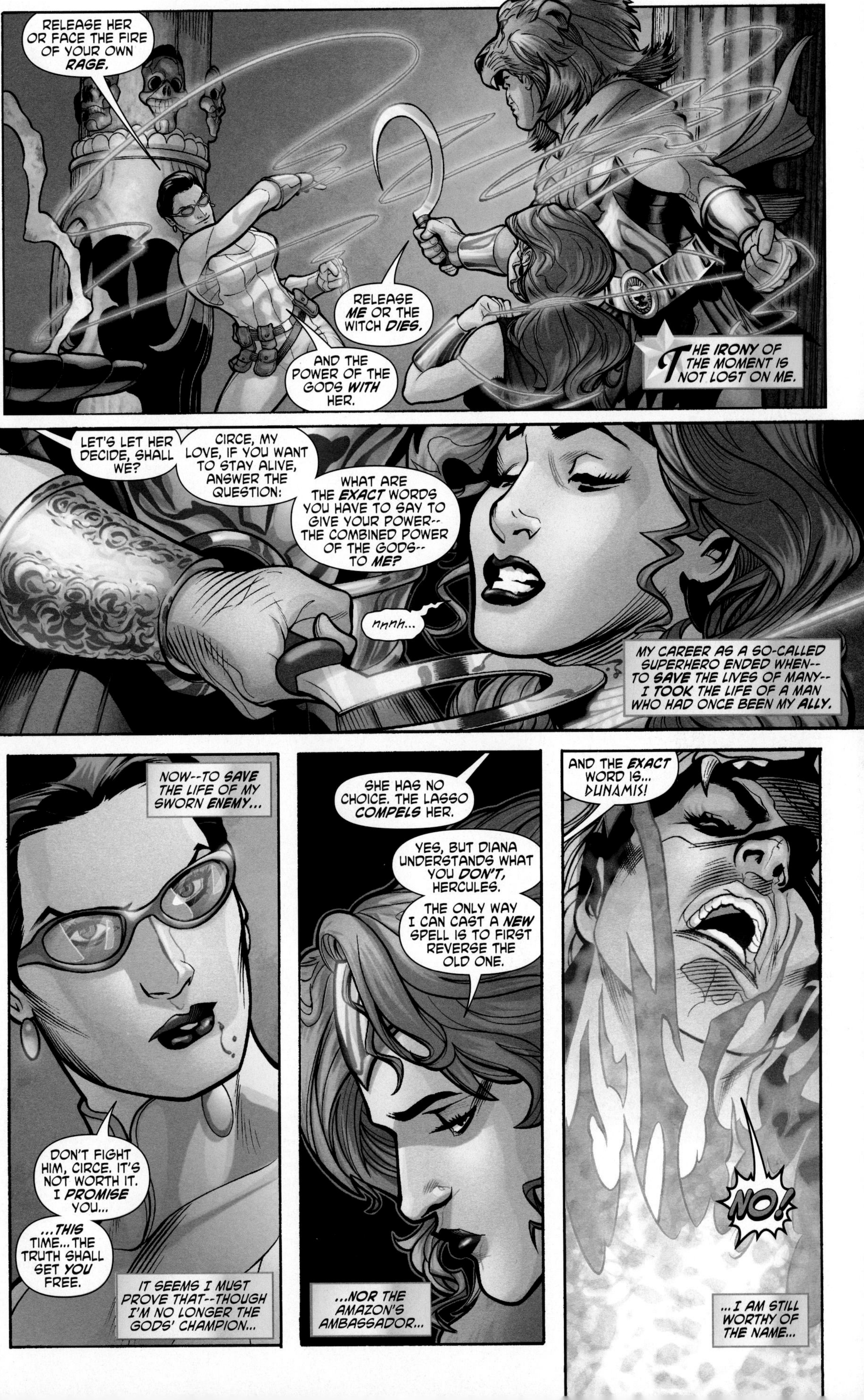

RELEASE HER OR FACE THE FIRE OF YOUR OWN RAGE.
RELEASE ME OR THE WITCH DIES.
AND THE POWER OF THE GODS WITH HER.
THE IRONY OF THE MOMENT IS NOT LOST ON ME.
LET'S LET HER DECIDE, SHALL WE?
CIRCE, MY LOVE, IF YOU WANT TO STAY ALIVE, ANSWER THE QUESTION:
WHAT ARE THE EXACT WORDS YOU HAVE TO SAY TO GIVE YOUR POWER-- THE COMBINED POWER OF THE GODS-- TO ME?
nnnh...
MY CAREER AS A SO-CALLED SUPERHERO ENDED WHEN-- TO SAVE THE LIVES OF MANY-- I TOOK THE LIFE OF A MAN WHO HAD ONCE BEEN MY ALLY.
NOW--TO SAVE THE LIFE OF MY SWORN ENEMY...
DON'T FIGHT HIM, CIRCE. IT'S NOT WORTH IT. I PROMISE YOU...
...THIS TIME...THE TRUTH SHALL SET YOU FREE.
IT SEEMS I MUST PROVE THAT--THOUGH I'M NO LONGER THE GODS' CHAMPION...
SHE HAS NO CHOICE. THE LASSO COMPELS HER.
YES, BUT DIANA UNDERSTANDS WHAT YOU DON'T, HERCULES.
THE ONLY WAY I CAN CAST A NEW SPELL IS TO FIRST REVERSE THE OLD ONE.
...NOR THE AMAZON'S AMBASSADOR...
AND THE EXACT WORD IS... DUNAMIS!
NO!
...I AM STILL WORTHY OF THE NAME...

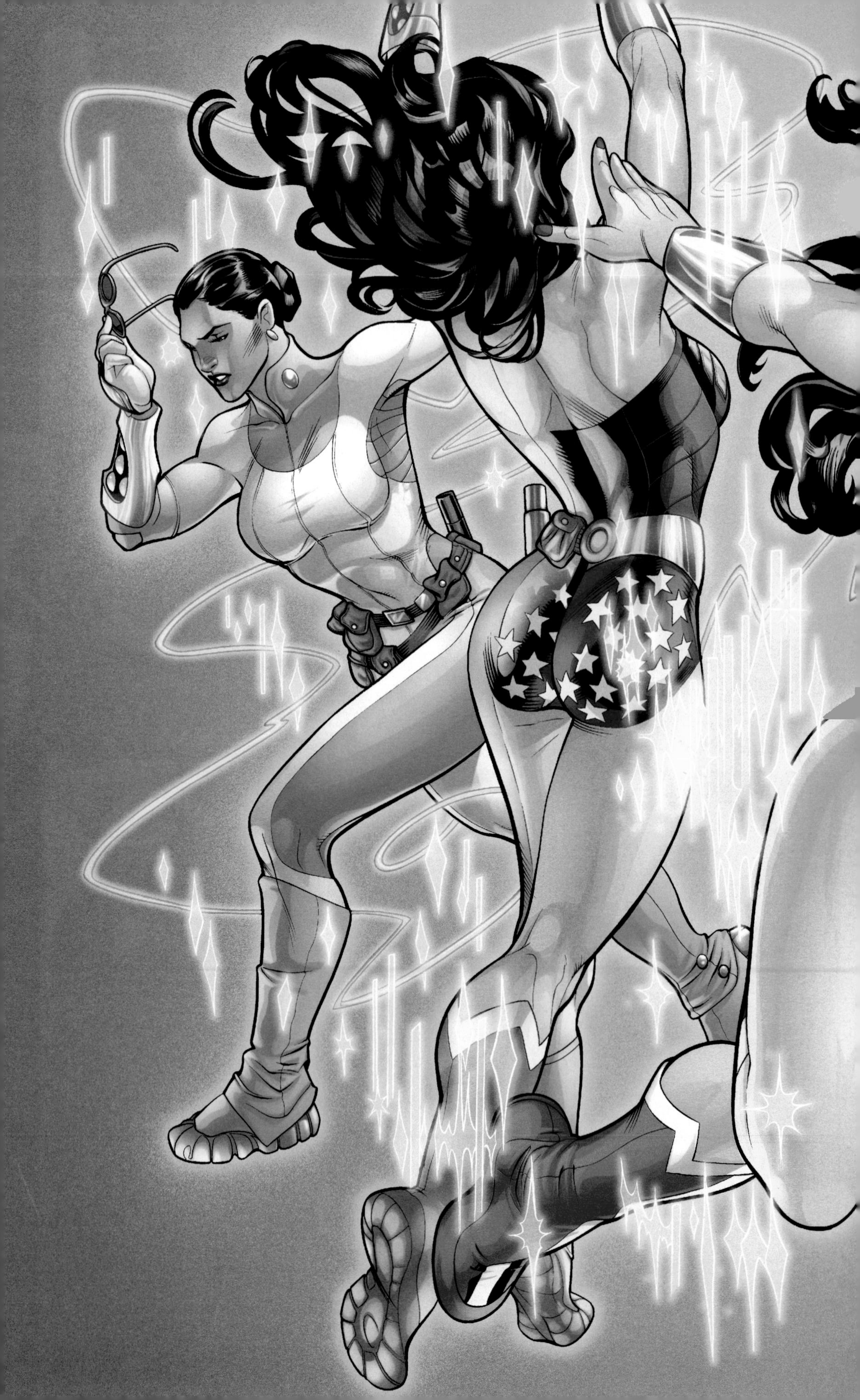

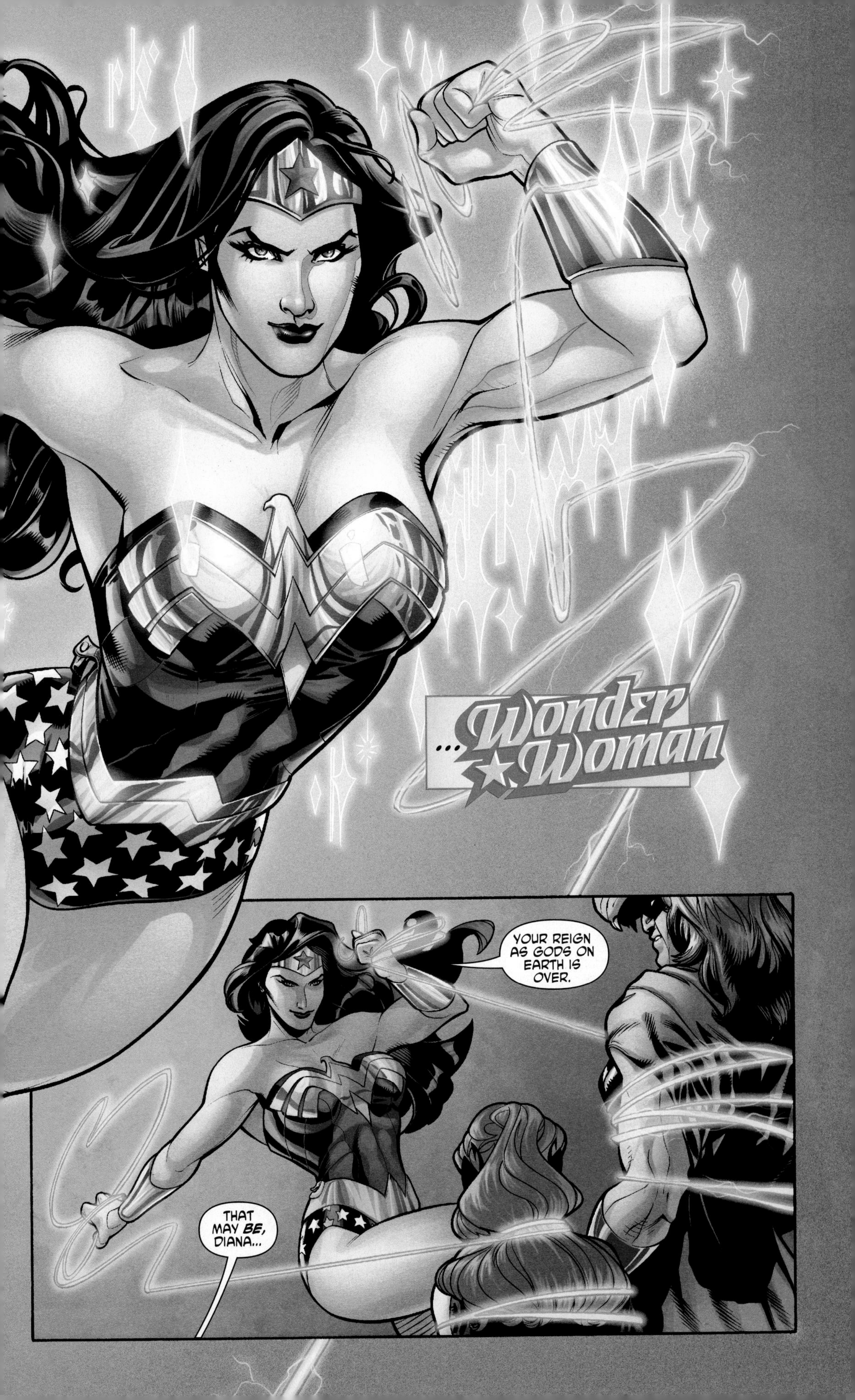

...Wonder Woman
YOUR REIGN AS GODS ON EARTH IS OVER.
THAT MAY BE, DIANA...

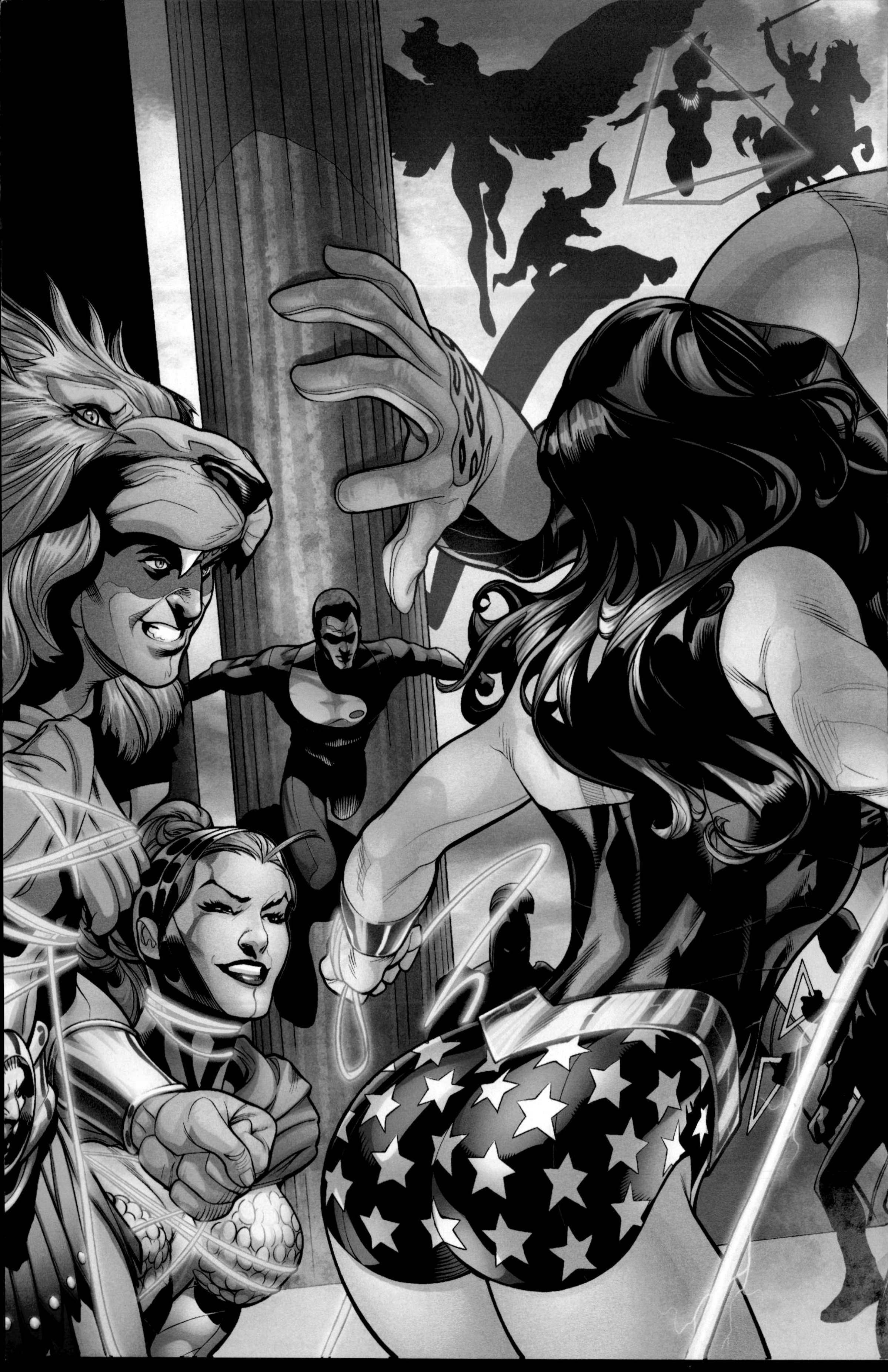

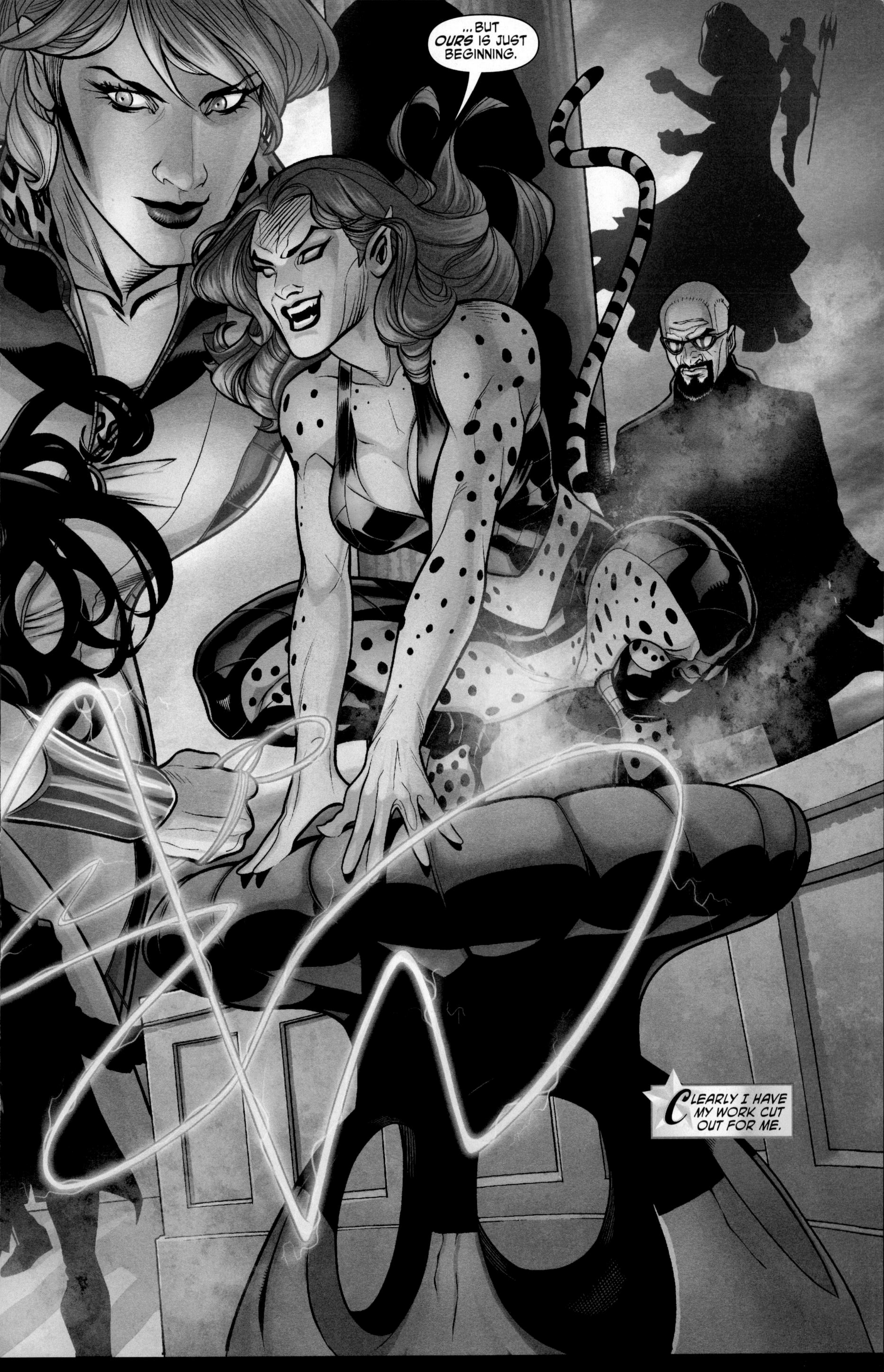
...BUT OURS IS JUST BEGINNING.
CLEARLY I HAVE MY WORK CUT OUT FOR ME.

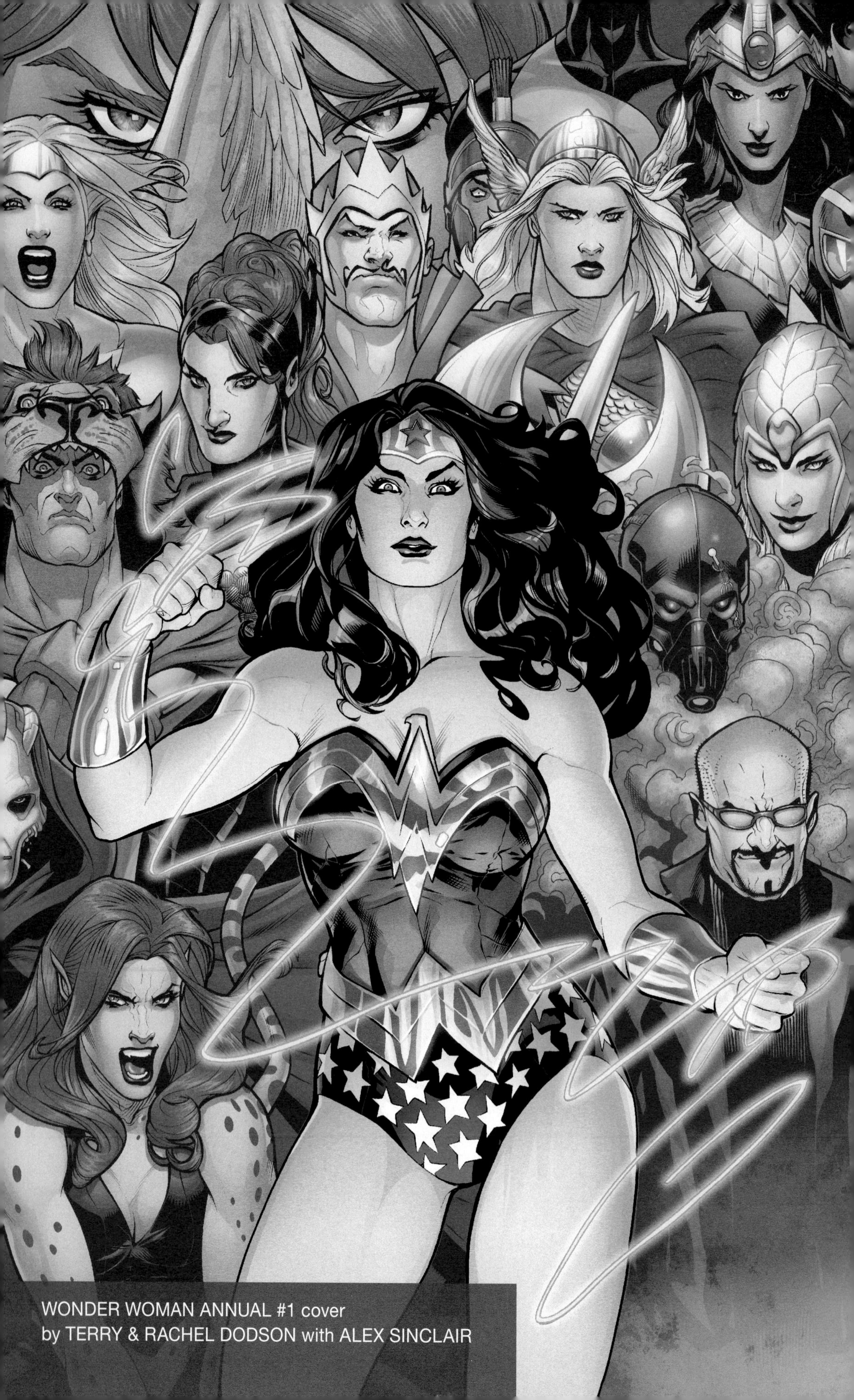

WONDER WOMAN ANNUAL #1 cover
by TERRY & RACHEL DODSON with ALEX SINCLAIR

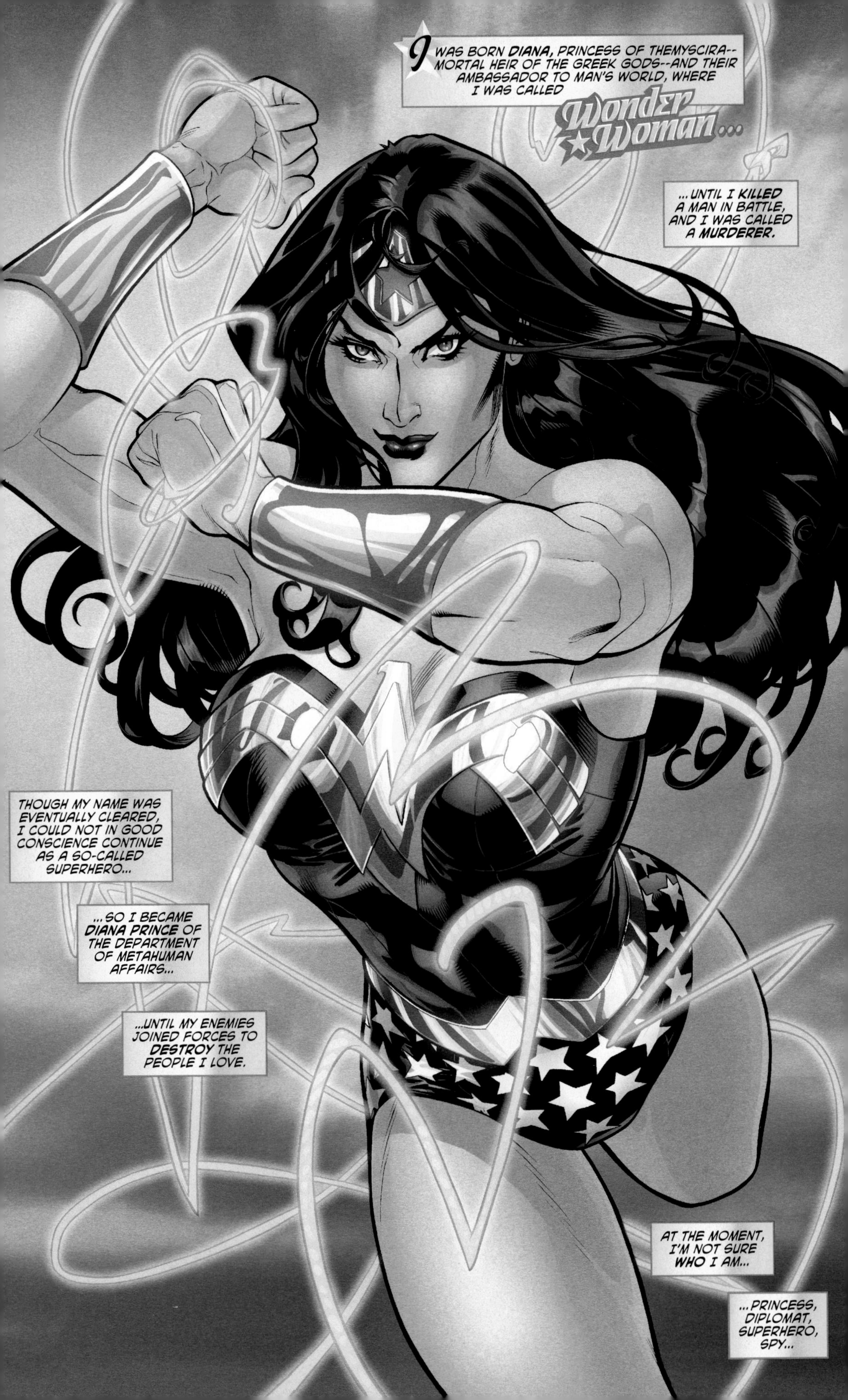
I WAS BORN DIANA, PRINCESS OF THEMYSCIRA-- MORTAL HEIR OF THE GREEK GODS--AND THEIR AMBASSADOR TO MAN'S WORLD, WHERE I WAS CALLED
Wonder Woman...
...UNTIL I KILLED A MAN IN BATTLE, AND I WAS CALLED A MURDERER.
THOUGH MY NAME WAS EVENTUALLY CLEARED, I COULD NOT IN GOOD CONSCIENCE CONTINUE AS A SO-CALLED SUPERHERO...
...SO I BECAME DIANA PRINCE OF THE DEPARTMENT OF METAHUMAN AFFAIRS...
...UNTIL MY ENEMIES JOINED FORCES TO DESTROY THE PEOPLE I LOVE.
AT THE MOMENT, I'M NOT SURE WHO I AM...
...PRINCESS, DIPLOMAT, SUPERHERO, SPY...

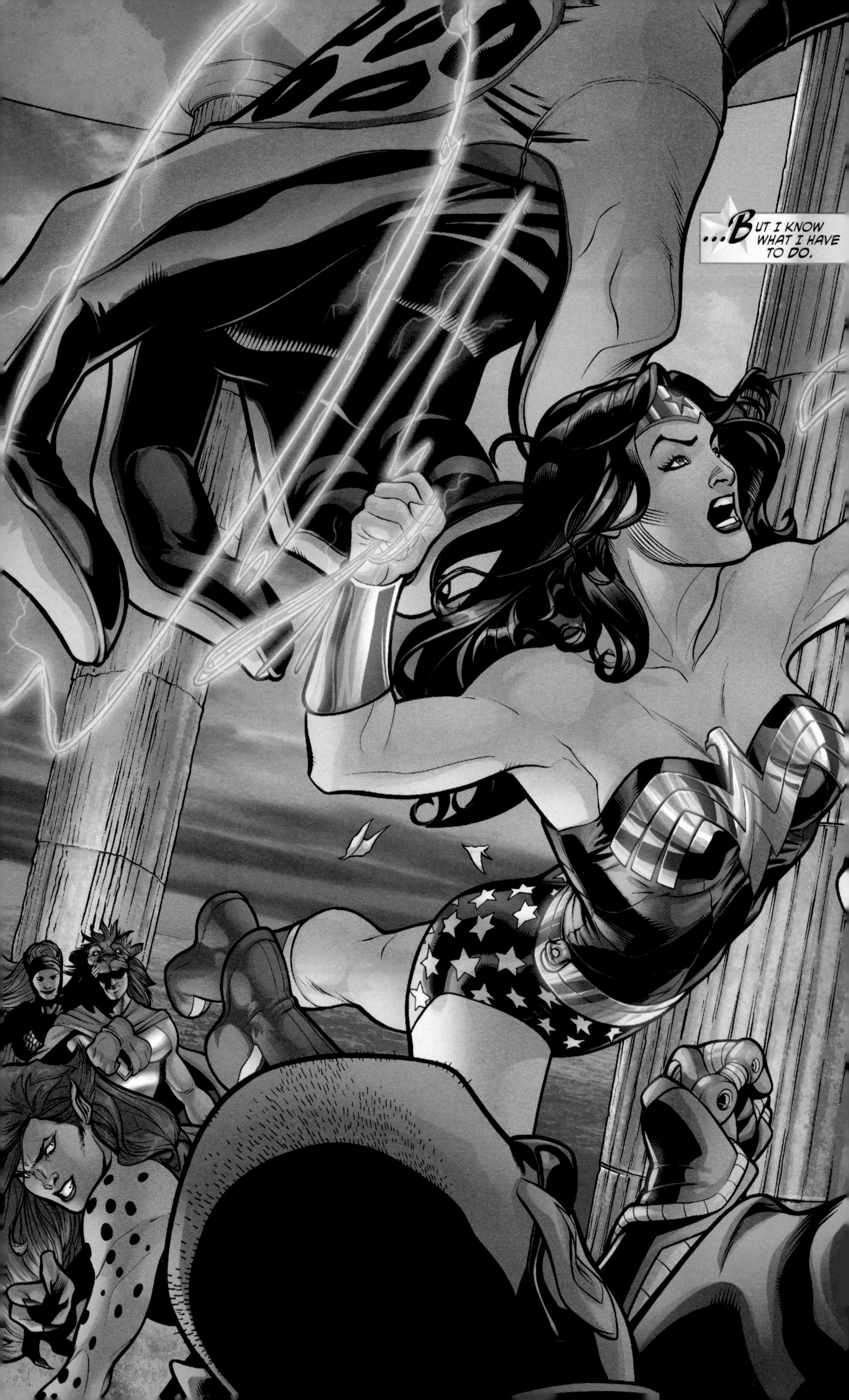
...BUT I KNOW WHAT I HAVE TO DO.

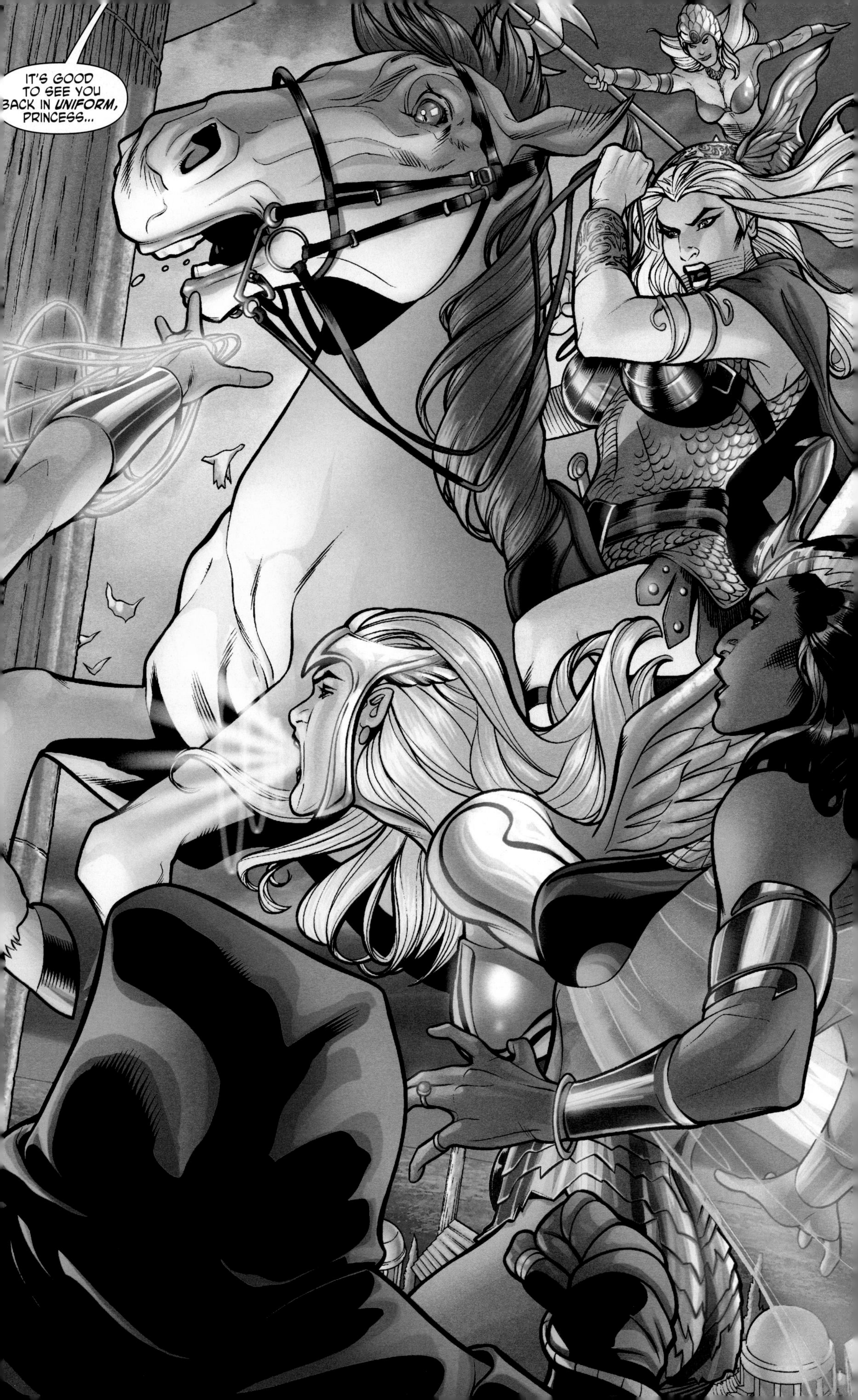
IT'S GOOD TO SEE YOU BACK IN UNIFORM, PRINCESS...

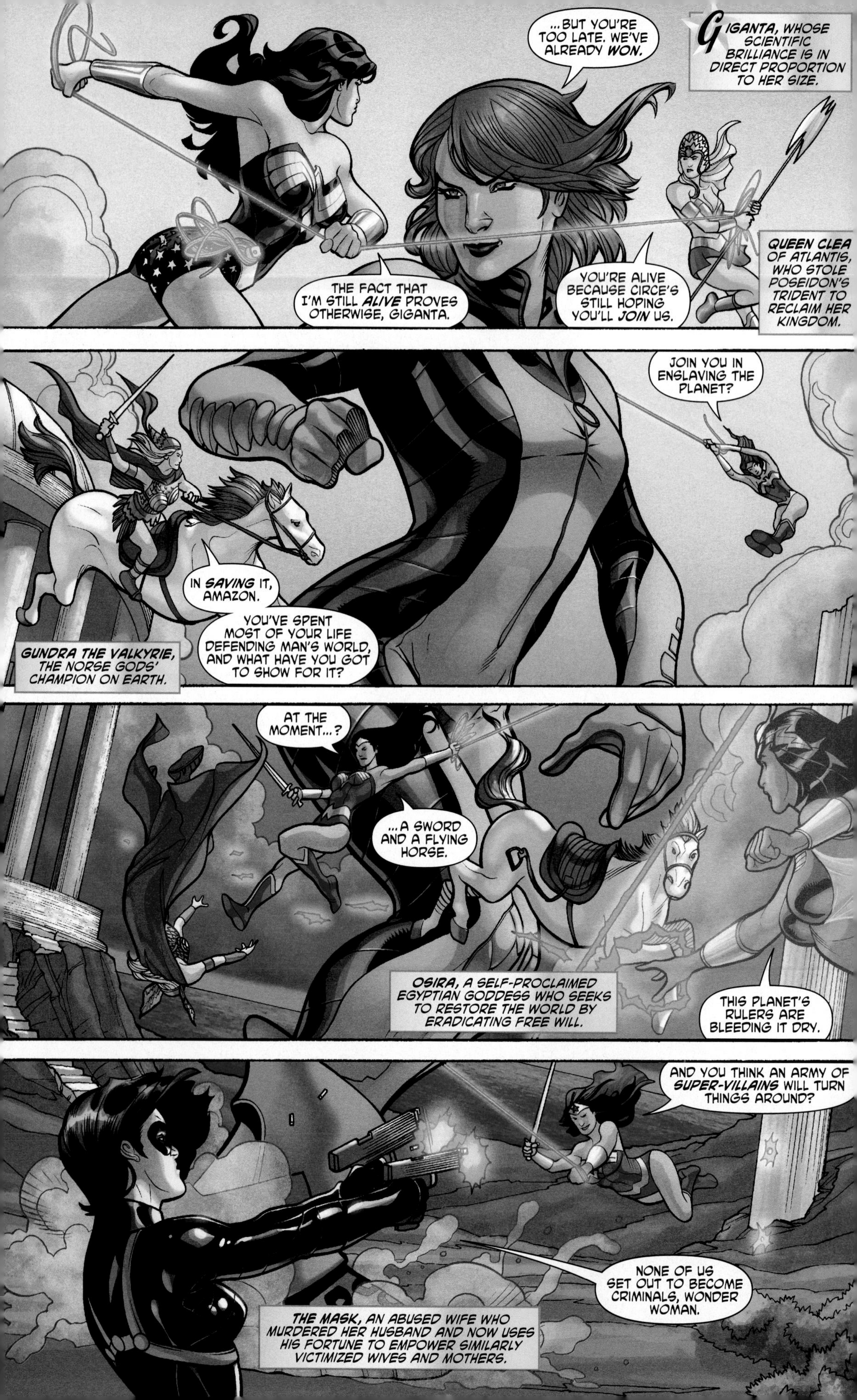

GIGANTA, WHOSE SCIENTIFIC BRILLIANCE IS IN DIRECT PROPORTION TO HER SIZE.
...BUT YOU'RE TOO LATE. WE'VE ALREADY WON.
THE FACT THAT I'M STILL ALIVE PROVES OTHERWISE, GIGANTA.
YOU'RE ALIVE BECAUSE CIRCE'S STILL HOPING YOU'LL JOIN US.
QUEEN CLEA OF ATLANTIS, WHO STOLE POSEIDON'S TRIDENT TO RECLAIM HER KINGDOM.
JOIN YOU IN ENSLAVING THE PLANET?
IN SAVING IT, AMAZON.
YOU'VE SPENT MOST OF YOUR LIFE DEFENDING MAN'S WORLD, AND WHAT HAVE YOU GOT TO SHOW FOR IT?
GUNDRA THE VALKYRIE, THE NORSE GODS' CHAMPION ON EARTH.
AT THE MOMENT...?
...A SWORD AND A FLYING HORSE.
OSIRA, A SELF-PROCLAIMED EGYPTIAN GODDESS WHO SEEKS TO RESTORE THE WORLD BY ERADICATING FREE WILL.
THIS PLANET'S RULERS ARE BLEEDING IT DRY.
AND YOU THINK AN ARMY OF SUPER-VILLAINS WILL TURN THINGS AROUND?
NONE OF US SET OUT TO BECOME CRIMINALS, WONDER WOMAN.
THE MASK, AN ABUSED WIFE WHO MURDERED HER HUSBAND AND NOW USES HIS FORTUNE TO EMPOWER SIMILARLY VICTIMIZED WIVES AND MOTHERS.

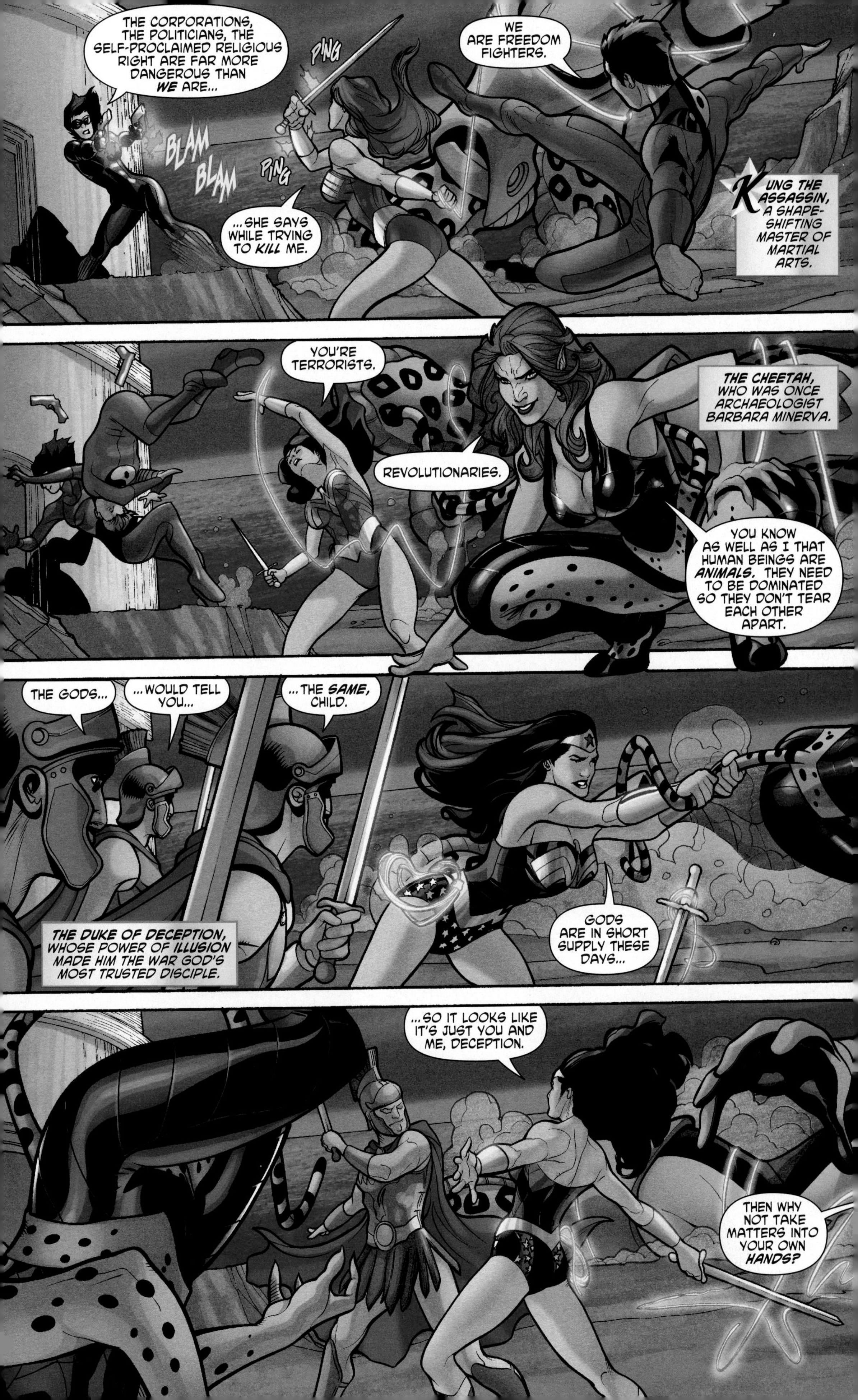
THE CORPORATIONS, THE POLITICIANS, THE SELF-PROCLAIMED RELIGIOUS RIGHT ARE FAR MORE DANGEROUS THAN WE ARE...
PING
BLAM
BLAM
PING
...SHE SAYS WHILE TRYING TO KILL ME.
WE ARE FREEDOM FIGHTERS.
KUNG THE KASSASSIN, A SHAPE-SHIFTING MASTER OF MARTIAL ARTS.
YOU'RE TERRORISTS.
REVOLUTIONARIES.
THE CHEETAH, WHO WAS ONCE ARCHAEOLOGIST BARBARA MINERVA.
YOU KNOW AS WELL AS I THAT HUMAN BEINGS ARE ANIMALS. THEY NEED TO BE DOMINATED SO THEY DON'T TEAR EACH OTHER APART.
THE GODS...
...WOULD TELL YOU...
...THE SAME, CHILD.
THE DUKE OF DECEPTION, WHOSE POWER OF ILLUSION MADE HIM THE WAR GOD'S MOST TRUSTED DISCIPLE.
GODS ARE IN SHORT SUPPLY THESE DAYS...
...SO IT LOOKS LIKE IT'S JUST YOU AND ME, DECEPTION.
THEN WHY NOT TAKE MATTERS INTO YOUR OWN HANDS?

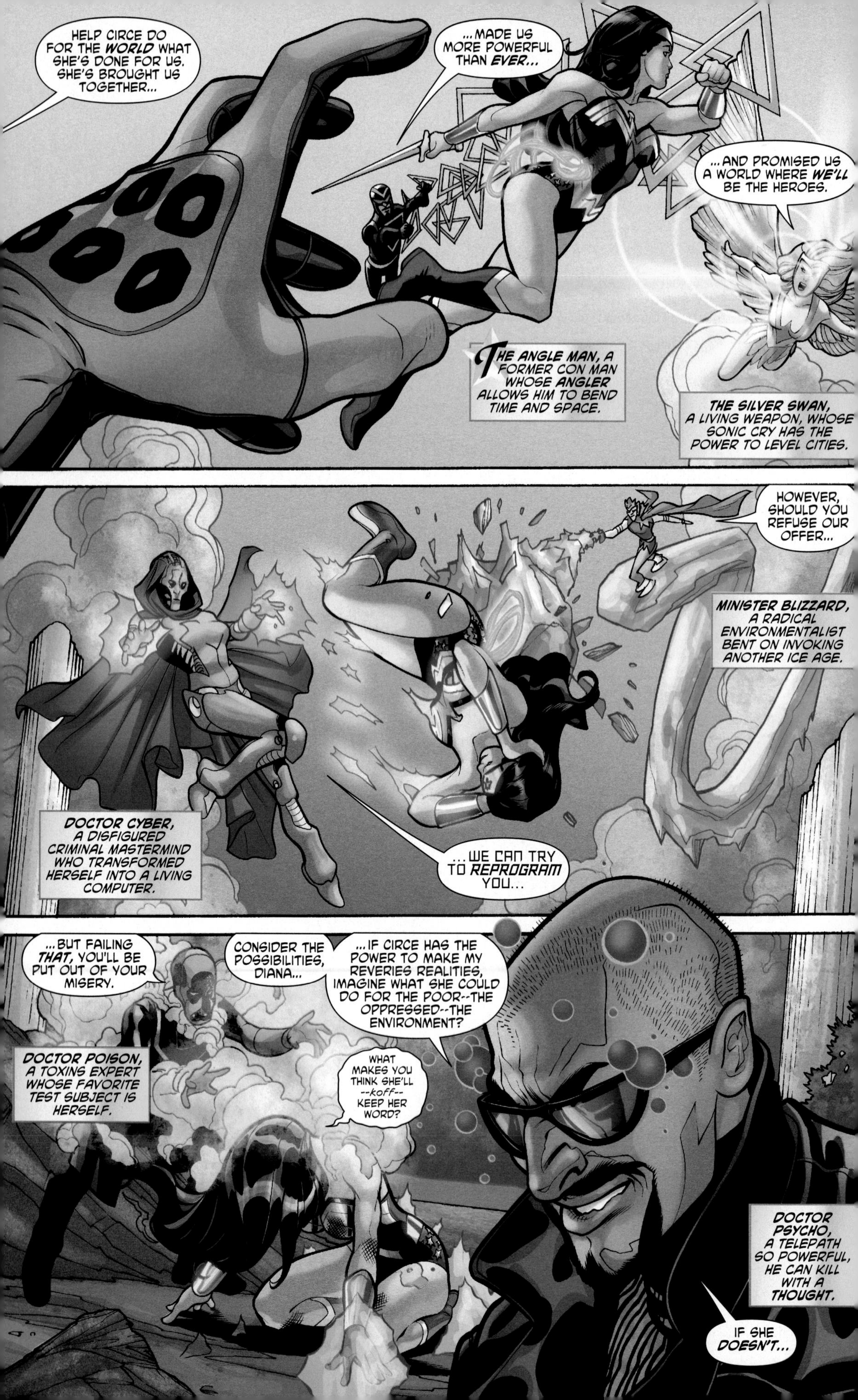
HELP CIRCE DO FOR THE WORLD WHAT SHE'S DONE FOR US. SHE'S BROUGHT US TOGETHER...
...MADE US MORE POWERFUL THAN EVER...
...AND PROMISED US A WORLD WHERE WE'LL BE THE HEROES.
THE ANGLE MAN, A FORMER CON MAN WHOSE ANGLER ALLOWS HIM TO BEND TIME AND SPACE.
THE SILVER SWAN, A LIVING WEAPON, WHOSE SONIC CRY HAS THE POWER TO LEVEL CITIES.
HOWEVER, SHOULD YOU REFUSE OUR OFFER...
MINISTER BLIZZARD, A RADICAL ENVIRONMENTALIST BENT ON INVOKING ANOTHER ICE AGE.
DOCTOR CYBER, A DISFIGURED CRIMINAL MASTERMIND WHO TRANSFORMED HERSELF INTO A LIVING COMPUTER.
...WE CAN TRY TO REPROGRAM YOU...
...BUT FAILING THAT, YOU'LL BE PUT OUT OF YOUR MISERY.
DOCTOR POISON, A TOXINS EXPERT WHOSE FAVORITE TEST SUBJECT IS HERSELF.
CONSIDER THE POSSIBILITIES, DIANA...
...IF CIRCE HAS THE POWER TO MAKE MY REVERIES REALITIES, IMAGINE WHAT SHE COULD DO FOR THE POOR--THE OPPRESSED--THE ENVIRONMENT?
WHAT MAKES YOU THINK SHE'LL --koff-- KEEP HER WORD?
DOCTOR PSYCHO, A TELEPATH SO POWERFUL, HE CAN KILL WITH A THOUGHT.
IF SHE DOESN'T...

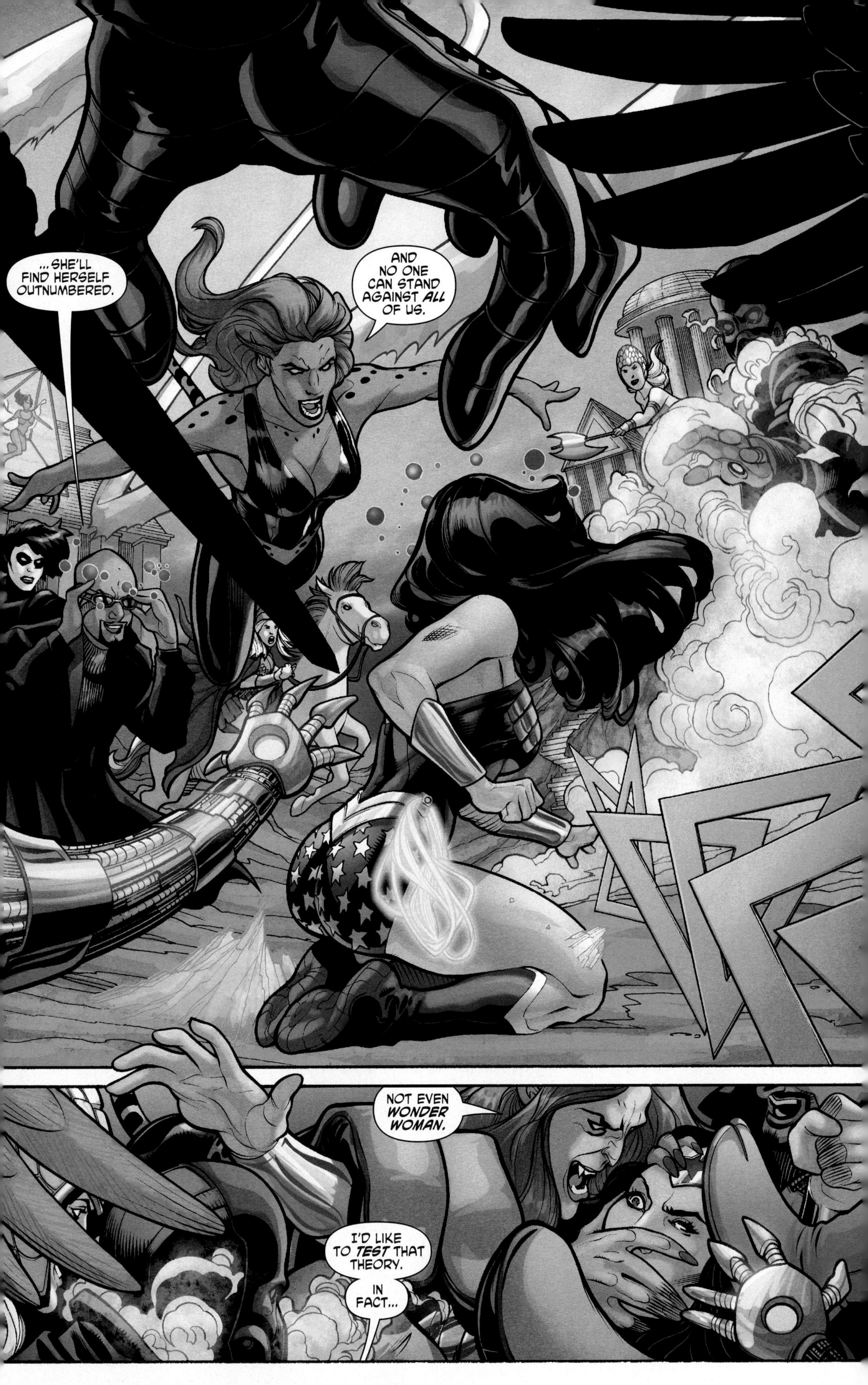
...SHE'LL FIND HERSELF OUTNUMBERED.
AND NO ONE CAN STAND AGAINST ALL OF US.
NOT EVEN WONDER WOMAN.
I'D LIKE TO TEST THAT THEORY.
IN FACT...

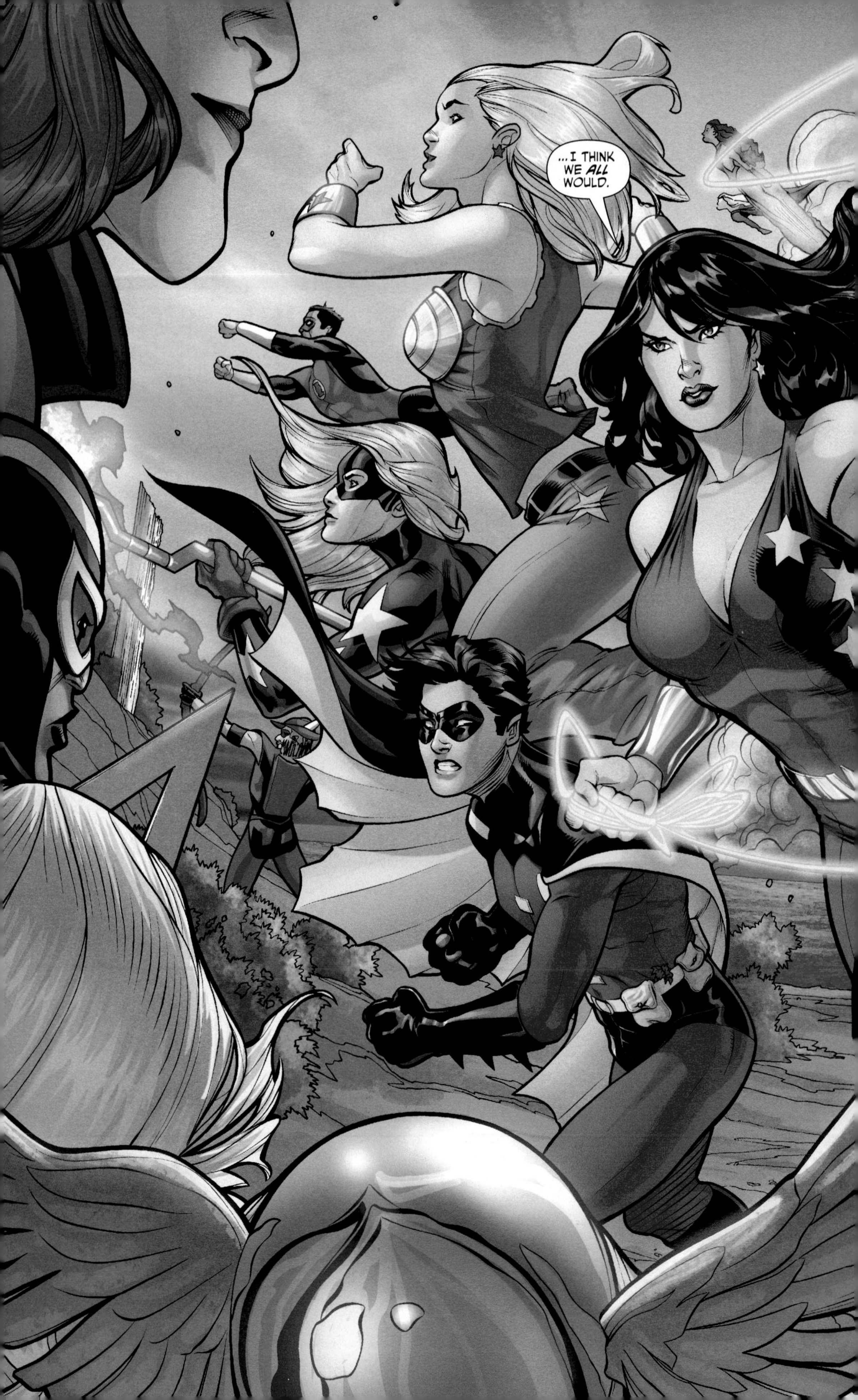
...I THINK WE ALL WOULD.

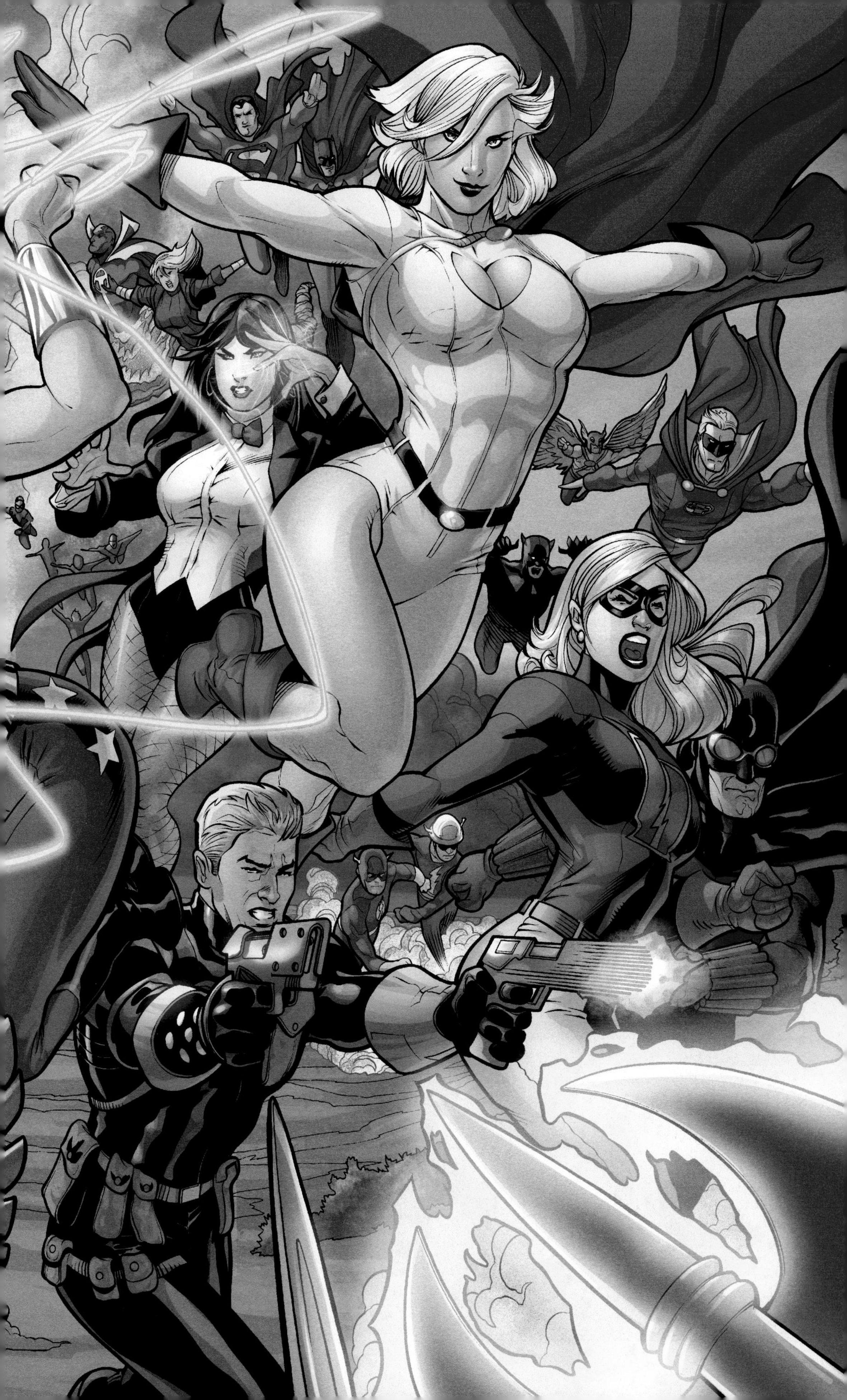

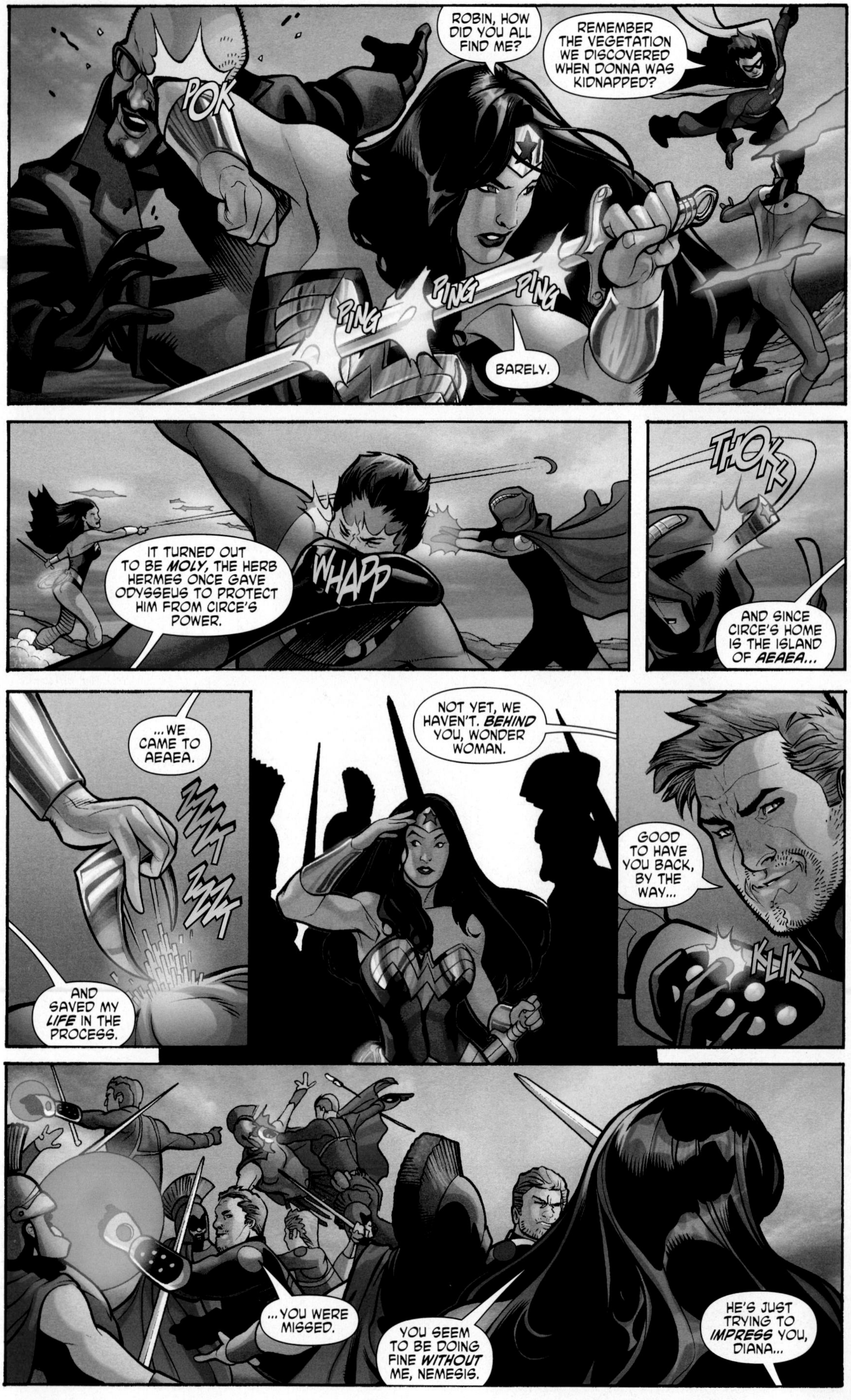
POK
ROBIN, HOW DID YOU ALL FIND ME?
REMEMBER THE VEGETATION WE DISCOVERED WHEN DONNA WAS KIDNAPPED?
PING PING PING
BARELY.
WHAPP
IT TURNED OUT TO BE *MOLY*, THE HERB HERMES ONCE GAVE ODYSSEUS TO PROTECT HIM FROM CIRCE'S POWER.
THOKK
AND SINCE CIRCE'S HOME IS THE ISLAND OF *AEAEA*...
...WE CAME TO AEAEA.
AND SAVED MY *LIFE* IN THE PROCESS.
NOT YET, WE HAVEN'T. *BEHIND* YOU, WONDER WOMAN.
GOOD TO HAVE YOU BACK, BY THE WAY...
KLIK
...YOU WERE MISSED.
YOU SEEM TO BE DOING FINE *WITHOUT* ME, NEMESIS.
HE'S JUST TRYING TO *IMPRESS* YOU, DIANA...

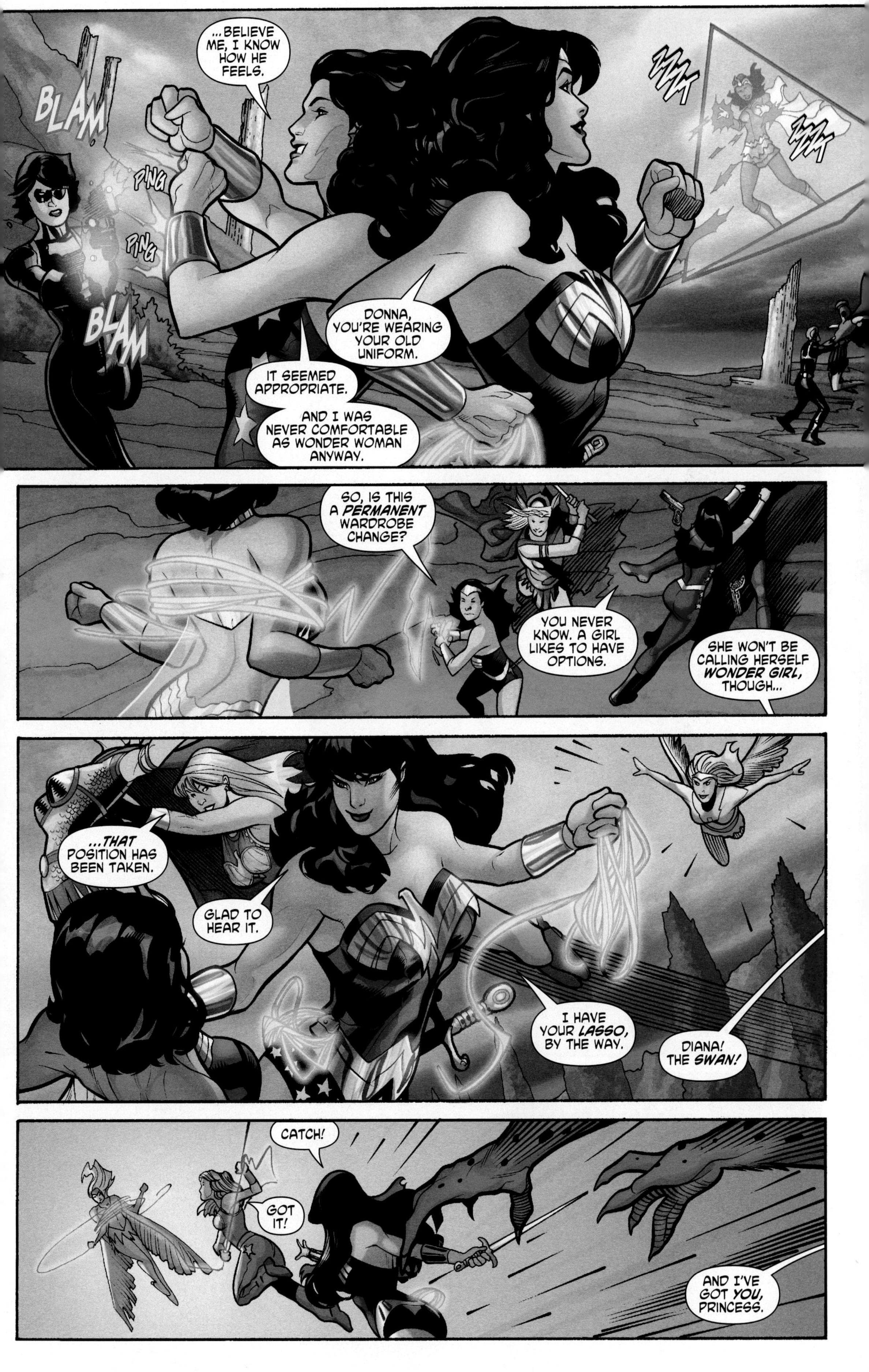
...BELIEVE ME, I KNOW HOW HE FEELS.
BLAM
PING
PING
BLAM
ZZAK
ZZAK
DONNA, YOU'RE WEARING YOUR OLD UNIFORM.
IT SEEMED APPROPRIATE.
AND I WAS NEVER COMFORTABLE AS WONDER WOMAN ANYWAY.
SO, IS THIS A *PERMANENT* WARDROBE CHANGE?
YOU NEVER KNOW. A GIRL LIKES TO HAVE OPTIONS.
SHE WON'T BE CALLING HERSELF *WONDER GIRL,* THOUGH...
...*THAT* POSITION HAS BEEN TAKEN.
GLAD TO HEAR IT.
I HAVE YOUR *LASSO,* BY THE WAY.
DIANA! THE *SWAN!*
CATCH!
GOT IT!
AND I'VE GOT *YOU,* PRINCESS.

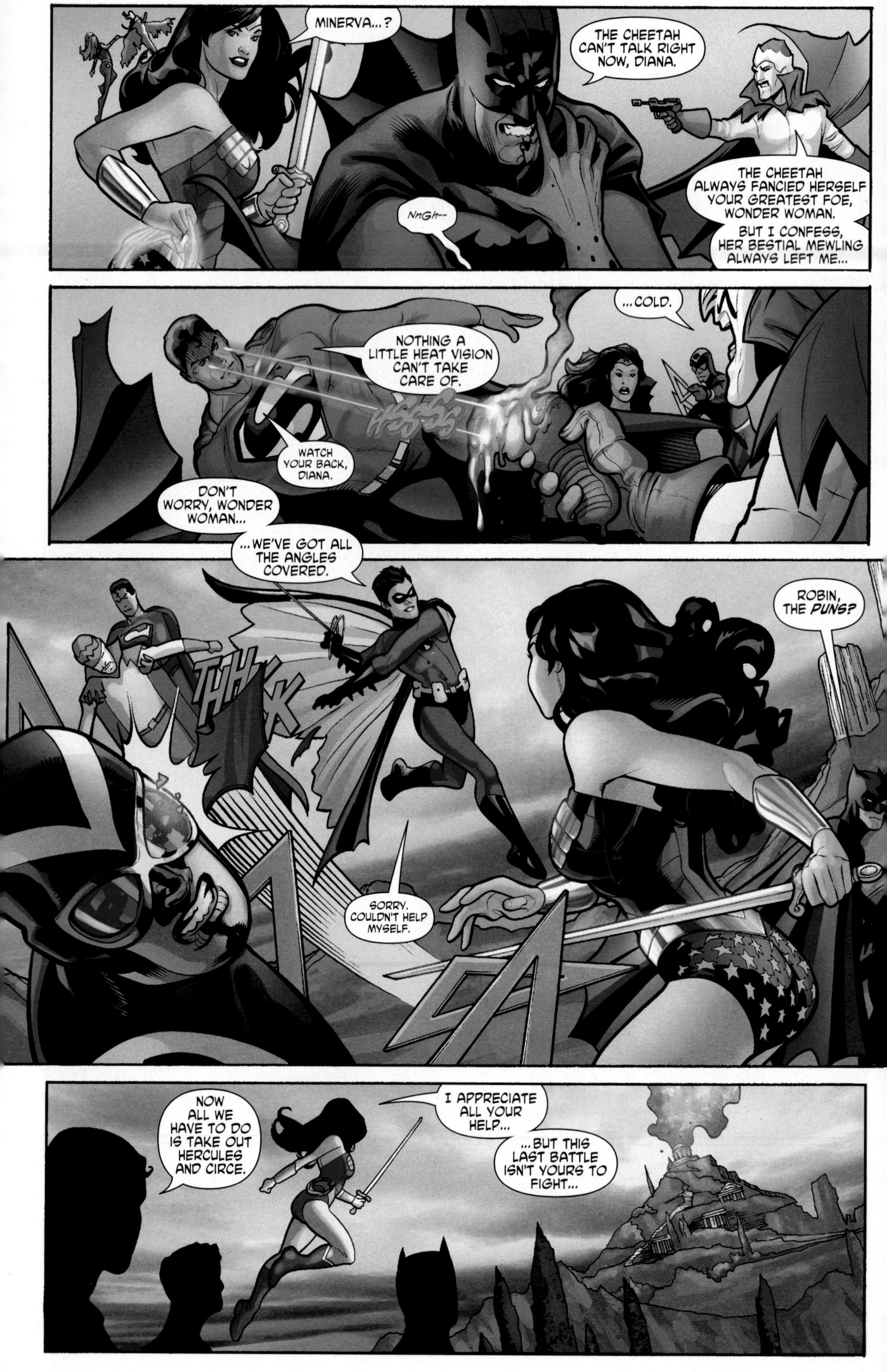
MINERVA...?
THE CHEETAH CAN'T TALK RIGHT NOW, DIANA.
NnGh--
THE CHEETAH ALWAYS FANCIED HERSELF YOUR GREATEST FOE, WONDER WOMAN.
BUT I CONFESS, HER BESTIAL MEWLING ALWAYS LEFT ME...
...COLD.
NOTHING A LITTLE HEAT VISION CAN'T TAKE CARE OF.
HSSSS
WATCH YOUR BACK, DIANA.
DON'T WORRY, WONDER WOMAN...
...WE'VE GOT ALL THE ANGLES COVERED.
ROBIN, THE *PUNS*?
THHK
SORRY. COULDN'T HELP MYSELF.
NOW ALL WE HAVE TO DO IS TAKE OUT HERCULES AND CIRCE.
I APPRECIATE ALL YOUR HELP...
...BUT THIS LAST BATTLE ISN'T YOURS TO FIGHT...

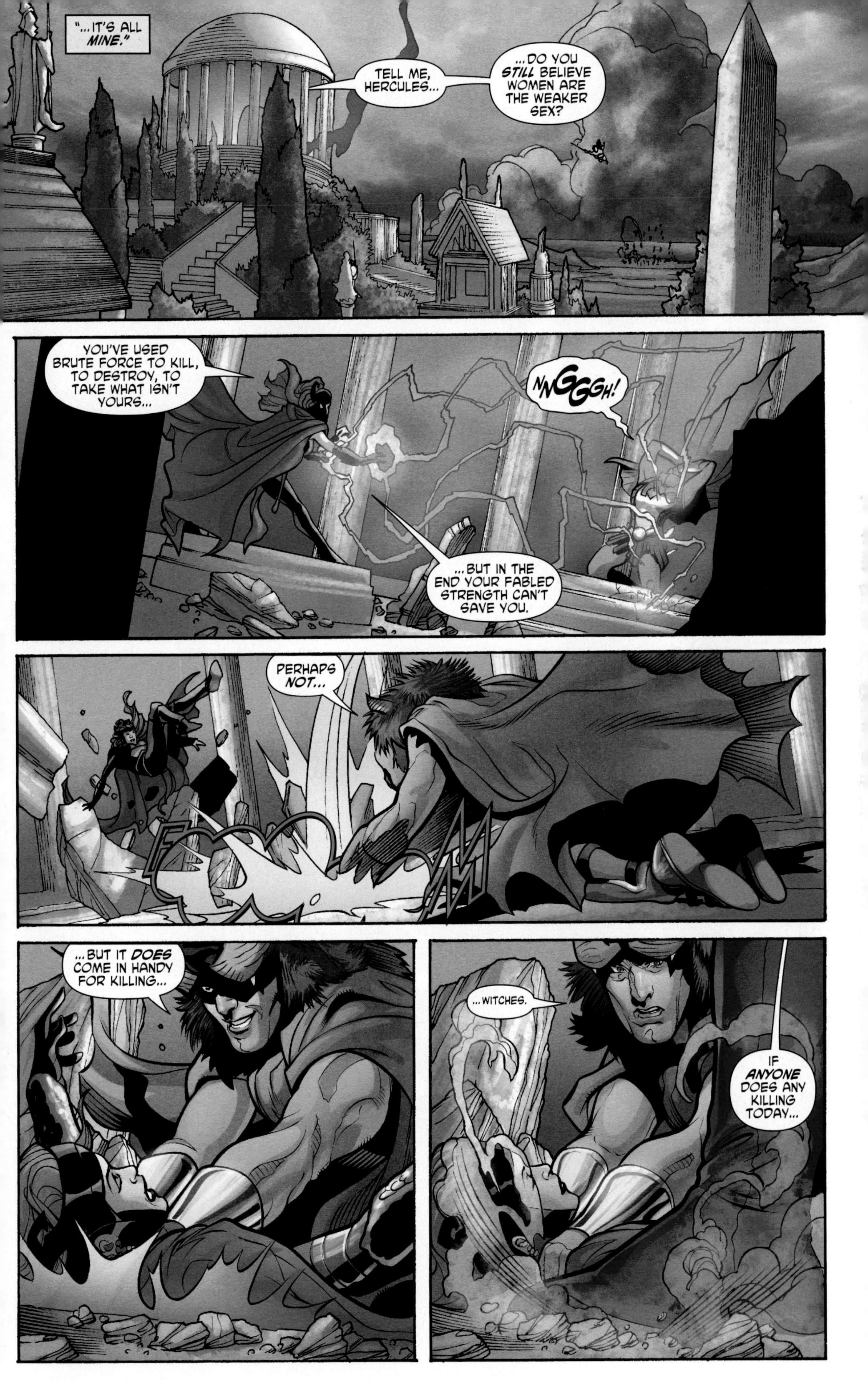
"...IT'S ALL MINE."
TELL ME, HERCULES...
...DO YOU STILL BELIEVE WOMEN ARE THE WEAKER SEX?
YOU'VE USED BRUTE FORCE TO KILL, TO DESTROY, TO TAKE WHAT ISN'T YOURS...
NNGGGH!
...BUT IN THE END YOUR FABLED STRENGTH CAN'T SAVE YOU.
PERHAPS NOT...
...BUT IT DOES COME IN HANDY FOR KILLING...
...WITCHES.
IF ANYONE DOES ANY KILLING TODAY...

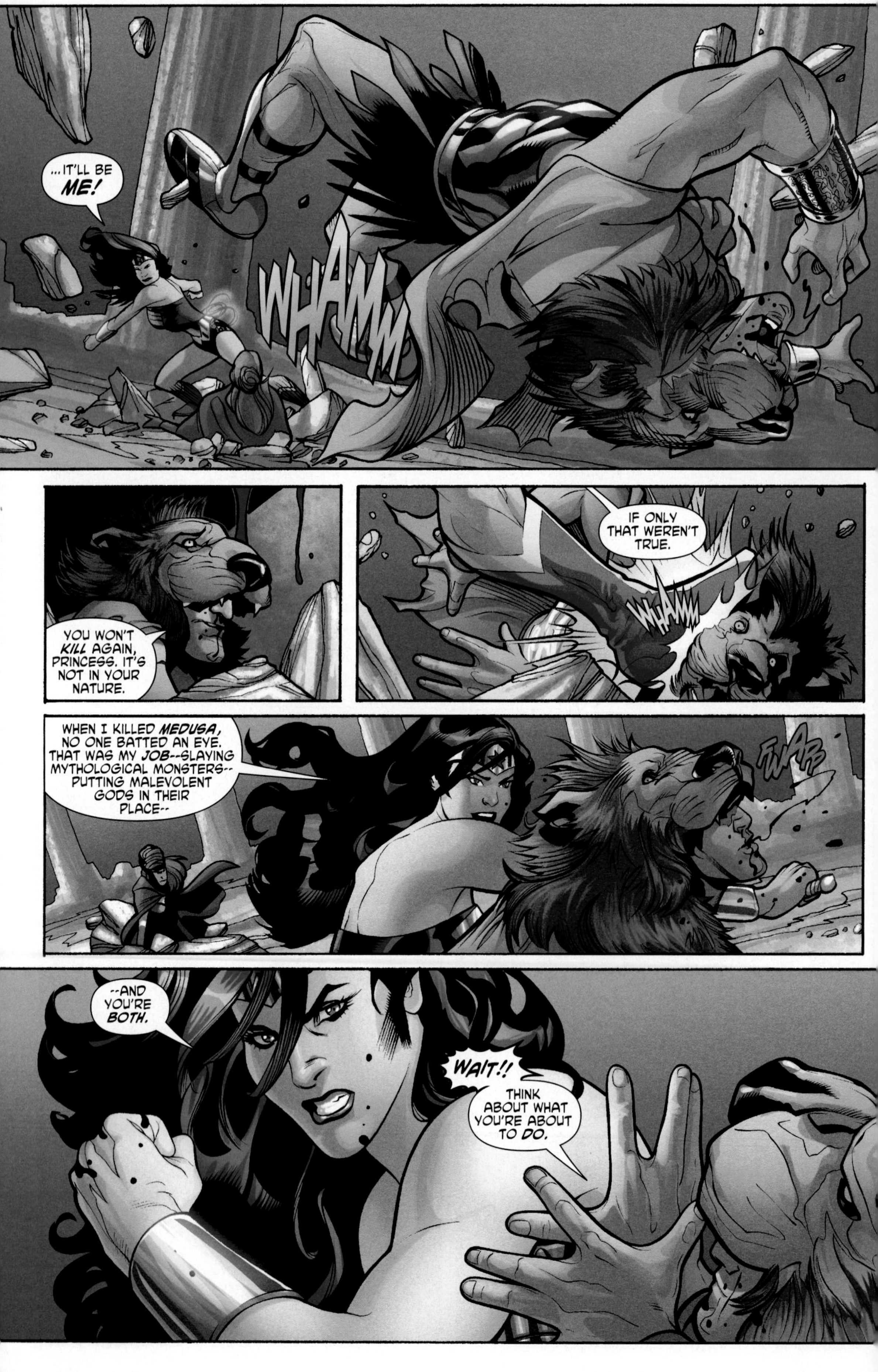
...IT'LL BE ME!
WHAMM
YOU WON'T KILL AGAIN, PRINCESS. IT'S NOT IN YOUR NATURE.
IF ONLY THAT WEREN'T TRUE.
WHAMM
WHEN I KILLED MEDUSA, NO ONE BATTED AN EYE. THAT WAS MY JOB--SLAYING MYTHOLOGICAL MONSTERS--PUTTING MALEVOLENT GODS IN THEIR PLACE--
FWAP
--AND YOU'RE BOTH.
WAIT!!
THINK ABOUT WHAT YOU'RE ABOUT TO DO.

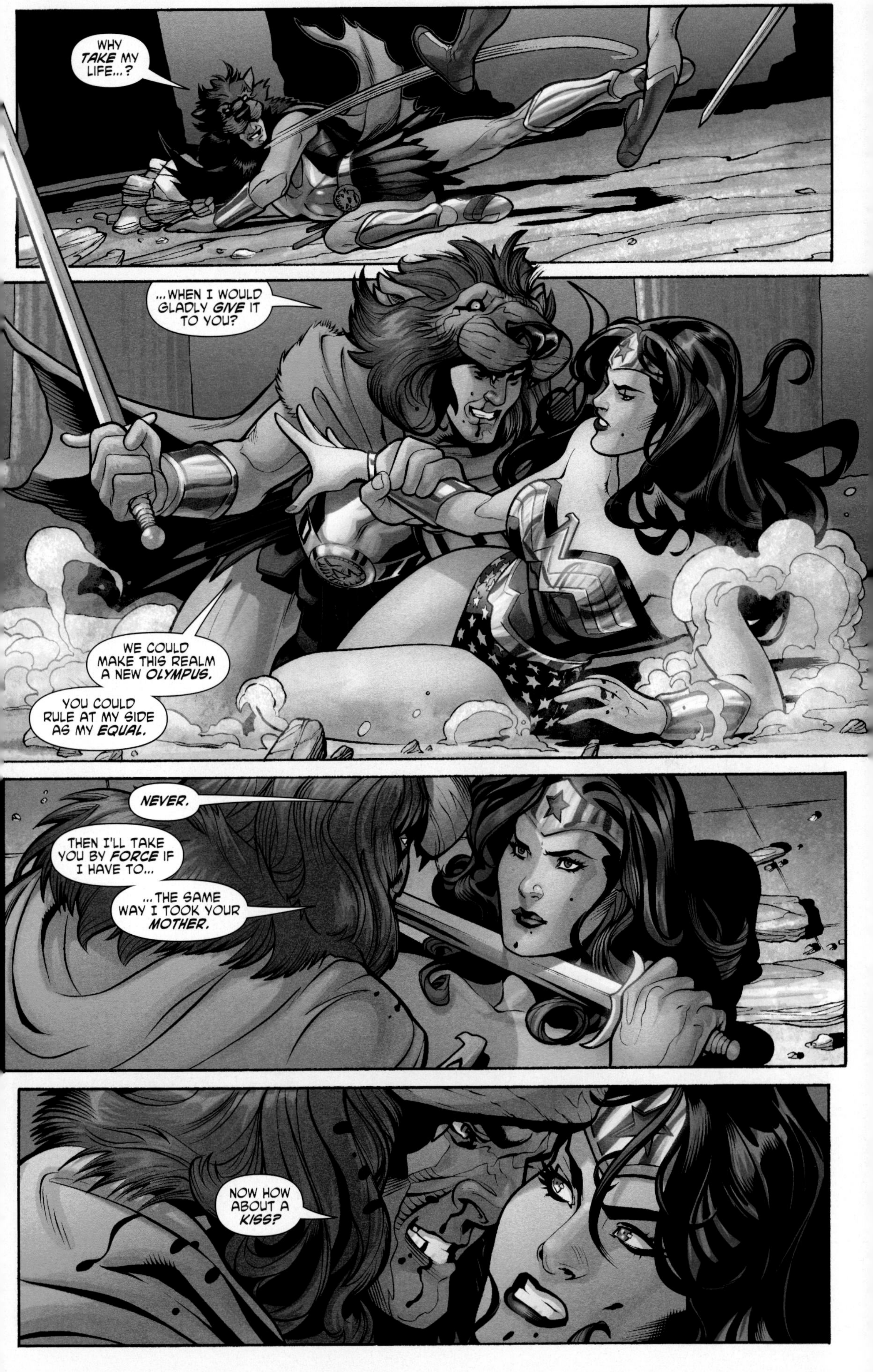
WHY TAKE MY LIFE...?
...WHEN I WOULD GLADLY GIVE IT TO YOU?
WE COULD MAKE THIS REALM A NEW OLYMPUS.
YOU COULD RULE AT MY SIDE AS MY EQUAL.
NEVER.
THEN I'LL TAKE YOU BY FORCE IF I HAVE TO...
...THE SAME WAY I TOOK YOUR MOTHER.
NOW HOW ABOUT A KISS?

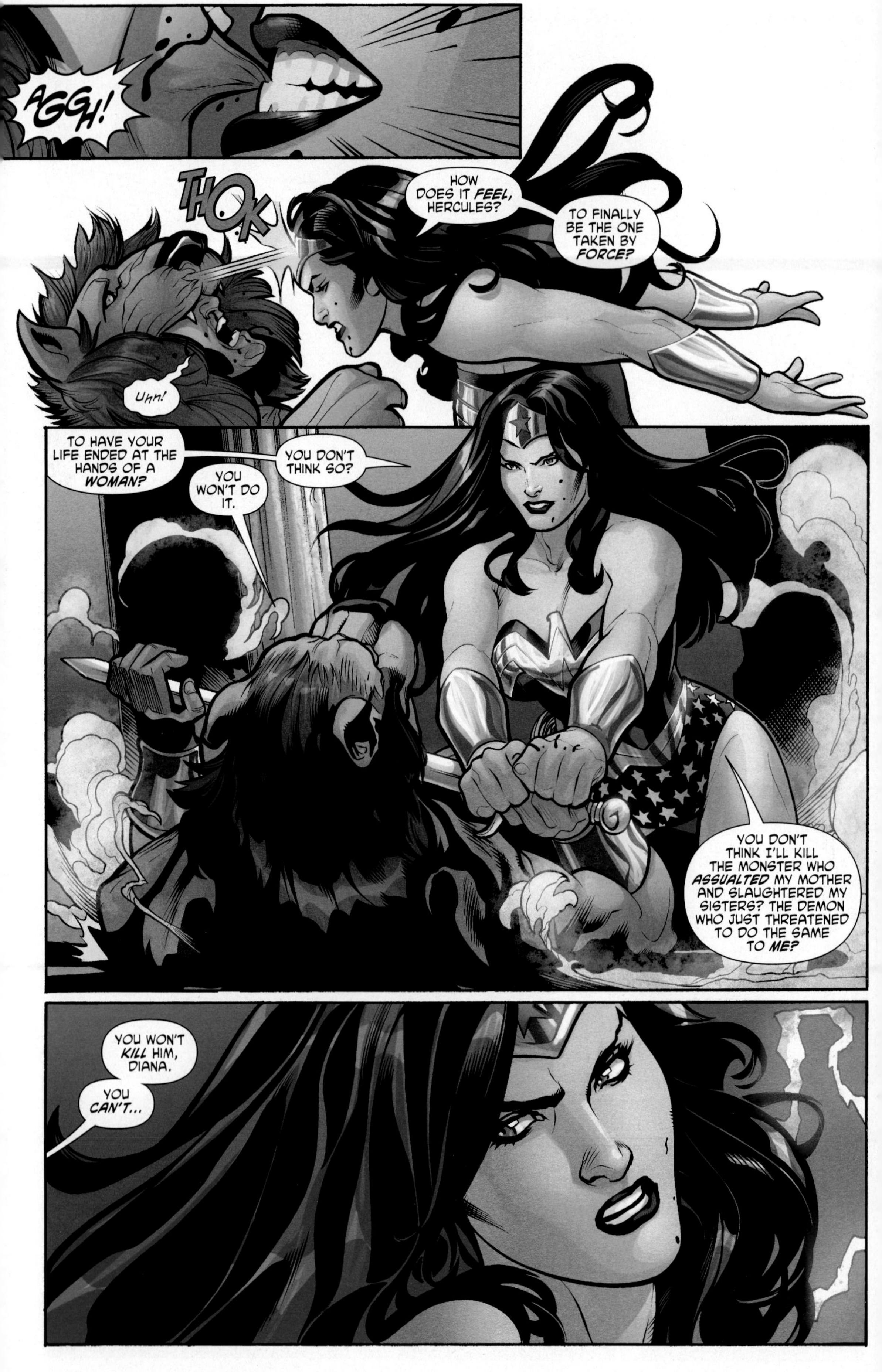
AGGH!
THOK
HOW DOES IT FEEL, HERCULES?
TO FINALLY BE THE ONE TAKEN BY FORCE?
Uhn!
TO HAVE YOUR LIFE ENDED AT THE HANDS OF A WOMAN?
YOU WON'T DO IT.
YOU DON'T THINK SO?
YOU DON'T THINK I'LL KILL THE MONSTER WHO ASSUALTED MY MOTHER AND SLAUGHTERED MY SISTERS? THE DEMON WHO JUST THREATENED TO DO THE SAME TO ME?
YOU WON'T KILL HIM, DIANA.
YOU CAN'T...

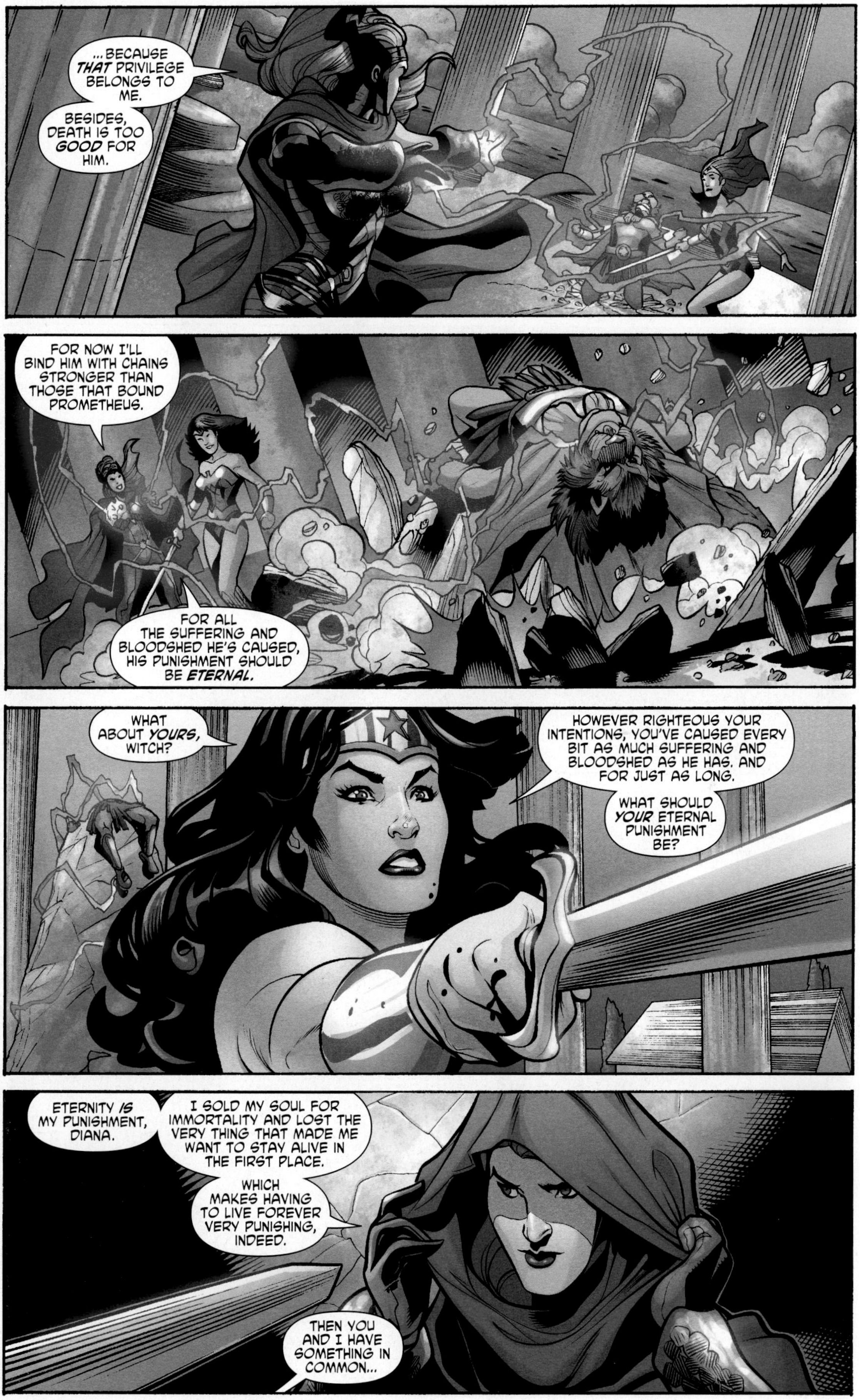
...BECAUSE *THAT* PRIVILEGE BELONGS TO ME.
BESIDES, DEATH IS TOO *GOOD* FOR HIM.
FOR NOW I'LL BIND HIM WITH CHAINS STRONGER THAN THOSE THAT BOUND PROMETHEUS.
FOR ALL THE SUFFERING AND BLOODSHED HE'S CAUSED, HIS PUNISHMENT SHOULD BE *ETERNAL.*
WHAT ABOUT *YOURS,* WITCH?
HOWEVER RIGHTEOUS YOUR INTENTIONS, YOU'VE CAUSED EVERY BIT AS MUCH SUFFERING AND BLOODSHED AS HE HAS. AND FOR JUST AS LONG.
WHAT SHOULD *YOUR* ETERNAL PUNISHMENT BE?
ETERNITY *IS* MY PUNISHMENT, DIANA.
I SOLD MY SOUL FOR IMMORTALITY AND LOST THE VERY THING THAT MADE ME WANT TO STAY ALIVE IN THE FIRST PLACE.
WHICH MAKES HAVING TO LIVE FOREVER VERY PUNISHING, INDEED.
THEN YOU AND I HAVE SOMETHING IN COMMON...

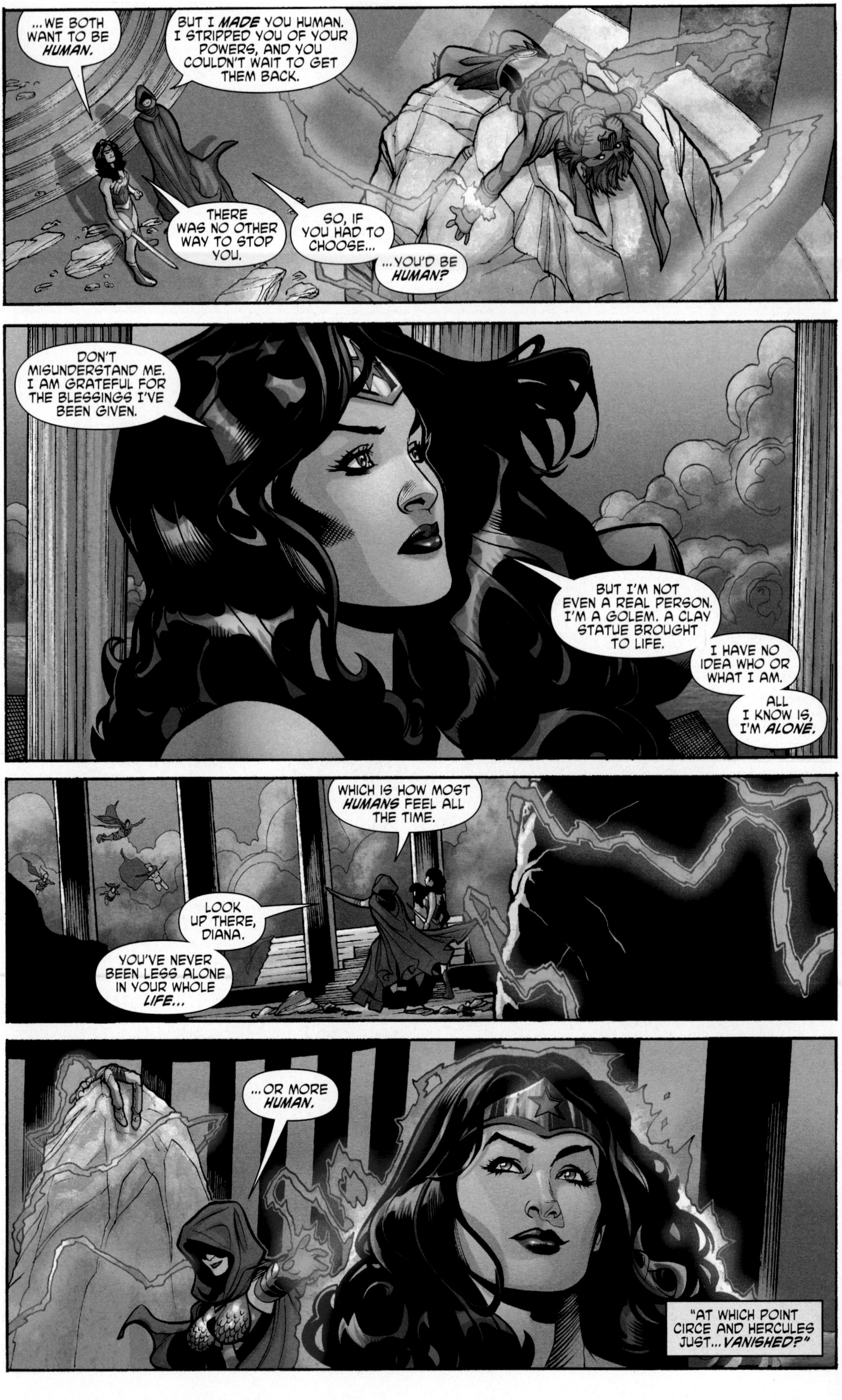
...WE BOTH WANT TO BE HUMAN.
BUT I MADE YOU HUMAN. I STRIPPED YOU OF YOUR POWERS, AND YOU COULDN'T WAIT TO GET THEM BACK.
THERE WAS NO OTHER WAY TO STOP YOU.
SO, IF YOU HAD TO CHOOSE...
...YOU'D BE HUMAN?
DON'T MISUNDERSTAND ME. I AM GRATEFUL FOR THE BLESSINGS I'VE BEEN GIVEN.
BUT I'M NOT EVEN A REAL PERSON. I'M A GOLEM. A CLAY STATUE BROUGHT TO LIFE.
I HAVE NO IDEA WHO OR WHAT I AM.
ALL I KNOW IS, I'M ALONE.
WHICH IS HOW MOST HUMANS FEEL ALL THE TIME.
LOOK UP THERE, DIANA.
YOU'VE NEVER BEEN LESS ALONE IN YOUR WHOLE LIFE...
...OR MORE HUMAN.
"AT WHICH POINT CIRCE AND HERCULES JUST...VANISHED?"

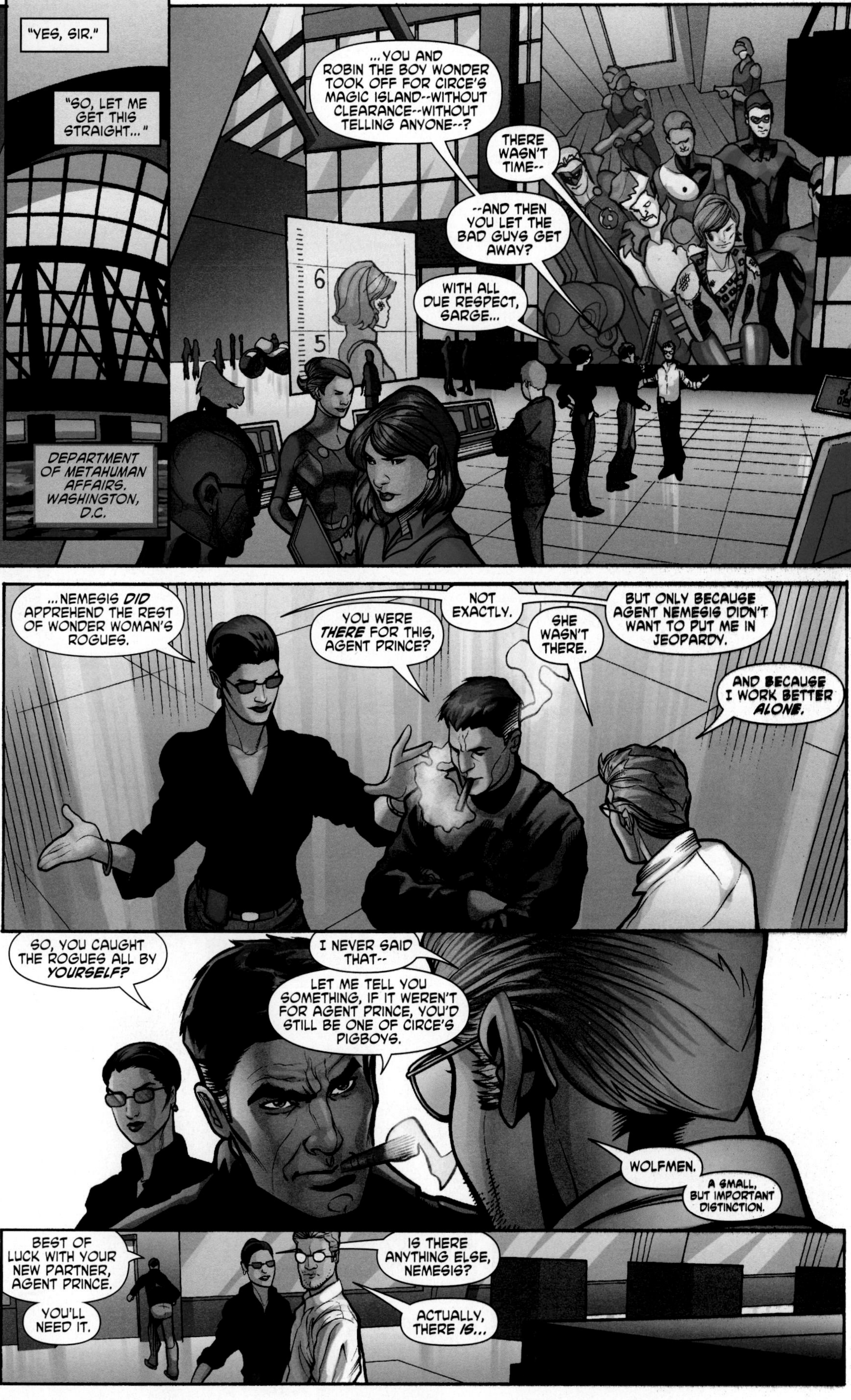
"YES, SIR."
"SO, LET ME GET THIS STRAIGHT..."
DEPARTMENT OF METAHUMAN AFFAIRS. WASHINGTON, D.C.
...YOU AND ROBIN THE BOY WONDER TOOK OFF FOR CIRCE'S MAGIC ISLAND--WITHOUT CLEARANCE--WITHOUT TELLING ANYONE--?
THERE WASN'T TIME--
--AND THEN YOU LET THE BAD GUYS GET AWAY?
WITH ALL DUE RESPECT, SARGE...
...NEMESIS *DID* APPREHEND THE REST OF WONDER WOMAN'S ROGUES.
YOU WERE *THERE* FOR THIS, AGENT PRINCE?
NOT EXACTLY.
SHE WASN'T THERE.
BUT ONLY BECAUSE AGENT NEMESIS DIDN'T WANT TO PUT ME IN JEOPARDY.
AND BECAUSE I WORK BETTER *ALONE*.
SO, YOU CAUGHT THE ROGUES ALL BY *YOURSELF?*
I NEVER SAID THAT--
LET ME TELL YOU SOMETHING, IF IT WEREN'T FOR AGENT PRINCE, YOU'D STILL BE ONE OF CIRCE'S PIGBOYS.
WOLFMEN.
A SMALL, BUT IMPORTANT DISTINCTION.
BEST OF LUCK WITH YOUR NEW PARTNER, AGENT PRINCE.
YOU'LL NEED IT.
IS THERE ANYTHING ELSE, NEMESIS?
ACTUALLY, THERE *IS*...

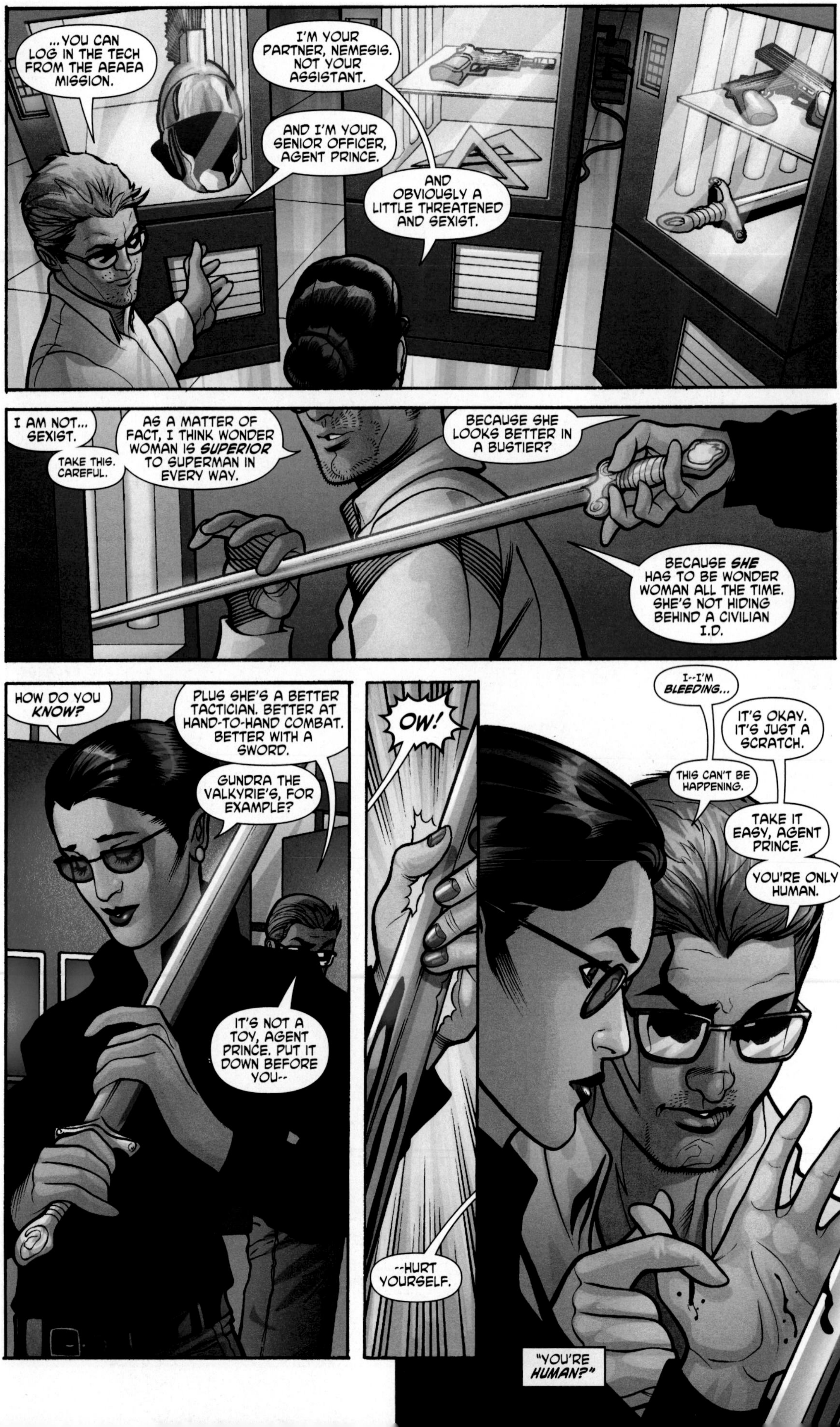
...YOU CAN LOG IN THE TECH FROM THE AEAEA MISSION.
I'M YOUR PARTNER, NEMESIS. NOT YOUR ASSISTANT.
AND I'M YOUR SENIOR OFFICER, AGENT PRINCE.
AND OBVIOUSLY A LITTLE THREATENED AND SEXIST.
I AM NOT... SEXIST.
TAKE THIS. CAREFUL.
AS A MATTER OF FACT, I THINK WONDER WOMAN IS SUPERIOR TO SUPERMAN IN EVERY WAY.
BECAUSE SHE LOOKS BETTER IN A BUSTIER?
BECAUSE SHE HAS TO BE WONDER WOMAN ALL THE TIME. SHE'S NOT HIDING BEHIND A CIVILIAN I.D.
HOW DO YOU KNOW?
PLUS SHE'S A BETTER TACTICIAN. BETTER AT HAND-TO-HAND COMBAT. BETTER WITH A SWORD.
GUNDRA THE VALKYRIE'S, FOR EXAMPLE?
IT'S NOT A TOY, AGENT PRINCE. PUT IT DOWN BEFORE YOU--
OW!
--HURT YOURSELF.
I--I'M BLEEDING...
IT'S OKAY. IT'S JUST A SCRATCH.
THIS CAN'T BE HAPPENING.
TAKE IT EASY, AGENT PRINCE.
YOU'RE ONLY HUMAN.
"YOU'RE HUMAN?"

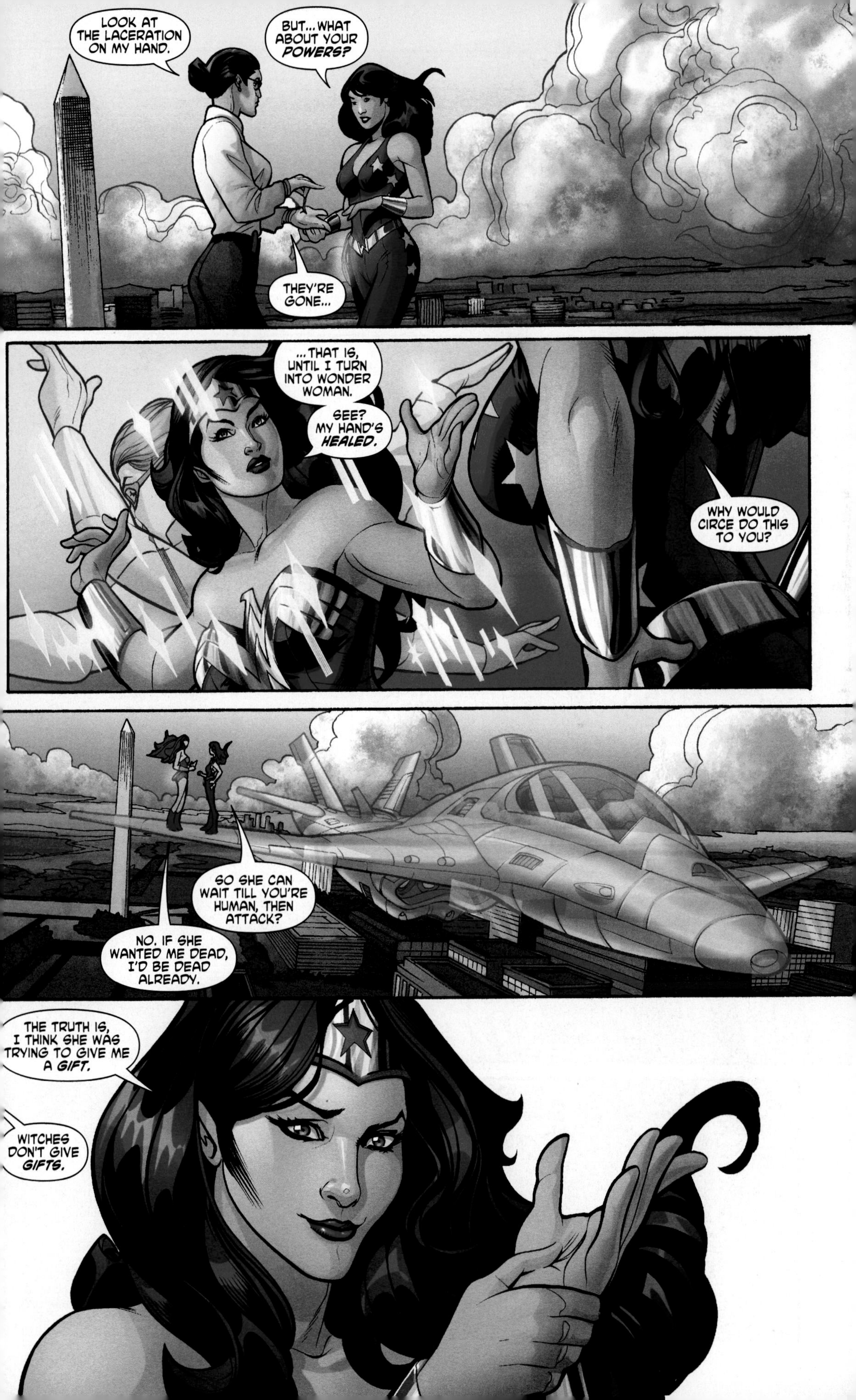
LOOK AT THE LACERATION ON MY HAND.
BUT...WHAT ABOUT YOUR *POWERS?*
THEY'RE GONE...
...THAT IS, UNTIL I TURN INTO WONDER WOMAN.
SEE? MY HAND'S *HEALED.*
WHY WOULD CIRCE DO THIS TO YOU?
SO SHE CAN WAIT TILL YOU'RE HUMAN, THEN ATTACK?
NO. IF SHE WANTED ME DEAD, I'D BE DEAD ALREADY.
THE TRUTH IS, I THINK SHE WAS TRYING TO GIVE ME A *GIFT.*
WITCHES DON'T GIVE *GIFTS.*

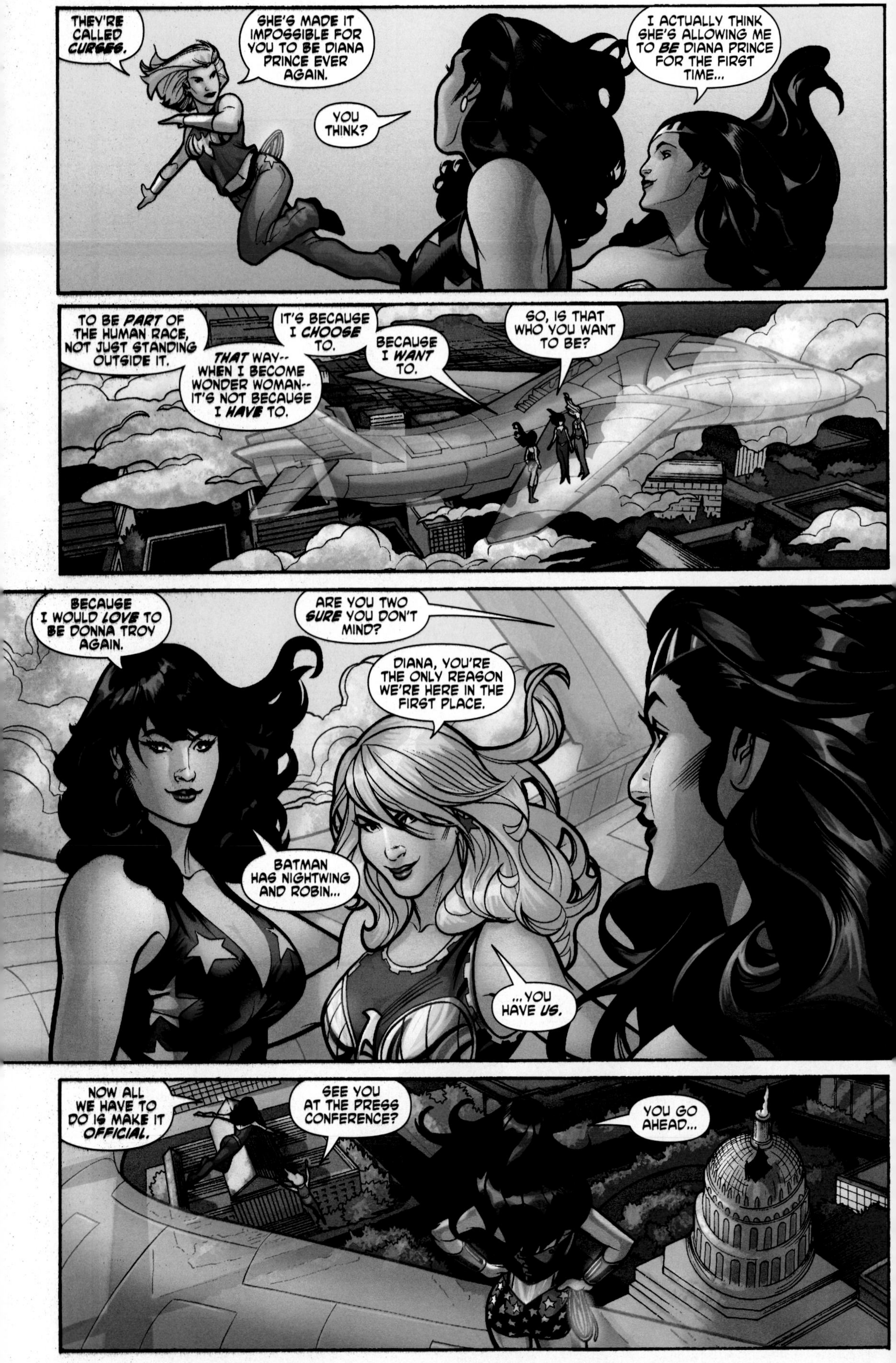
THEY'RE CALLED *CURSES*.
SHE'S MADE IT IMPOSSIBLE FOR YOU TO BE DIANA PRINCE EVER AGAIN.
YOU THINK?
I ACTUALLY THINK SHE'S ALLOWING ME TO *BE* DIANA PRINCE FOR THE FIRST TIME...
TO BE *PART* OF THE HUMAN RACE, NOT JUST STANDING OUTSIDE IT.
THAT WAY-- WHEN I BECOME WONDER WOMAN-- IT'S NOT BECAUSE I *HAVE* TO.
IT'S BECAUSE I *CHOOSE* TO.
BECAUSE I *WANT* TO.
SO, IS THAT WHO YOU WANT TO BE?
BECAUSE I WOULD *LOVE* TO BE DONNA TROY AGAIN.
ARE YOU TWO *SURE* YOU DON'T MIND?
DIANA, YOU'RE THE ONLY REASON WE'RE HERE IN THE FIRST PLACE.
BATMAN HAS NIGHTWING AND ROBIN...
...YOU HAVE *US*.
NOW ALL WE HAVE TO DO IS MAKE IT *OFFICIAL*.
SEE YOU AT THE PRESS CONFERENCE?
YOU GO AHEAD...

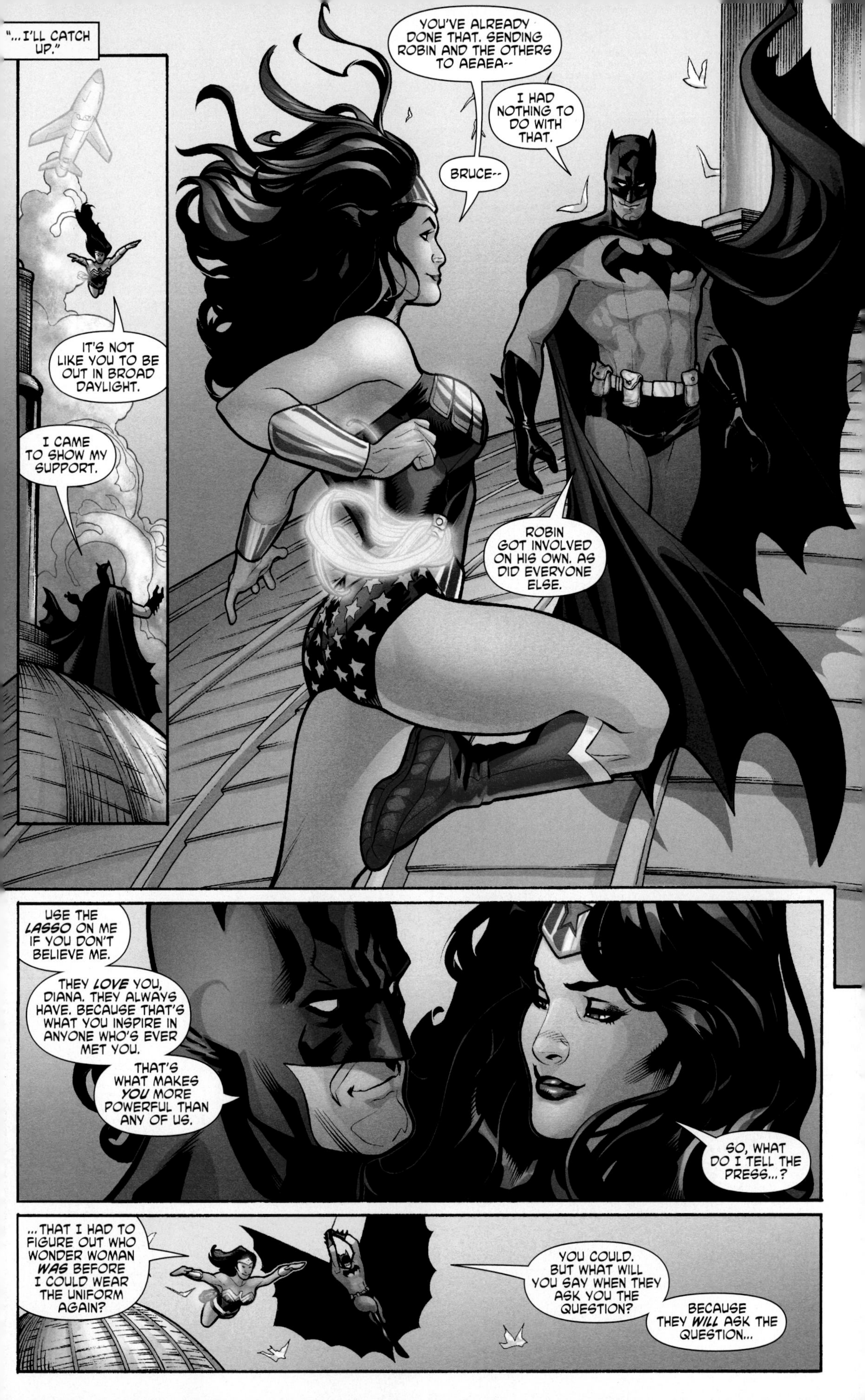
"...I'LL CATCH UP."
IT'S NOT LIKE YOU TO BE OUT IN BROAD DAYLIGHT.
I CAME TO SHOW MY SUPPORT.
YOU'VE ALREADY DONE THAT. SENDING ROBIN AND THE OTHERS TO AEAEA--
BRUCE--
I HAD NOTHING TO DO WITH THAT.
ROBIN GOT INVOLVED ON HIS OWN. AS DID EVERYONE ELSE.
USE THE *LASSO* ON ME IF YOU DON'T BELIEVE ME.
THEY *LOVE* YOU, DIANA. THEY ALWAYS HAVE. BECAUSE THAT'S WHAT YOU INSPIRE IN ANYONE WHO'S EVER MET YOU.
THAT'S WHAT MAKES *YOU* MORE POWERFUL THAN ANY OF US.
SO, WHAT DO I TELL THE PRESS...?
...THAT I HAD TO FIGURE OUT WHO WONDER WOMAN *WAS* BEFORE I COULD WEAR THE UNIFORM AGAIN?
YOU COULD. BUT WHAT WILL YOU SAY WHEN THEY ASK YOU THE QUESTION?
BECAUSE THEY *WILL* ASK THE QUESTION...

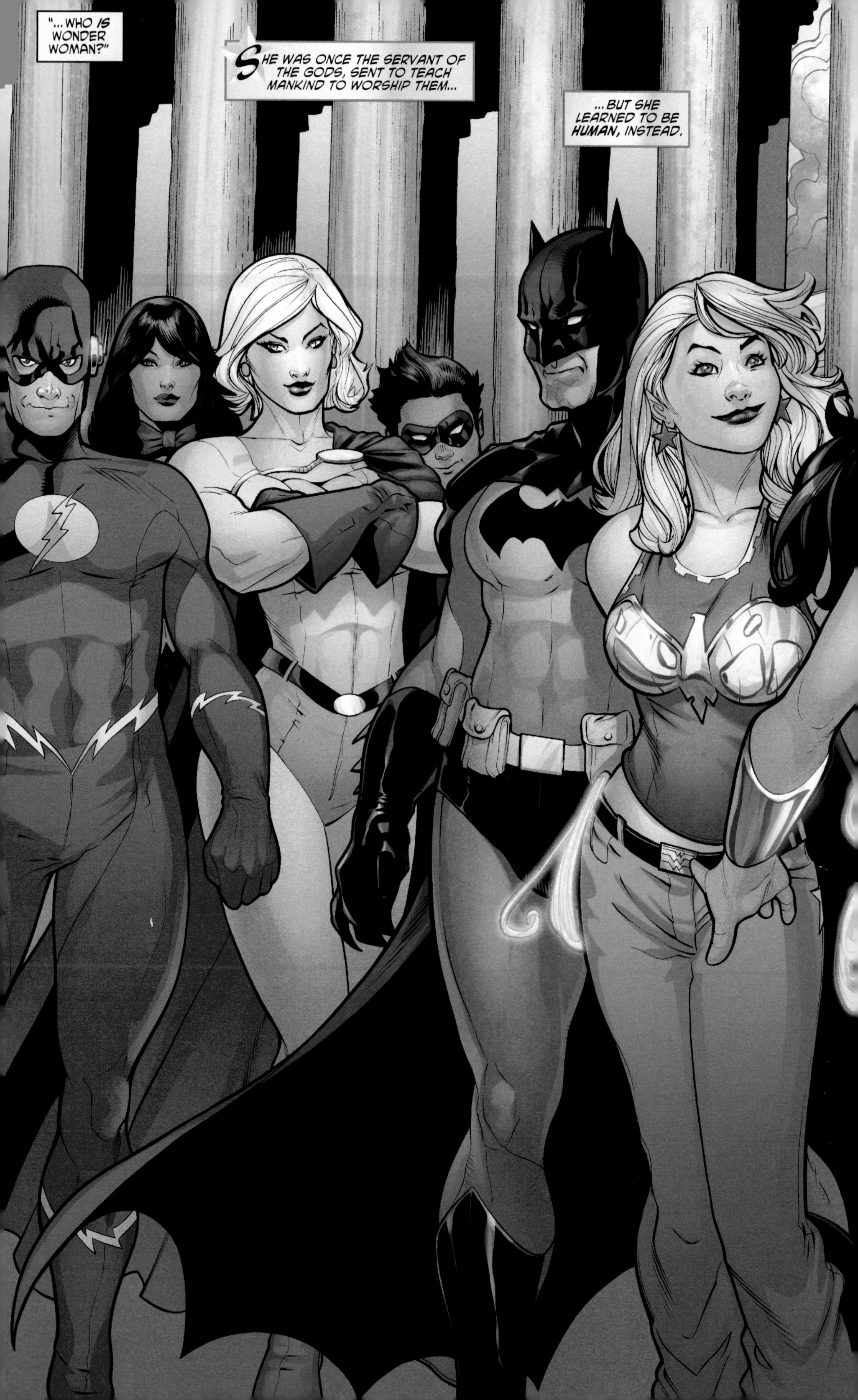
"...WHO IS WONDER WOMAN?"
SHE WAS ONCE THE SERVANT OF THE GODS, SENT TO TEACH MANKIND TO WORSHIP THEM...
...BUT SHE LEARNED TO BE HUMAN, INSTEAD.

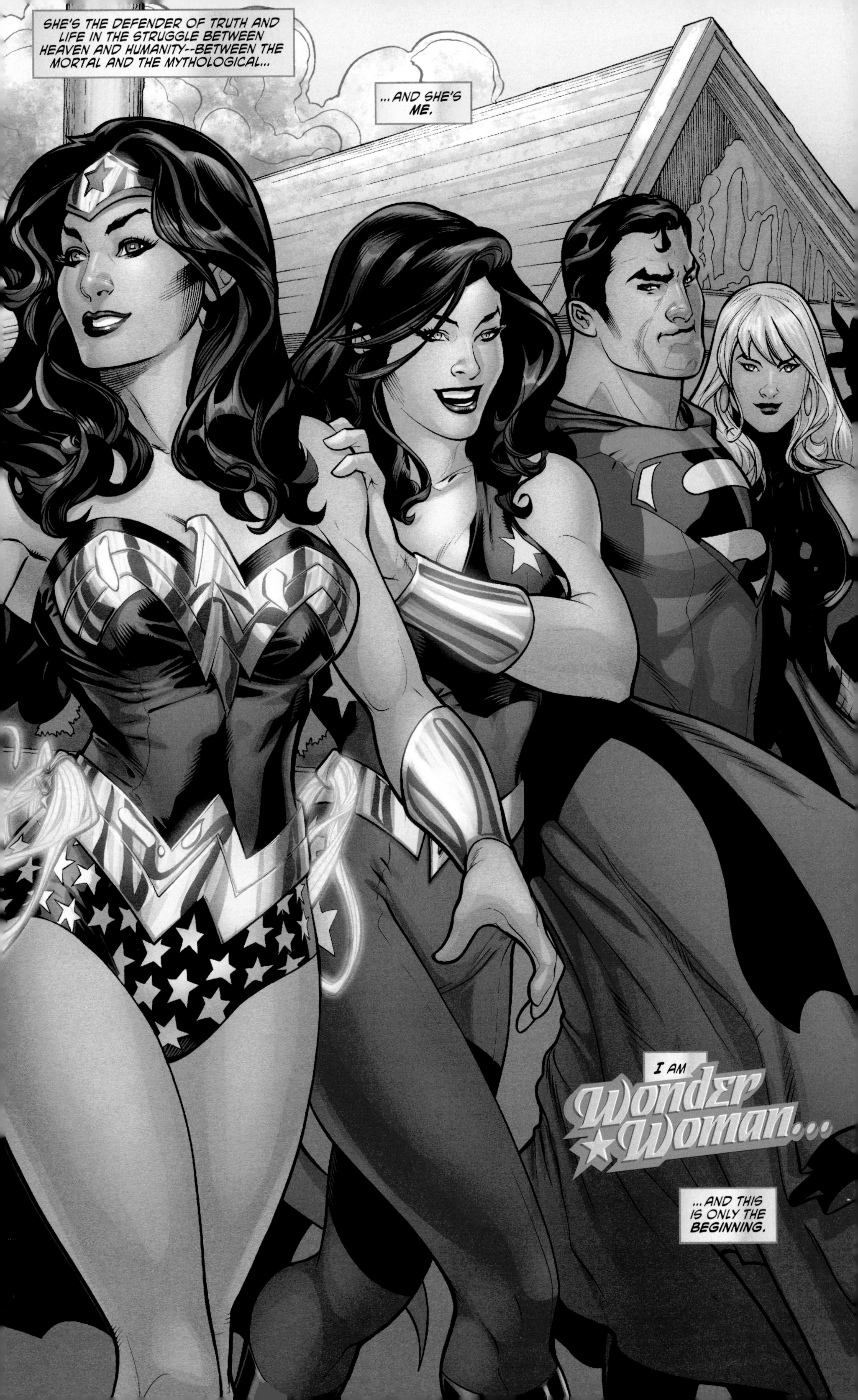
SHE'S THE DEFENDER OF TRUTH AND LIFE IN THE STRUGGLE BETWEEN HEAVEN AND HUMANITY--BETWEEN THE MORTAL AND THE MYTHOLOGICAL...
...AND SHE'S ME.
I AM Wonder Woman...
...AND THIS IS ONLY THE BEGINNING.

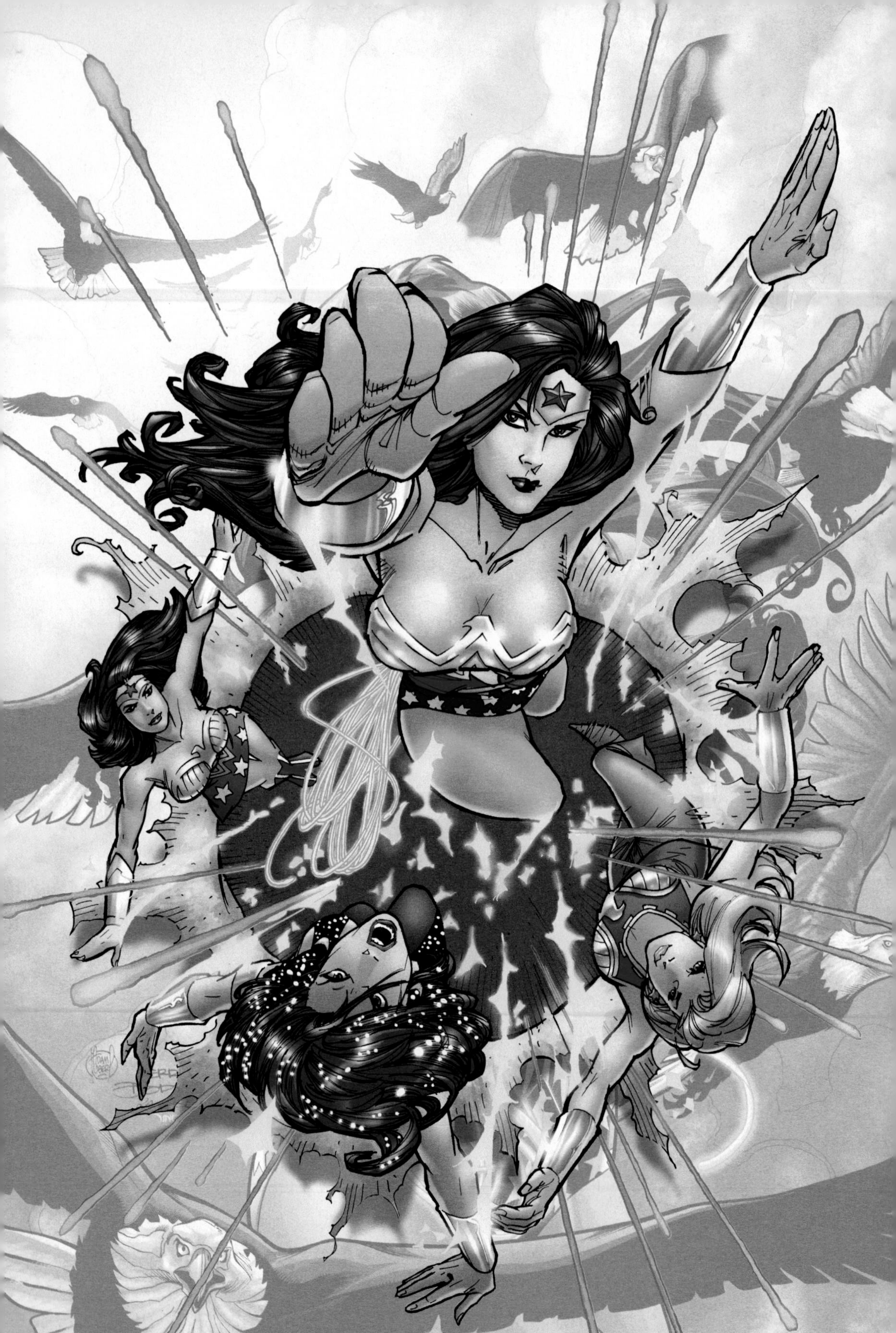

WONDER WOMAN #1 variant cover
by ADAM KUBERT with ALEX SINCLAIR

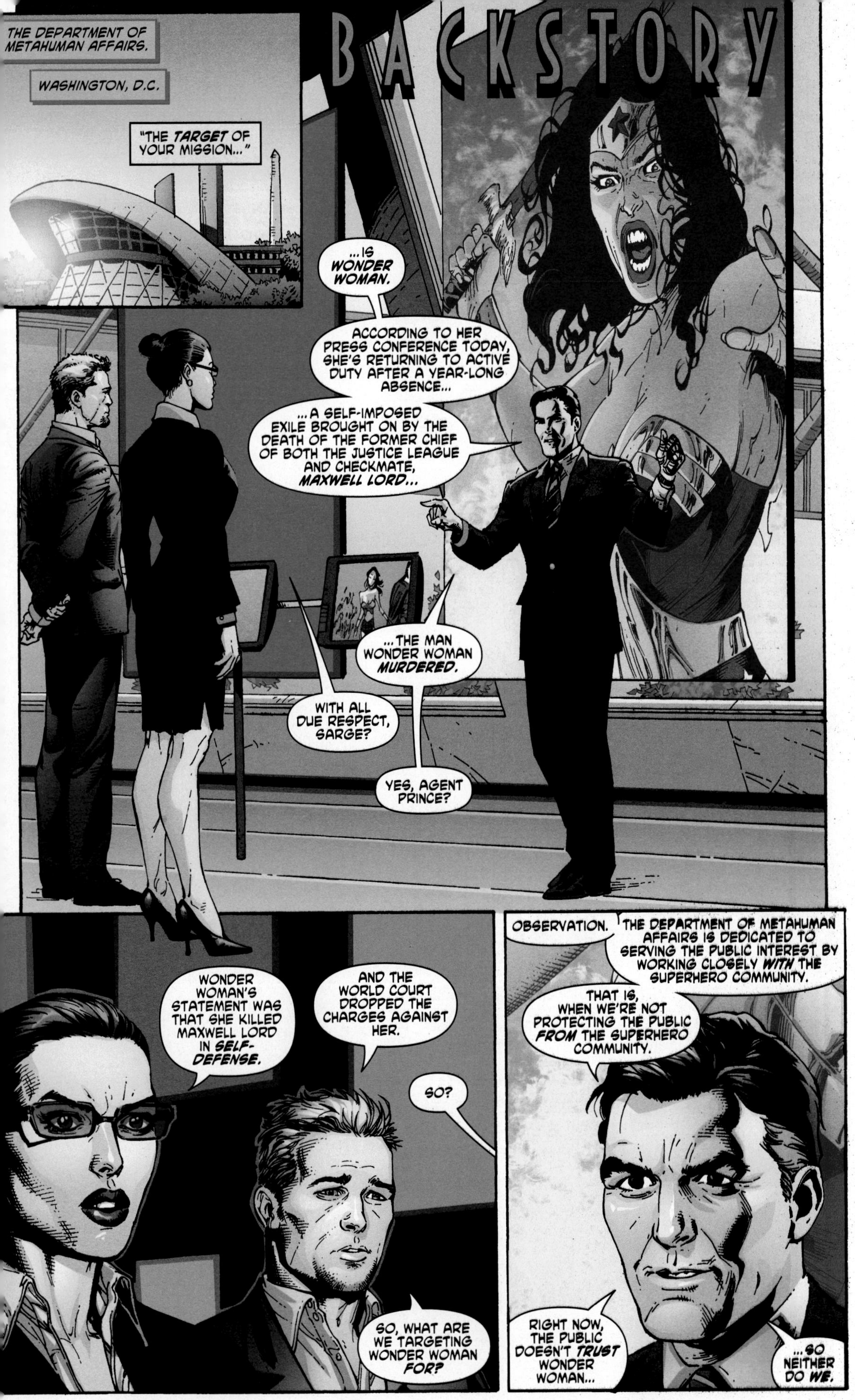
BACKSTORY
THE DEPARTMENT OF METAHUMAN AFFAIRS.
WASHINGTON, D.C.
"THE TARGET OF YOUR MISSION..."
...IS WONDER WOMAN.
ACCORDING TO HER PRESS CONFERENCE TODAY, SHE'S RETURNING TO ACTIVE DUTY AFTER A YEAR-LONG ABSENCE...
...A SELF-IMPOSED EXILE BROUGHT ON BY THE DEATH OF THE FORMER CHIEF OF BOTH THE JUSTICE LEAGUE AND CHECKMATE, MAXWELL LORD...
...THE MAN WONDER WOMAN MURDERED.
WITH ALL DUE RESPECT, SARGE?
YES, AGENT PRINCE?
WONDER WOMAN'S STATEMENT WAS THAT SHE KILLED MAXWELL LORD IN SELF-DEFENSE.
AND THE WORLD COURT DROPPED THE CHARGES AGAINST HER.
SO?
SO, WHAT ARE WE TARGETING WONDER WOMAN FOR?
OBSERVATION.
THE DEPARTMENT OF METAHUMAN AFFAIRS IS DEDICATED TO SERVING THE PUBLIC INTEREST BY WORKING CLOSELY WITH THE SUPERHERO COMMUNITY.
THAT IS, WHEN WE'RE NOT PROTECTING THE PUBLIC FROM THE SUPERHERO COMMUNITY.
RIGHT NOW, THE PUBLIC DOESN'T TRUST WONDER WOMAN...
...SO NEITHER DO WE.

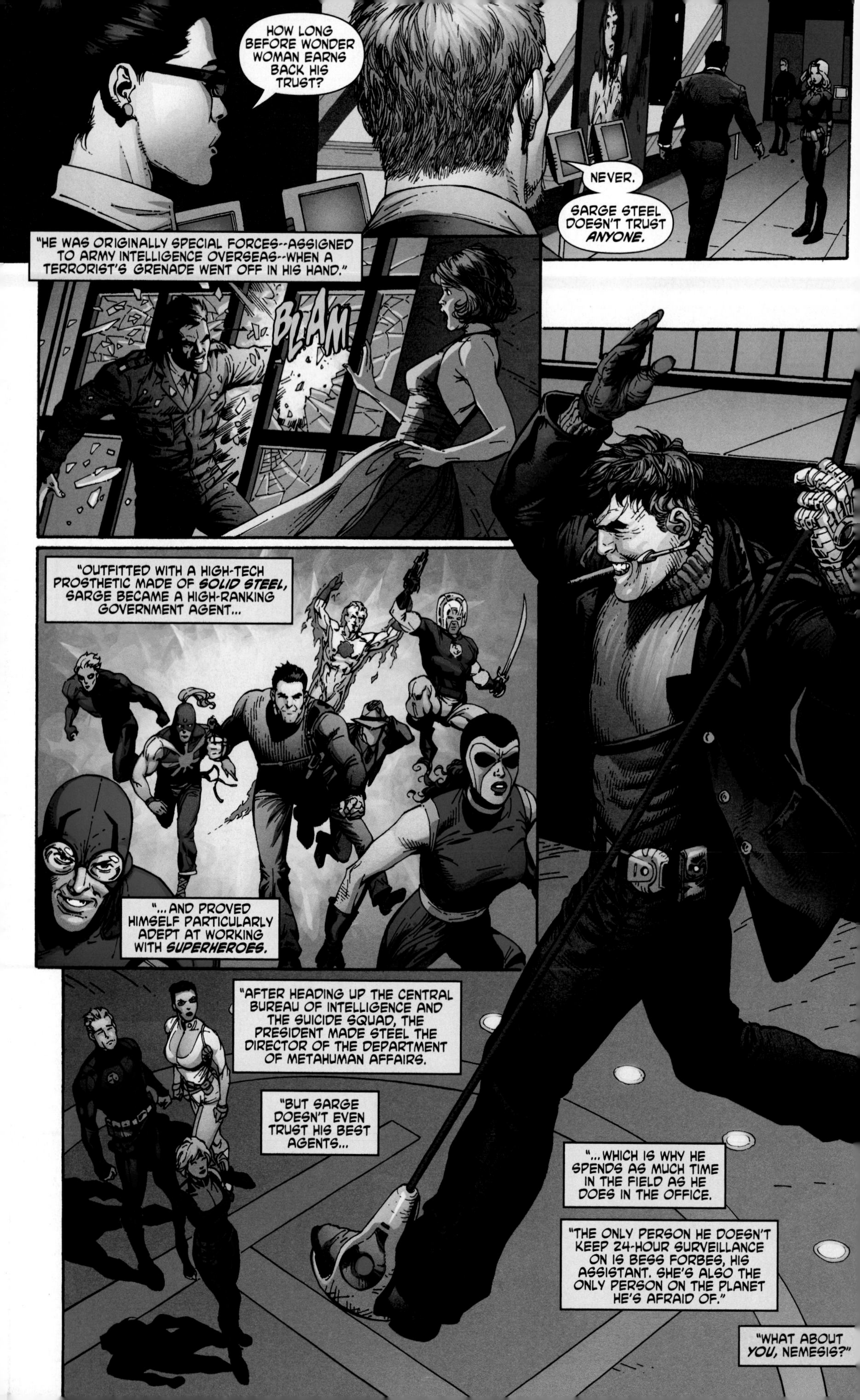

HOW LONG BEFORE WONDER WOMAN EARNS BACK HIS TRUST?
NEVER.
SARGE STEEL DOESN'T TRUST ANYONE.
"HE WAS ORIGINALLY SPECIAL FORCES--ASSIGNED TO ARMY INTELLIGENCE OVERSEAS--WHEN A TERRORIST'S GRENADE WENT OFF IN HIS HAND."
BLAM
"OUTFITTED WITH A HIGH-TECH PROSTHETIC MADE OF SOLID STEEL, SARGE BECAME A HIGH-RANKING GOVERNMENT AGENT...
"...AND PROVED HIMSELF PARTICULARLY ADEPT AT WORKING WITH SUPERHEROES.
"AFTER HEADING UP THE CENTRAL BUREAU OF INTELLIGENCE AND THE SUICIDE SQUAD, THE PRESIDENT MADE STEEL THE DIRECTOR OF THE DEPARTMENT OF METAHUMAN AFFAIRS.
"BUT SARGE DOESN'T EVEN TRUST HIS BEST AGENTS...
"...WHICH IS WHY HE SPENDS AS MUCH TIME IN THE FIELD AS HE DOES IN THE OFFICE.
"THE ONLY PERSON HE DOESN'T KEEP 24-HOUR SURVEILLANCE ON IS BESS FORBES, HIS ASSISTANT. SHE'S ALSO THE ONLY PERSON ON THE PLANET HE'S AFRAID OF."
"WHAT ABOUT YOU, NEMESIS?"

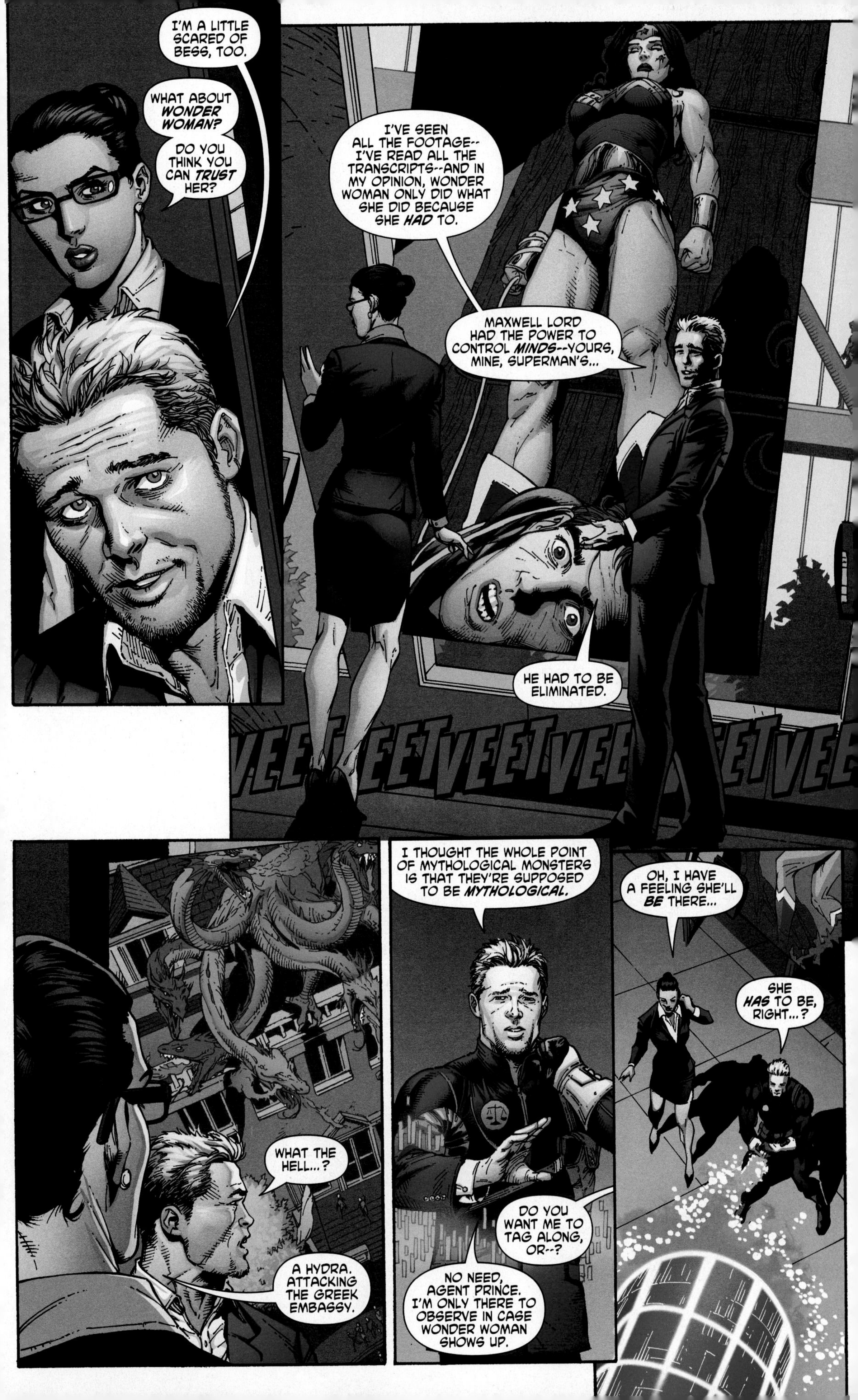
I'M A LITTLE SCARED OF BESS, TOO.
WHAT ABOUT *WONDER WOMAN?*
DO YOU THINK YOU CAN *TRUST* HER?
I'VE SEEN ALL THE FOOTAGE--I'VE READ ALL THE TRANSCRIPTS--AND IN MY OPINION, WONDER WOMAN ONLY DID WHAT SHE DID BECAUSE SHE *HAD* TO.
MAXWELL LORD HAD THE POWER TO CONTROL *MINDS*--YOURS, MINE, SUPERMAN'S...
HE HAD TO BE ELIMINATED.
VEETVEETVEETVEETVEETVEE
WHAT THE HELL...?
A HYDRA. ATTACKING THE GREEK EMBASSY.
I THOUGHT THE WHOLE POINT OF MYTHOLOGICAL MONSTERS IS THAT THEY'RE SUPPOSED TO BE *MYTHOLOGICAL.*
DO YOU WANT ME TO TAG ALONG, OR--?
NO NEED, AGENT PRINCE. I'M ONLY THERE TO OBSERVE IN CASE WONDER WOMAN SHOWS UP.
OH, I HAVE A FEELING SHE'LL *BE* THERE...
SHE *HAS* TO BE, RIGHT...?

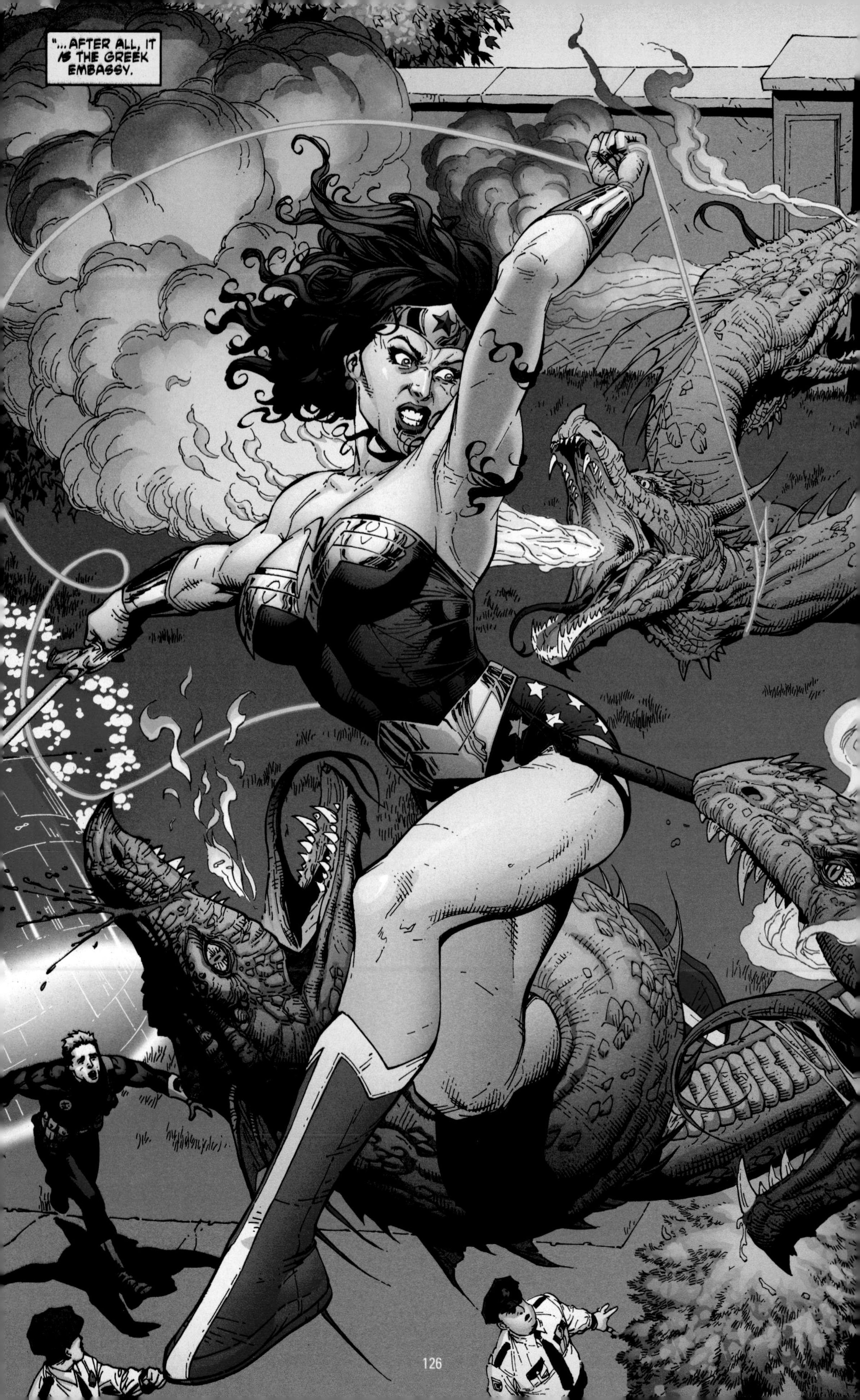
"...AFTER ALL, IT IS THE GREEK EMBASSY.

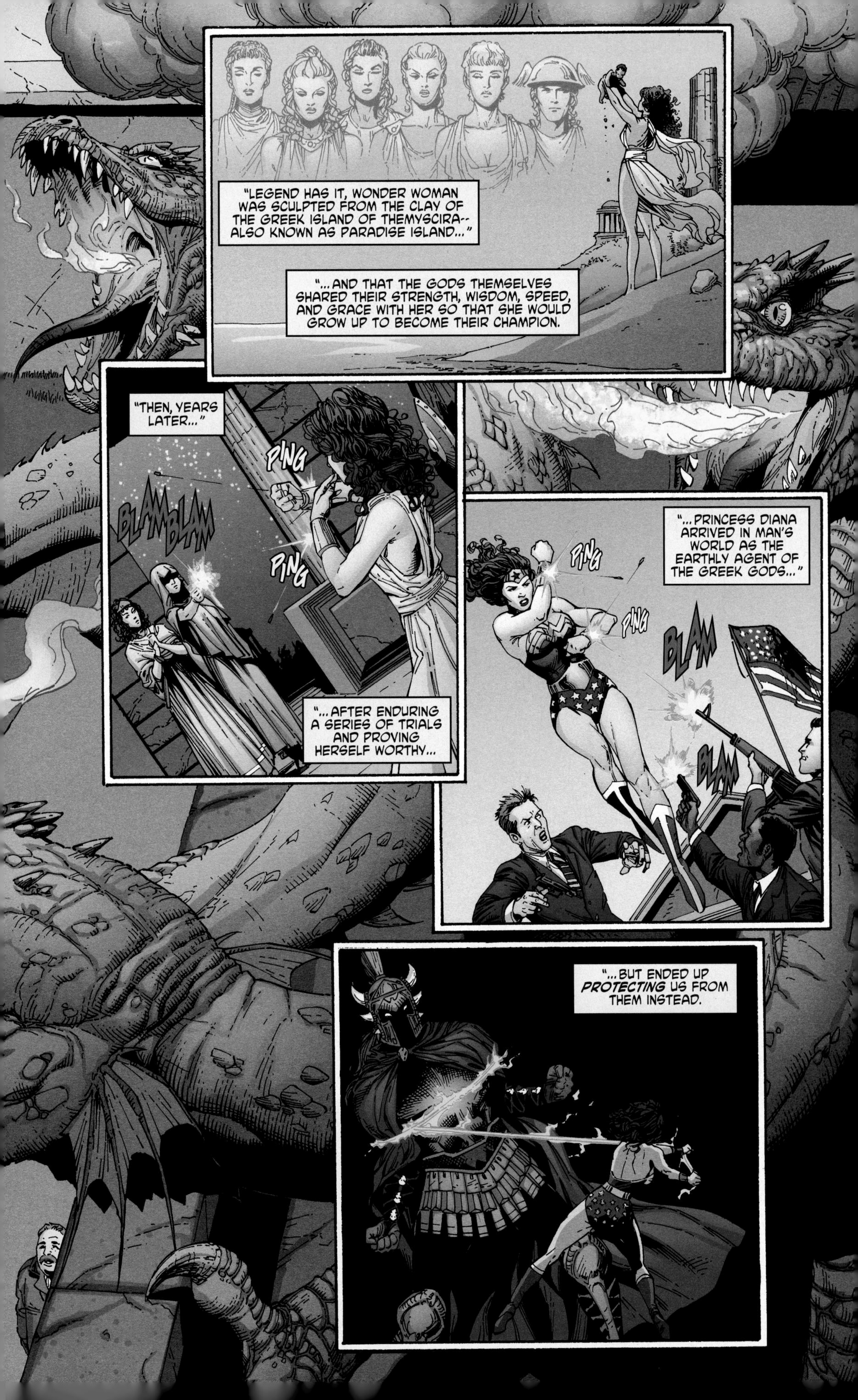
"LEGEND HAS IT, WONDER WOMAN WAS SCULPTED FROM THE CLAY OF THE GREEK ISLAND OF THEMYSCIRA-- ALSO KNOWN AS PARADISE ISLAND..."
"...AND THAT THE GODS THEMSELVES SHARED THEIR STRENGTH, WISDOM, SPEED, AND GRACE WITH HER SO THAT SHE WOULD GROW UP TO BECOME THEIR CHAMPION.
"THEN, YEARS LATER..."
PING
BLAM BLAM
PING
"...AFTER ENDURING A SERIES OF TRIALS AND PROVING HERSELF WORTHY...
"...PRINCESS DIANA ARRIVED IN MAN'S WORLD AS THE EARTHLY AGENT OF THE GREEK GODS..."
PING
PING
BLAM
BLAM
"...BUT ENDED UP PROTECTING US FROM THEM INSTEAD.

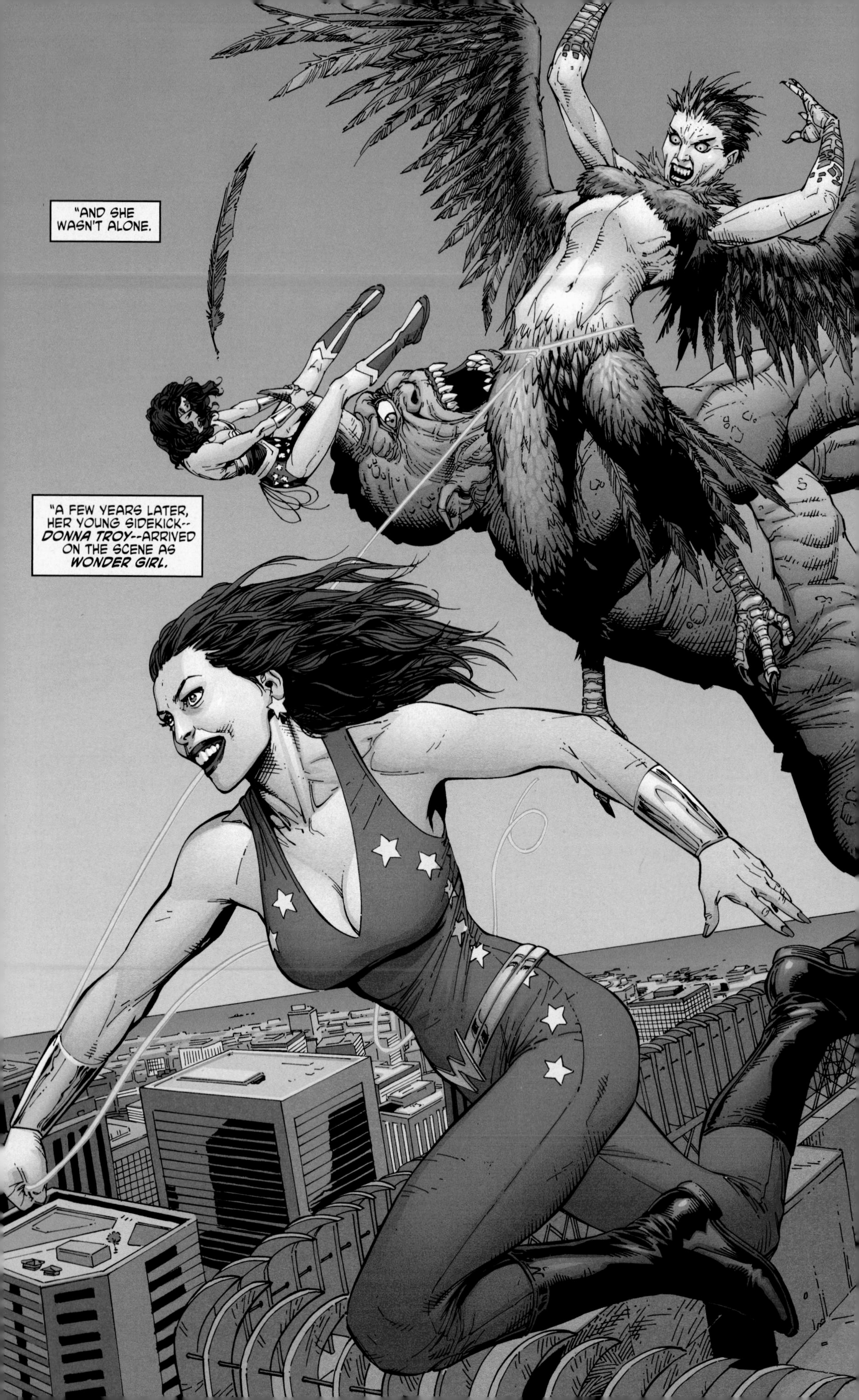
"AND SHE WASN'T ALONE.
"A FEW YEARS LATER, HER YOUNG SIDEKICK-- *DONNA TROY*--ARRIVED ON THE SCENE AS *WONDER GIRL.*

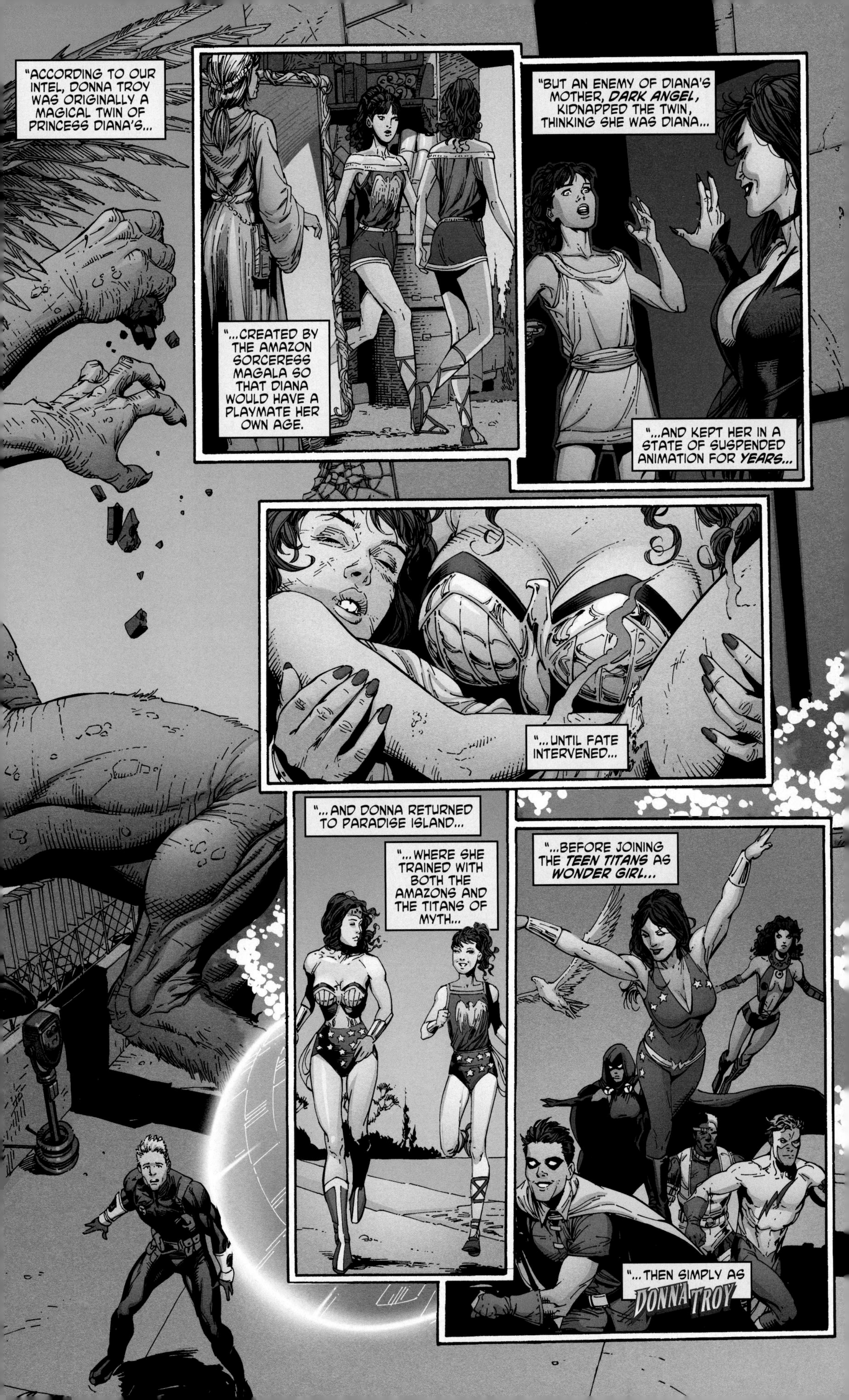
"ACCORDING TO OUR INTEL, DONNA TROY WAS ORIGINALLY A MAGICAL TWIN OF PRINCESS DIANA'S...
"...CREATED BY THE AMAZON SORCERESS MAGALA SO THAT DIANA WOULD HAVE A PLAYMATE HER OWN AGE.
"BUT AN ENEMY OF DIANA'S MOTHER, DARK ANGEL, KIDNAPPED THE TWIN, THINKING SHE WAS DIANA...
"...AND KEPT HER IN A STATE OF SUSPENDED ANIMATION FOR YEARS...
"...UNTIL FATE INTERVENED...
"...AND DONNA RETURNED TO PARADISE ISLAND...
"...WHERE SHE TRAINED WITH BOTH THE AMAZONS AND THE TITANS OF MYTH...
"...BEFORE JOINING THE TEEN TITANS AS WONDER GIRL...
"...THEN SIMPLY AS
DONNA TROY

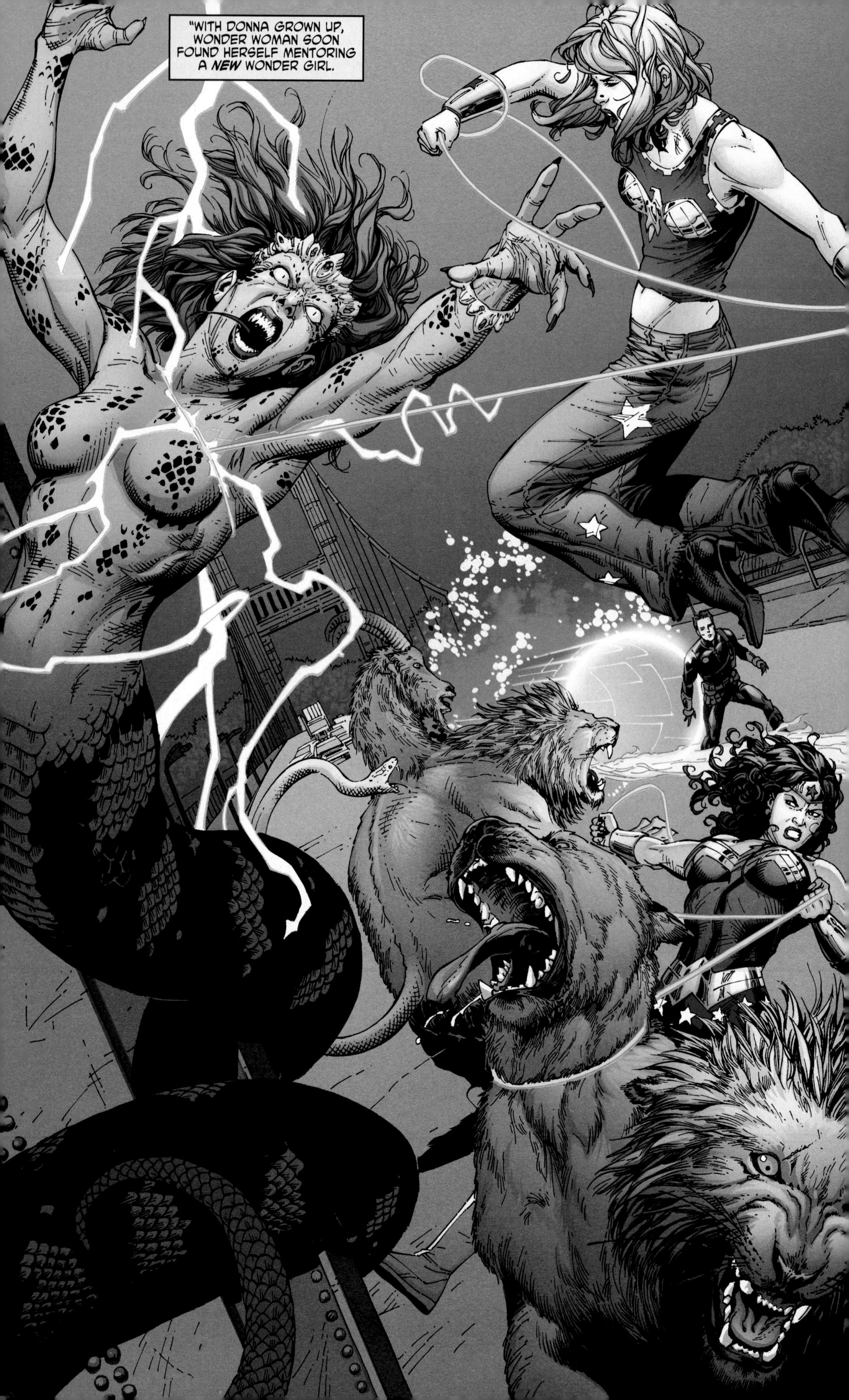
"WITH DONNA GROWN UP, WONDER WOMAN SOON FOUND HERSELF MENTORING A *NEW* WONDER GIRL.

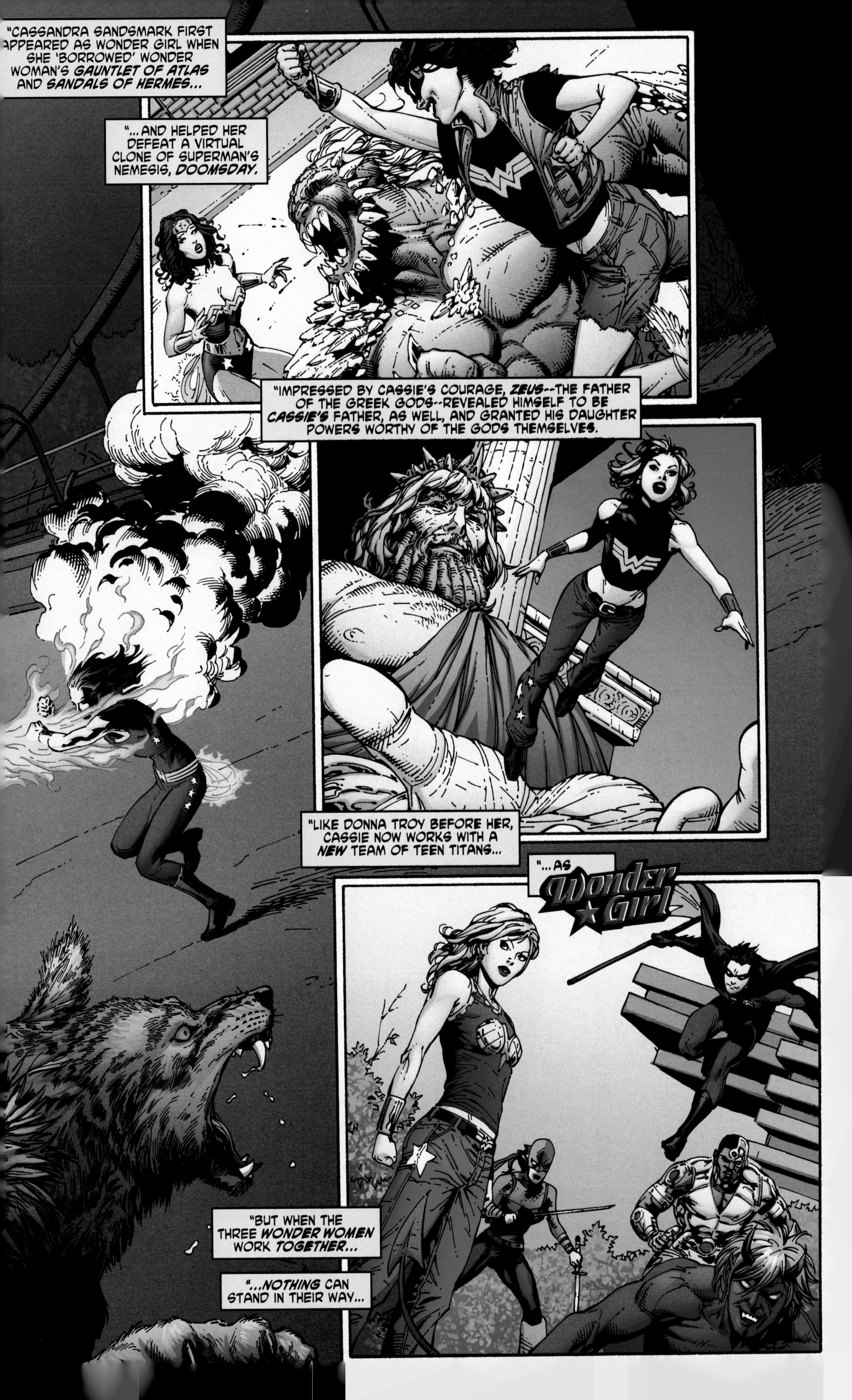
"CASSANDRA SANDSMARK FIRST APPEARED AS WONDER GIRL WHEN SHE 'BORROWED' WONDER WOMAN'S GAUNTLET OF ATLAS AND SANDALS OF HERMES...
"...AND HELPED HER DEFEAT A VIRTUAL CLONE OF SUPERMAN'S NEMESIS, DOOMSDAY.
"IMPRESSED BY CASSIE'S COURAGE, ZEUS--THE FATHER OF THE GREEK GODS--REVEALED HIMSELF TO BE CASSIE'S FATHER, AS WELL, AND GRANTED HIS DAUGHTER POWERS WORTHY OF THE GODS THEMSELVES.
"LIKE DONNA TROY BEFORE HER, CASSIE NOW WORKS WITH A NEW TEAM OF TEEN TITANS...
"...AS Wonder Girl
"BUT WHEN THE THREE WONDER WOMEN WORK TOGETHER...
"...NOTHING CAN STAND IN THEIR WAY...

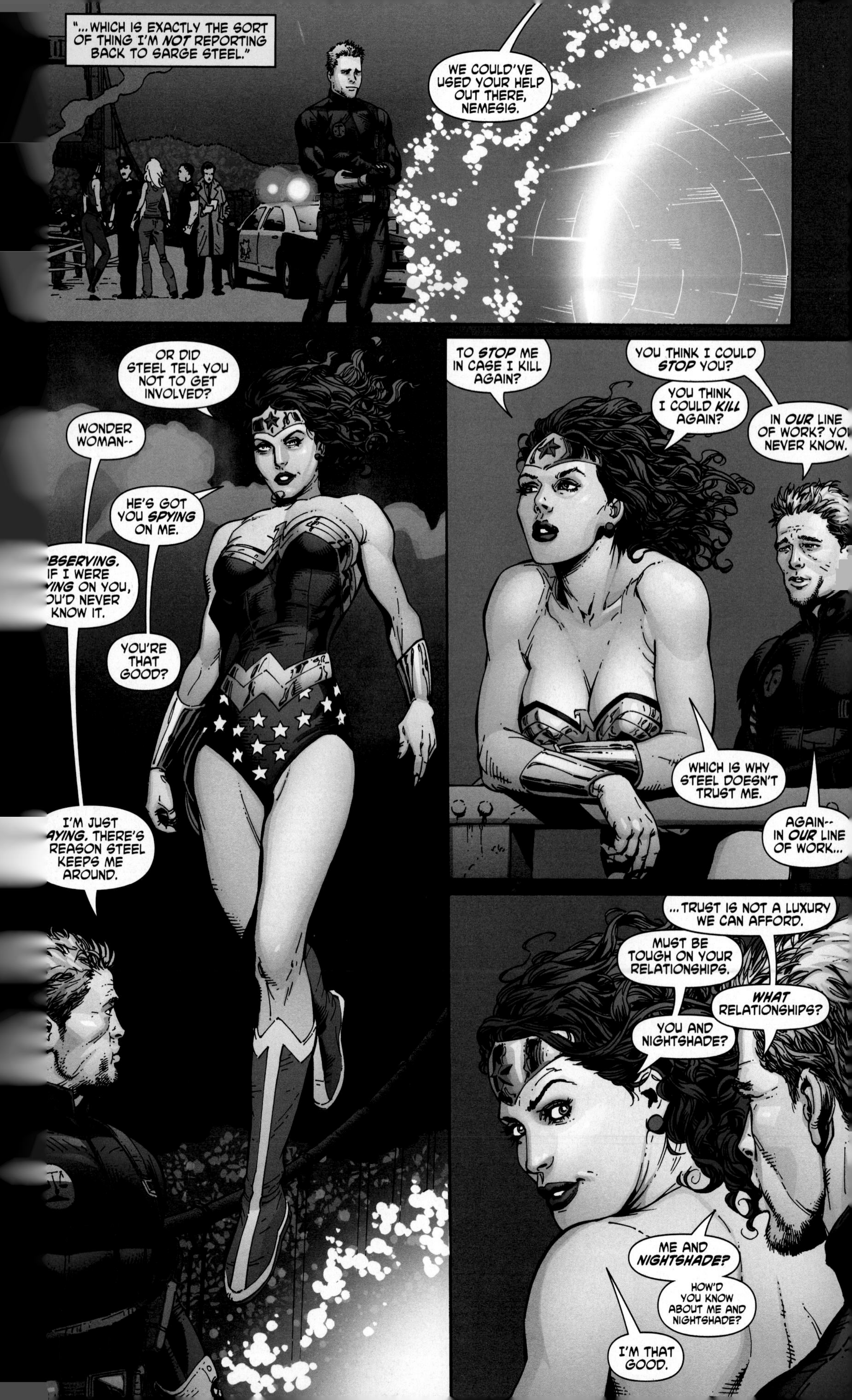
"...WHICH IS EXACTLY THE SORT OF THING I'M *NOT* REPORTING BACK TO SARGE STEEL."
WE COULD'VE USED YOUR HELP OUT THERE, NEMESIS.
OR DID STEEL TELL YOU NOT TO GET INVOLVED?
WONDER WOMAN--
HE'S GOT YOU *SPYING* ON ME.
BSERVING. F I WERE *YING* ON YOU, OU'D NEVER KNOW IT.
YOU'RE THAT GOOD?
I'M JUST *AYING.* THERE'S REASON STEEL KEEPS ME AROUND.
TO *STOP* ME IN CASE I KILL AGAIN?
YOU THINK I COULD *STOP* YOU?
YOU THINK I COULD *KILL* AGAIN?
IN *OUR* LINE OF WORK? YO NEVER KNOW.
WHICH IS WHY STEEL DOESN'T TRUST ME.
AGAIN-- IN *OUR* LINE OF WORK...
...TRUST IS NOT A LUXURY WE CAN AFFORD.
MUST BE TOUGH ON YOUR RELATIONSHIPS.
WHAT RELATIONSHIPS?
YOU AND NIGHTSHADE?
ME AND *NIGHTSHADE?*
HOW'D YOU KNOW ABOUT ME AND NIGHTSHADE?
I'M THAT GOOD.

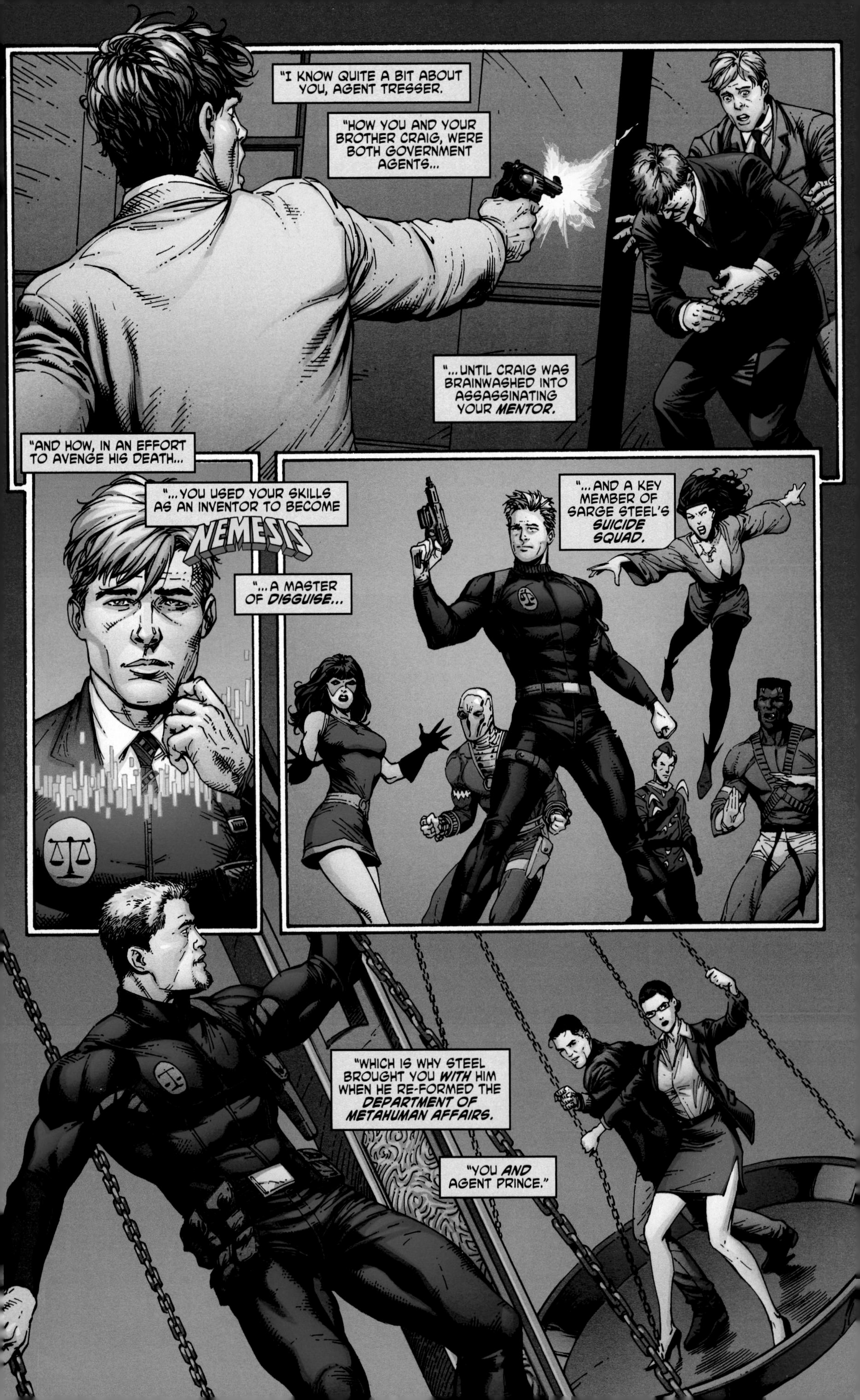
"I KNOW QUITE A BIT ABOUT YOU, AGENT TRESSER.
"HOW YOU AND YOUR BROTHER CRAIG, WERE BOTH GOVERNMENT AGENTS...
"...UNTIL CRAIG WAS BRAINWASHED INTO ASSASSINATING YOUR MENTOR.
"AND HOW, IN AN EFFORT TO AVENGE HIS DEATH...
"...YOU USED YOUR SKILLS AS AN INVENTOR TO BECOME
NEMESIS
"...A MASTER OF DISGUISE...
"...AND A KEY MEMBER OF SARGE STEEL'S SUICIDE SQUAD.
"WHICH IS WHY STEEL BROUGHT YOU WITH HIM WHEN HE RE-FORMED THE DEPARTMENT OF METAHUMAN AFFAIRS.
"YOU AND AGENT PRINCE."

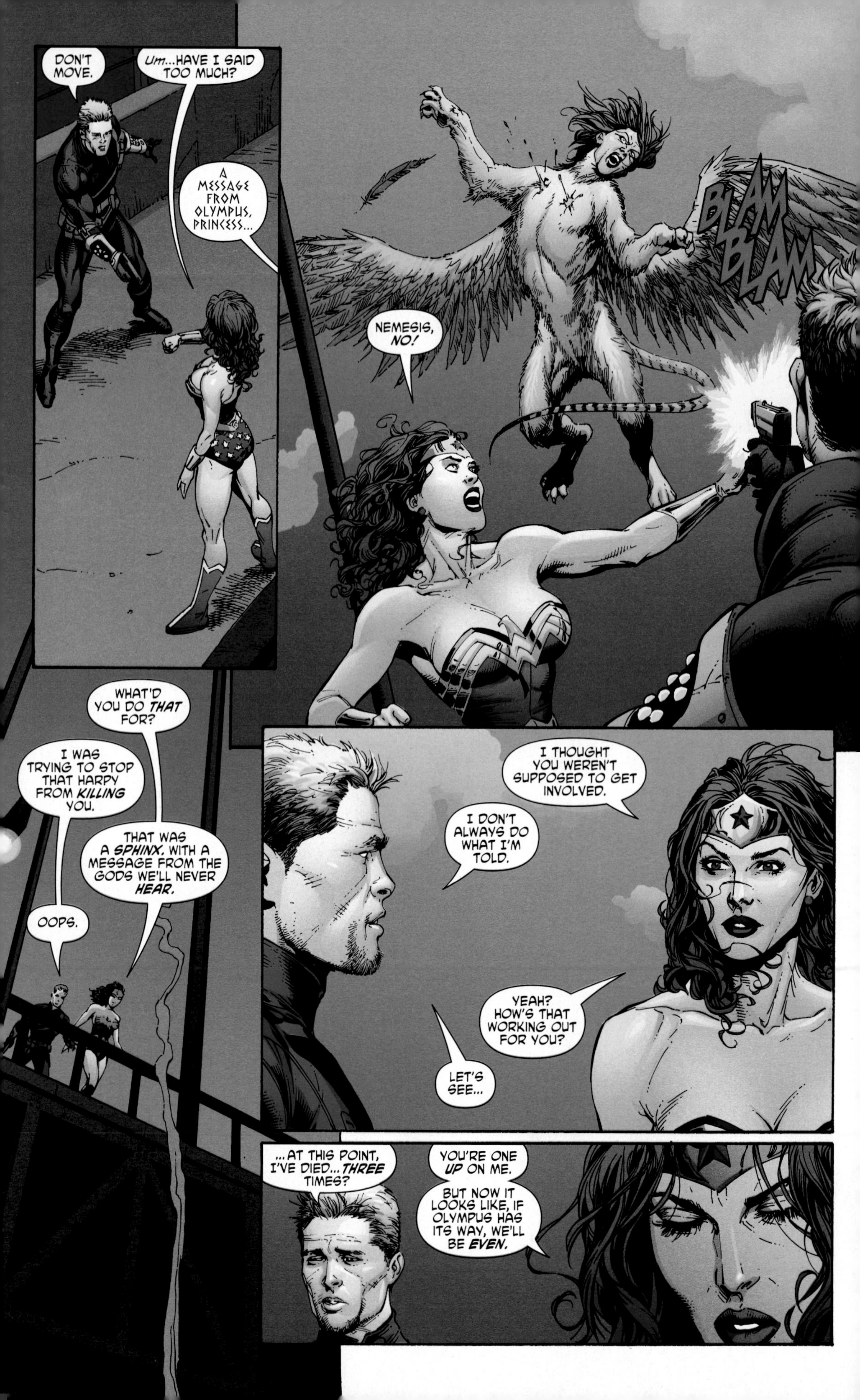
DON'T MOVE.
Um...HAVE I SAID TOO MUCH?
A MESSAGE FROM OLYMPUS, PRINCESS...
BLAM BLAM
NEMESIS, NO!
WHAT'D YOU DO THAT FOR?
I WAS TRYING TO STOP THAT HARPY FROM KILLING YOU.
THAT WAS A SPHINX. WITH A MESSAGE FROM THE GODS WE'LL NEVER HEAR.
OOPS.
I THOUGHT YOU WEREN'T SUPPOSED TO GET INVOLVED.
I DON'T ALWAYS DO WHAT I'M TOLD.
YEAH? HOW'S THAT WORKING OUT FOR YOU?
LET'S SEE...
...AT THIS POINT, I'VE DIED...THREE TIMES?
YOU'RE ONE UP ON ME.
BUT NOW IT LOOKS LIKE, IF OLYMPUS HAS ITS WAY, WE'LL BE EVEN.

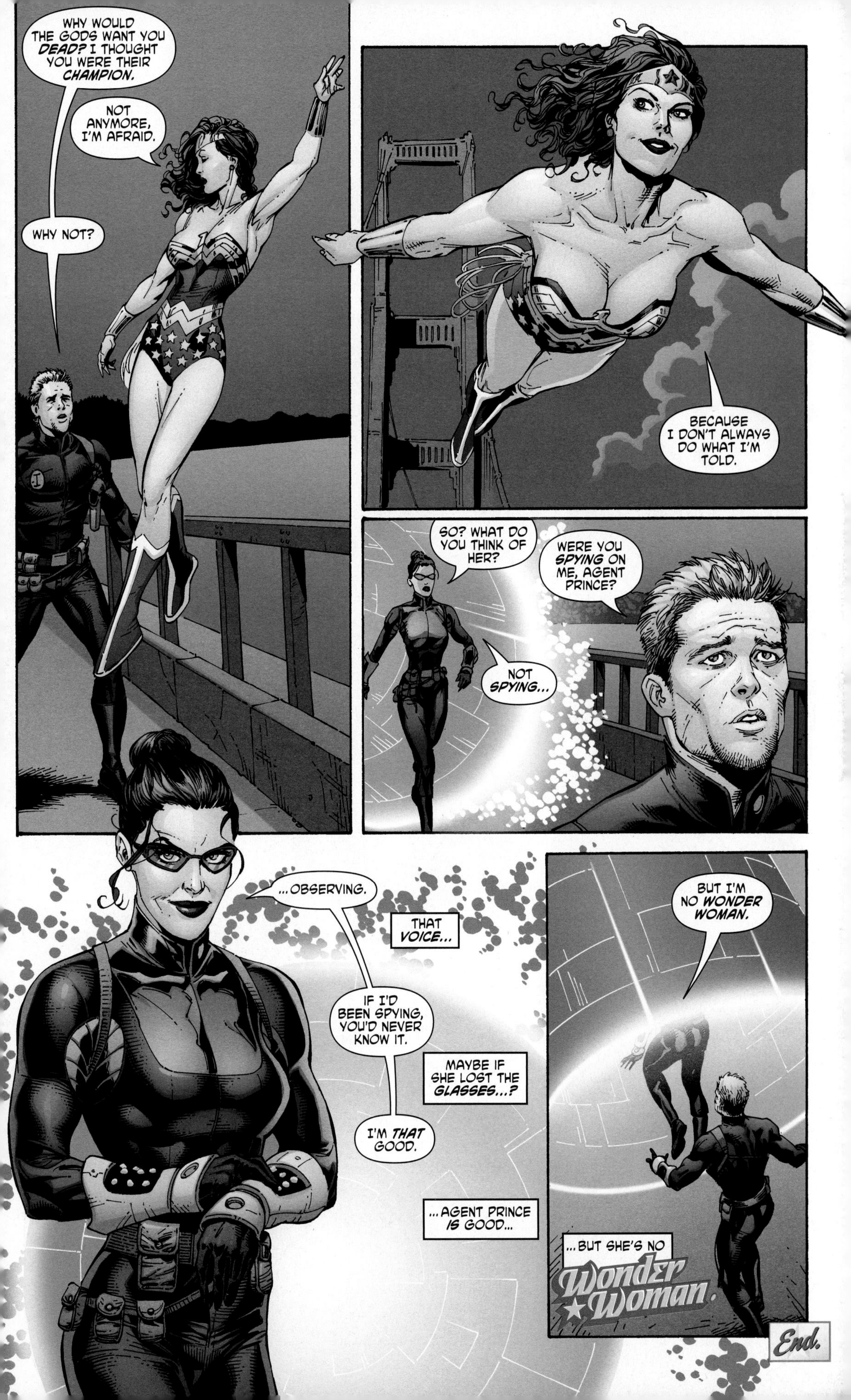
WHY WOULD THE GODS WANT YOU DEAD? I THOUGHT YOU WERE THEIR CHAMPION.
NOT ANYMORE, I'M AFRAID.
WHY NOT?
BECAUSE I DON'T ALWAYS DO WHAT I'M TOLD.
SO? WHAT DO YOU THINK OF HER?
WERE YOU SPYING ON ME, AGENT PRINCE?
NOT SPYING...
...OBSERVING.
THAT VOICE...
IF I'D BEEN SPYING, YOU'D NEVER KNOW IT.
MAYBE IF SHE LOST THE GLASSES...?
I'M THAT GOOD.
...AGENT PRINCE IS GOOD...
BUT I'M NO WONDER WOMAN.
...BUT SHE'S NO
Wonder Woman.
End.

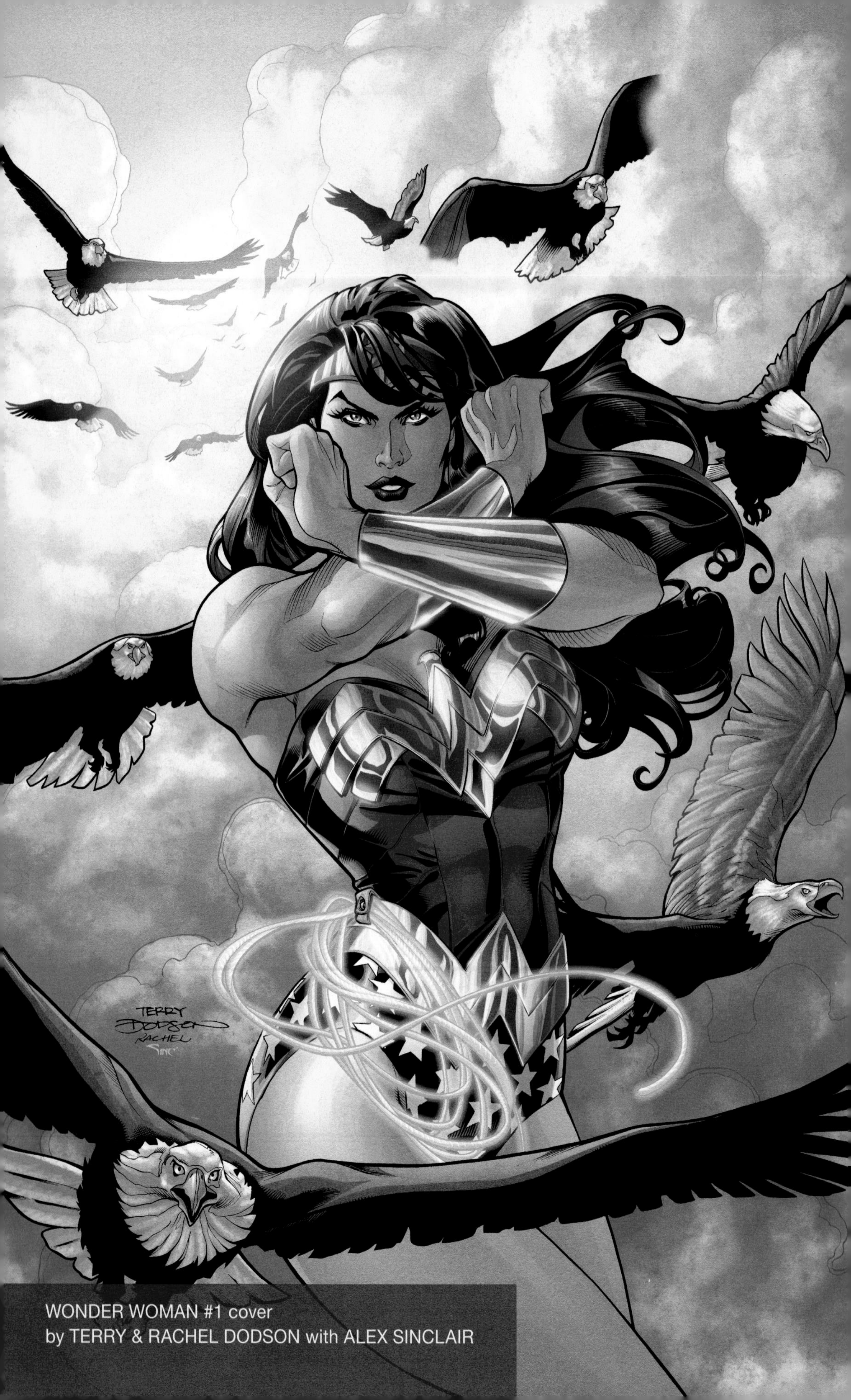
TERRY
DODSON
RACHEL

WONDER WOMAN #1 cover
by TERRY & RACHEL DODSON with ALEX SINCLAIR

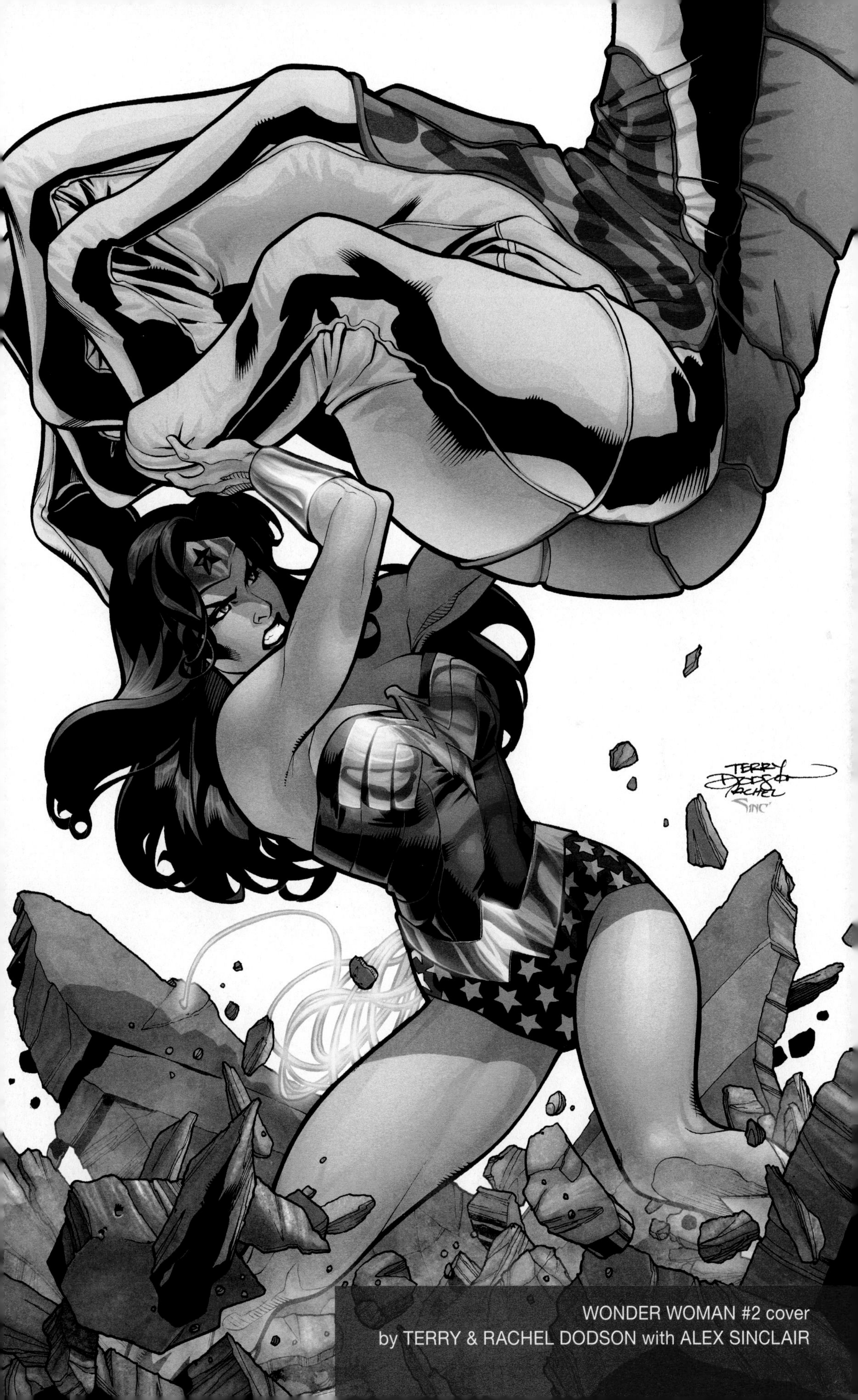

WONDER WOMAN #2 cover
by TERRY & RACHEL DODSON with ALEX SINCLAIR

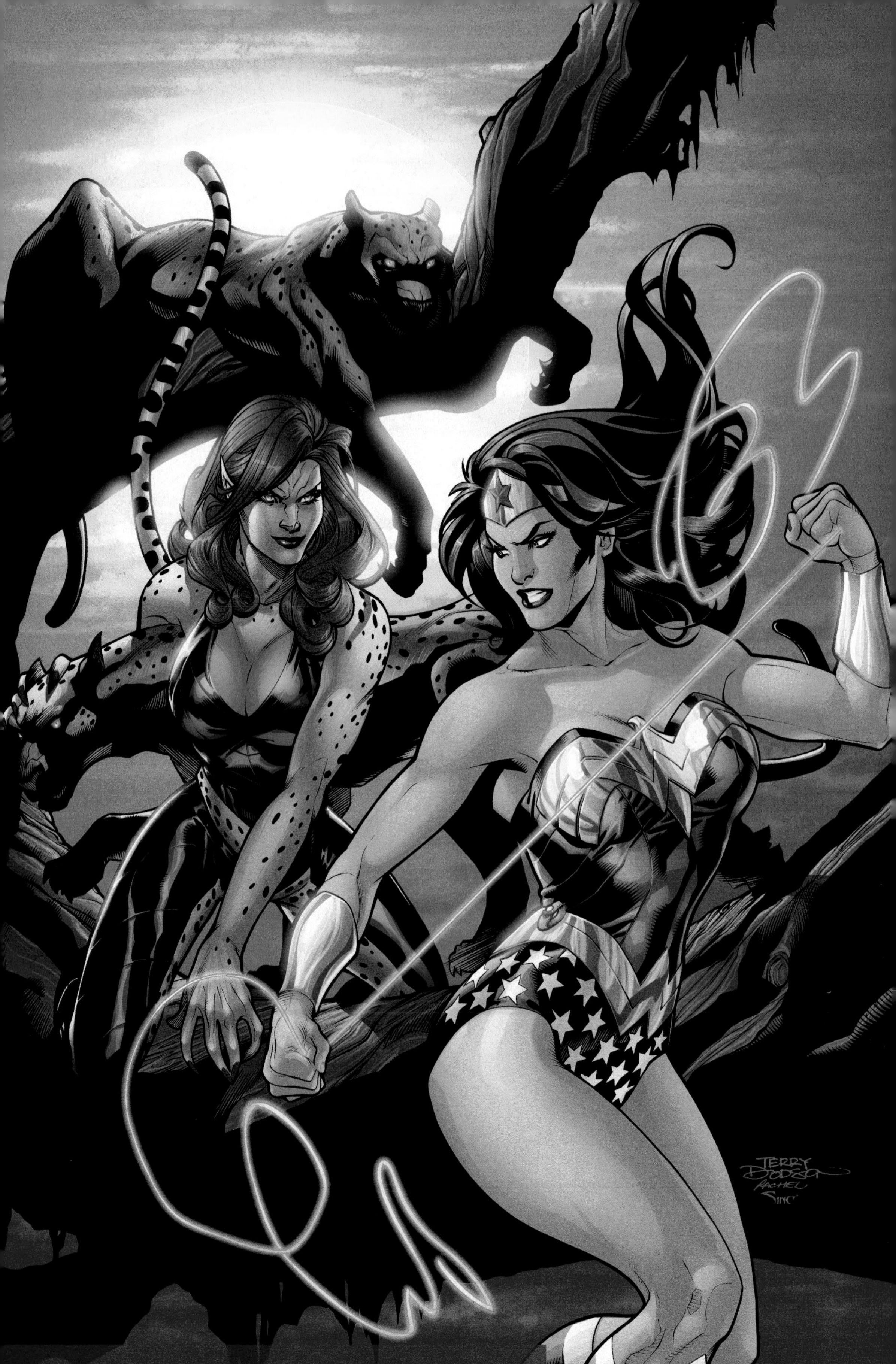

WONDER WOMAN #3 cover
by TERRY & RACHEL DODSON with ALEX SINCLAIR

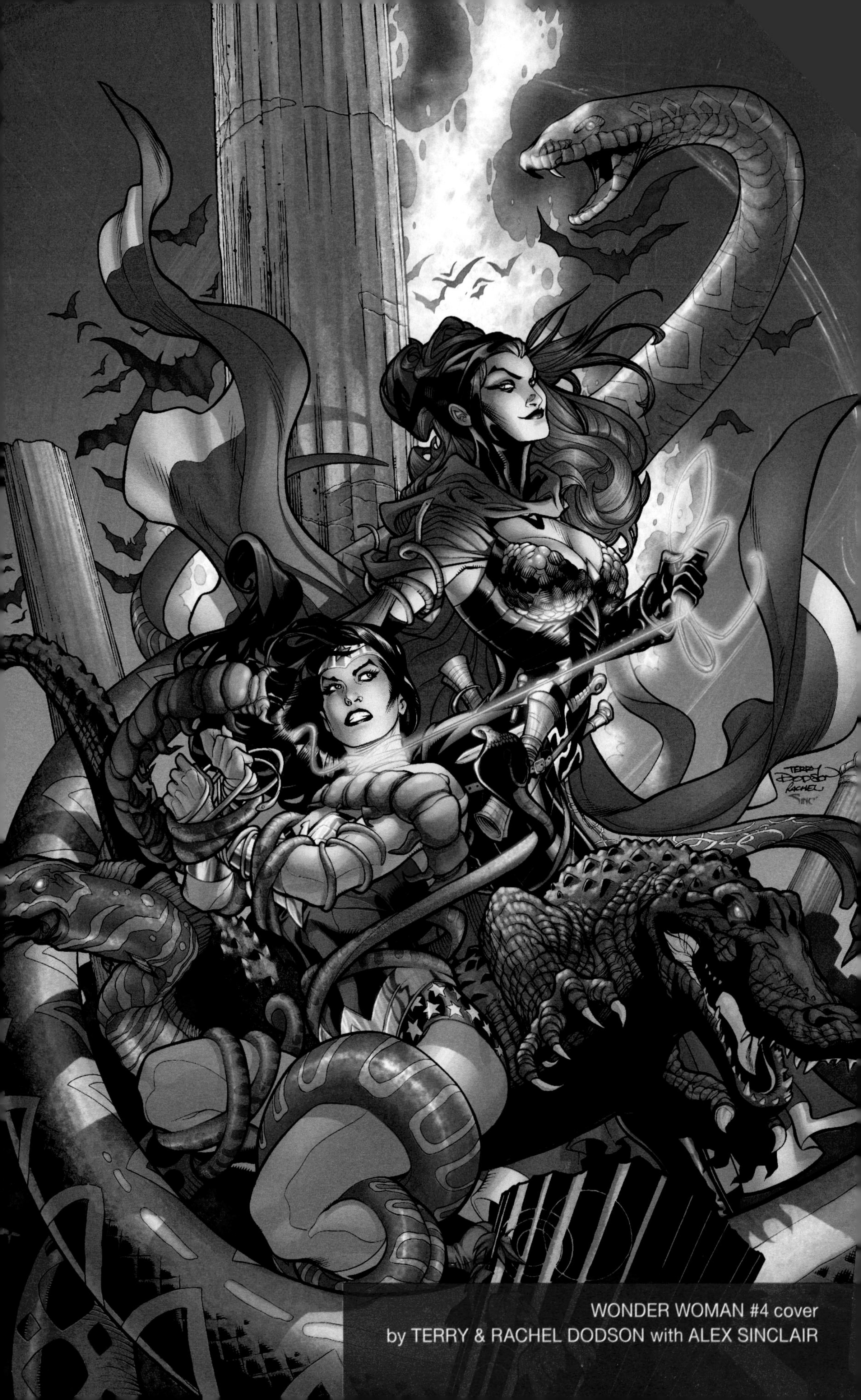

WONDER WOMAN #4 cover
by TERRY & RACHEL DODSON with ALEX SINCLAIR

sketchbook

by TERRY DODSON

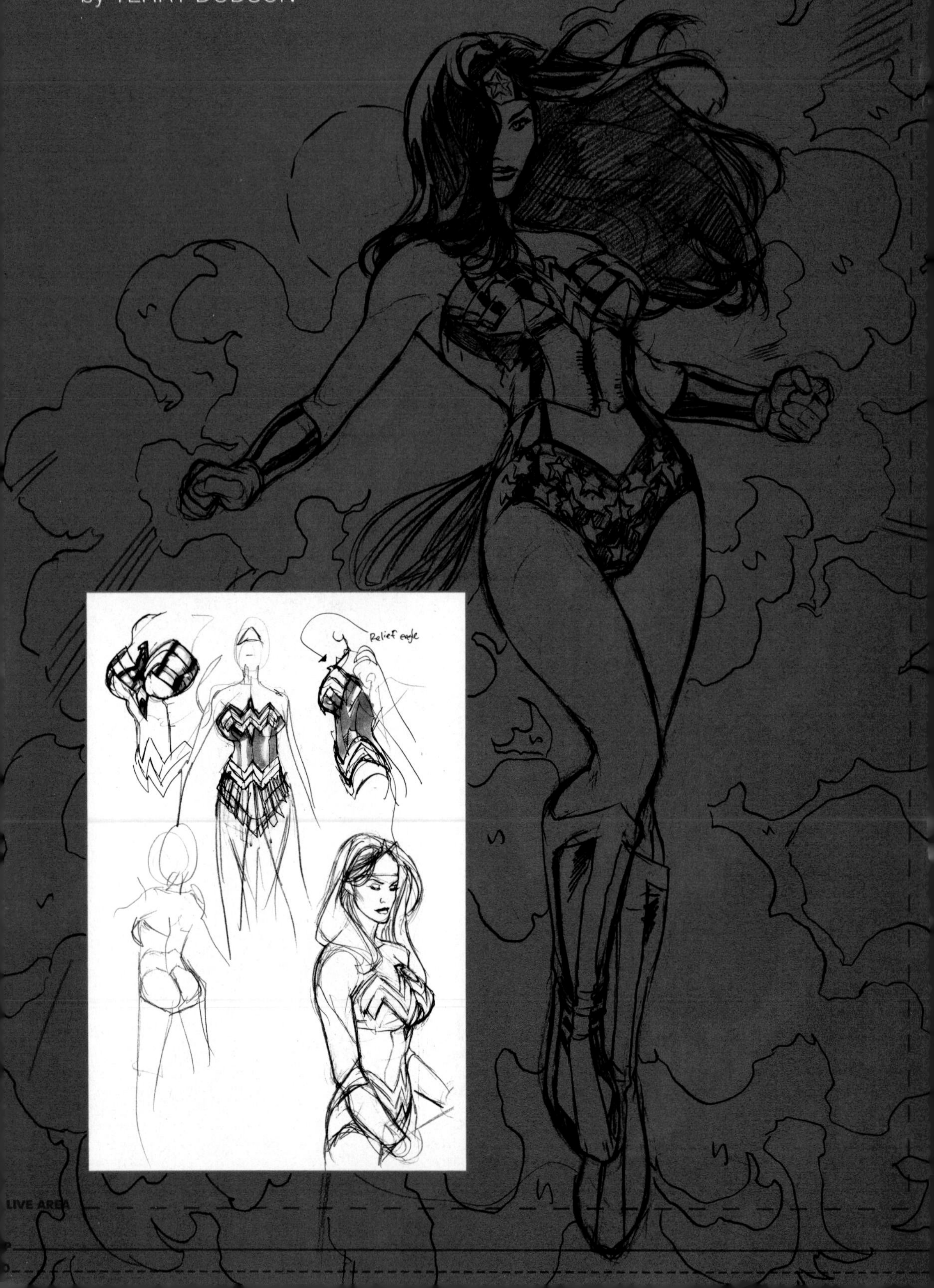
Relief eagle
LIVE AREA

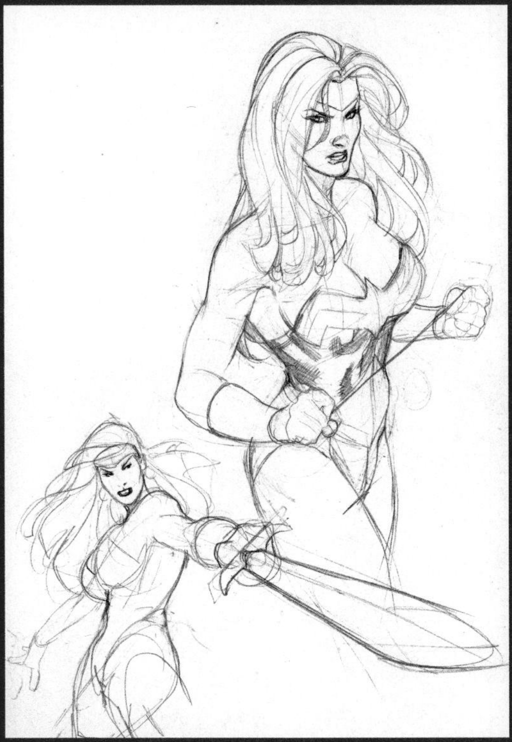

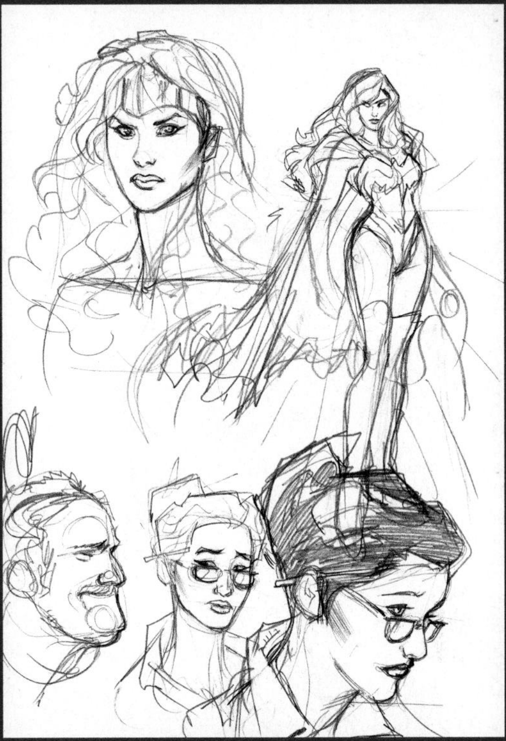

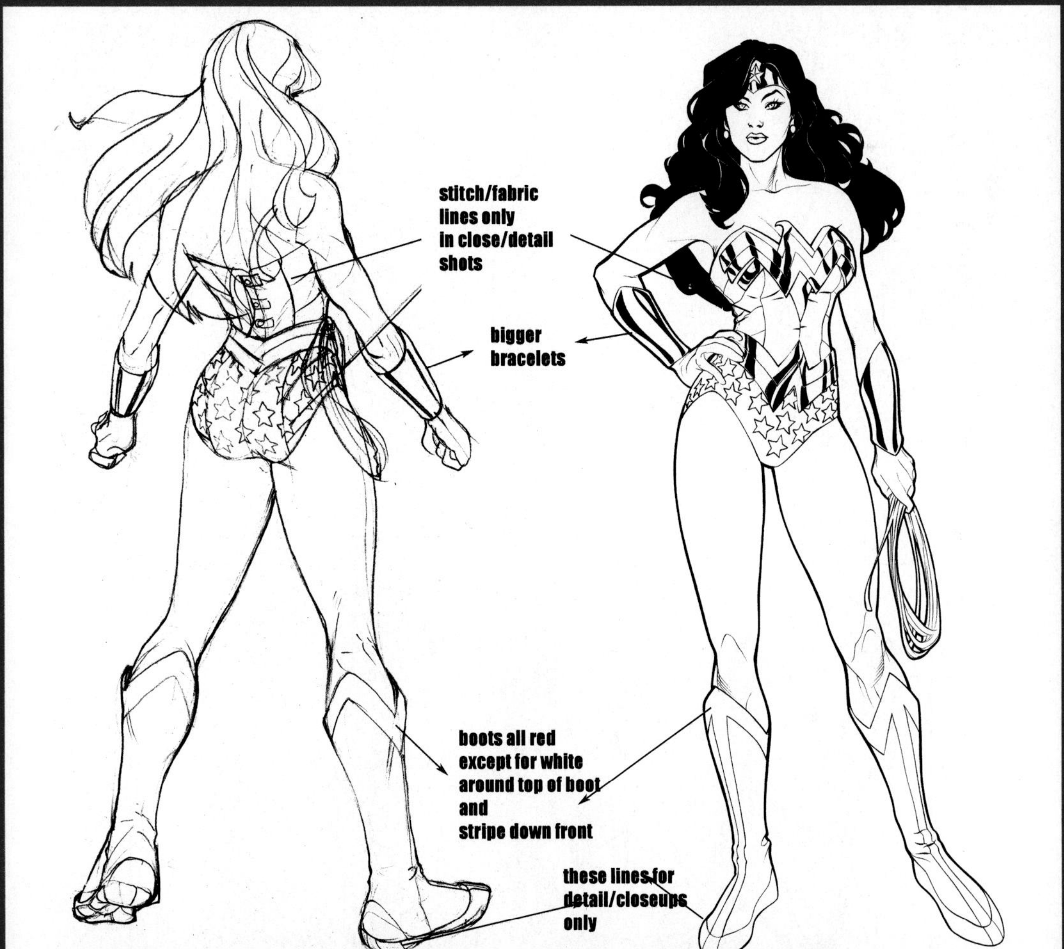
stitch/fabric
lines only
in close/detail
shots
bigger
bracelets
boots all red
except for white
around top of boot
and
stripe down front
these lines for
detail/closeups
only

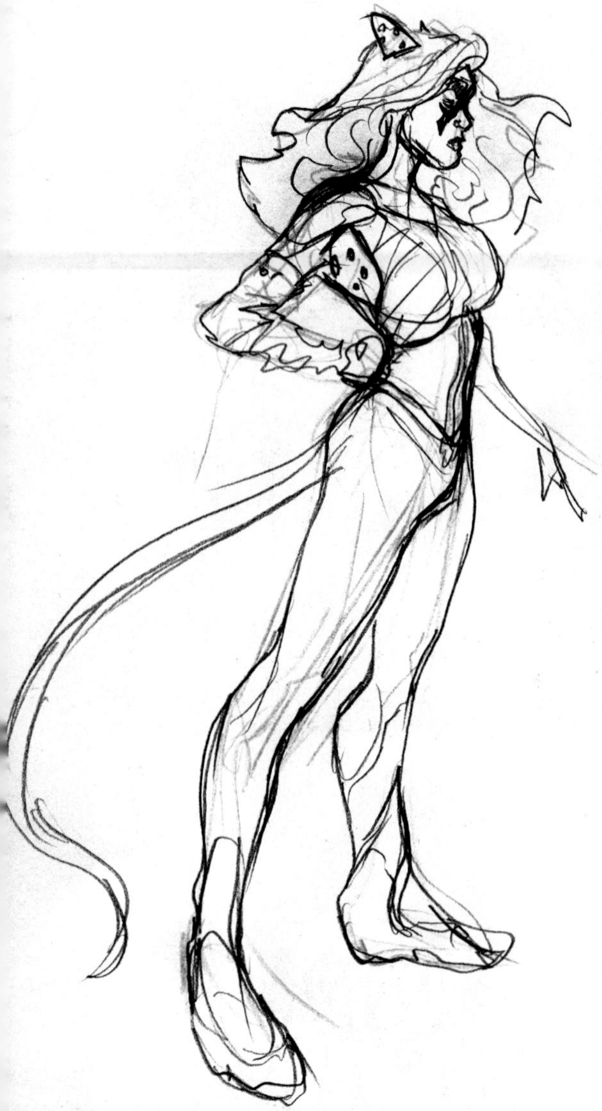

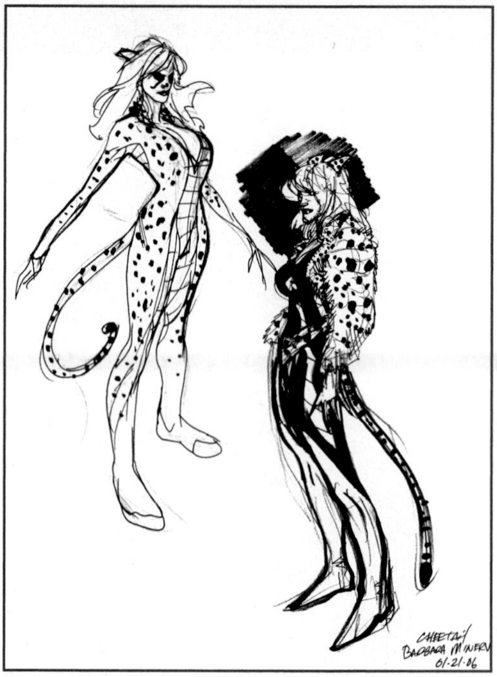

CHEETAH/
BARBARA MINERV
01-21-06

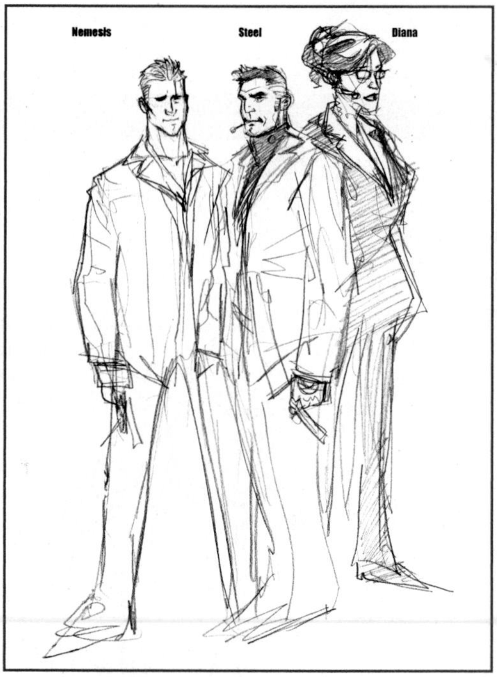

Nemesis
Steel
Diana

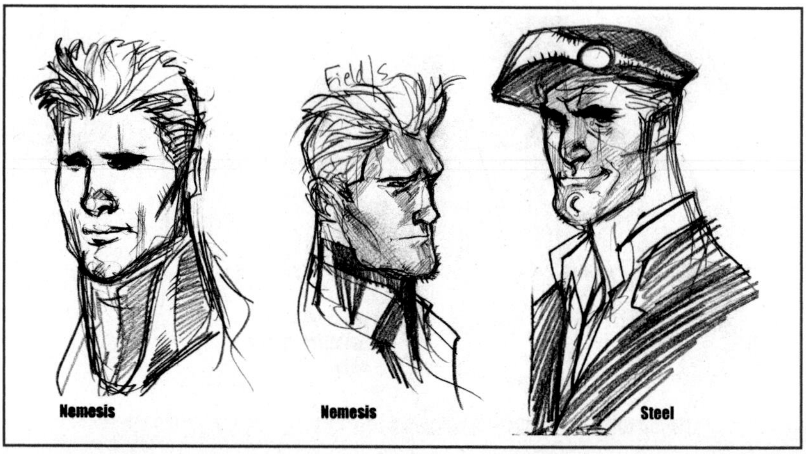

Fields
Nemesis
Nemesis
Steel

GIGANTA

A: pencils to ANNUAL #1 cover
B: pencils to issue #1 cover
C-E: sketch proposals for collection cover